Education and Training 14-18: a survey of new initiatives

by
Gloria Hitchcock

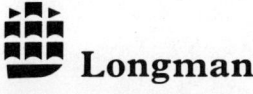
Longman

LONGMAN GROUP UK LIMITED
*Longman House, Burnt Mill, Harlow, Essex, CM20 2JE, England
and Associated Companies throughout the World*

© Longman Group UK Ltd 1988

*All rights reserved. No part of this publication may be
reproduced, stored in a retrieval system, or transmitted in
any form or by any means, electronic, mechanical, photocopying
recording or otherwise, without the prior written permission
of the publishers.*

First published 1988

ISBN 0 582 36222 9

Set in 10/12pt Monophoto Plantin

*Printed and bound in Great Britain by
Butler & Tanner Ltd, Frome and London*

Contents

Acknowledgements   vii
List of abbreviations   xi

SECTION A: MAJOR INITIATIVES

Chapter 1   *Technical and Vocational Education Initiative (TVEI)*
1.1	Background	1
1.2	Aims	2
1.3	Structure	3
1.4	Criteria	8
1.5	Impact on individuals and organisations	10
1.6	Benefits	12
1.7	Drawbacks	13
1.8	Political rationale	14
1.9	First-hand experience	15
	Summary	17

Chapter 2   *TVEI-Related In-Service training (TRIST)*
2.1	Background	19
2.2	Aims	20
2.3	Structure	20
2.4	Criteria	21
2.5	Impact on individuals and organisations	22
2.6	Benefits	23
2.7	Drawbacks	24
2.8	Political rationale	26
2.9	First-hand experience	27
	Summary	34

Chapter 3   *The Certificate of Pre-vocational Education (CPVE)*
3.1	Background	43
3.2	Aims	45

3.3	Structure	46
3.4	Criteria	48
3.5	Impact on individuals and organisations	50
3.6	Benefits	53
3.7	Drawbacks	54
3.8	Political rationale	55
3.9	First-hand experience	57
	Summary	67

Chapter 4 *The Youth Training Scheme (YTS)*

4.1	Background	70
4.2	Aims	72
4.3	Structure	73
4.4	Criteria	75
4.5	Impact on individuals and organisations	76
4.6	Benefits	80
4.7	Drawbacks	82
4.8	Political rationale	83
4.9	First-hand experience	84
	Summary	86

Chapter 5 *The General Certificate of Secondary Education (GCSE)*

5.1	Background	88
5.2	Aims	89
5.3	Structure	90
5.4	Criteria	92
5.5	Impact on individuals and organisations	93
5.6	Benefits	94
5.7	Drawbacks	95
5.8	Political rationale	96
5.9	First-hand experience	97
	Summary	101

Chapter 6 *Profiles and records of achievement*

6.1	Background	105
6.2	Aims	106
6.3	Structure	107
6.4	Criteria	125
6.5	Impact on individuals and organisations	125
6.6	Benefits	139
6.7	Drawbacks	139
6.8	Political rationale	139
6.9	First-hand experience	140
	Summary	149

Chapter 7 The modular curriculum
7.1	Background	152
7.2	Aims	152
7.3	Structure	153
7.4	Criteria	155
7.5	Impact on individuals and organisations	156
7.6	Benefits	158
7.7	Drawbacks	160
7.8	Political rationale	161
7.9	First-hand experience	162
	Summary	168

SECTION B: PREPARING FOR LIFE AFTER SCHOOL – BRIDGING THE GAP

Chapter 8 Enterprise Education
8A	Young Enterprise	170
8A.1	Background	170
8A.2	Aims	171
8A.3	Organisation	171
8A.4	What do Young Achievers gain?	173
8A.5	What's in it for employers?	173
8A.6	First-hand experience	174
8B	The Mini Enterprise in Schools Project	177
8B.1	Aims	177
8B.2	Funding	179
8B.3	Organisation	179
8B.4	First-hand experience	180
	Summary	184

Chapter 9 Education-industry links
9.1	Background	186
9.2	Some major participants	187
9.3	What can education gain from links with industry?	194
9.4	What can industry gain from links with education?	204
	Summary	207

Chapter 10 The careers contribution
10.1	Making sense of the confusion	208
10.2	What should be done to rationalise the new trends?	208
10.3	The role of careers education	209
10.4	Functions of the careers teacher	209
10.5	The counter argument	212

10.6	First-hand experience	213
	Summary	217

Chapter 11   Common themes

11.1	Experiential learning	219
11.2	Changing teaching styles and student/teacher relationships	220
11.3	Cross-curricular issues	221
11.4	Links with industry	221
11.5	Modular developments	221
11.5	Integration	222
	Conclusion	222

Acknowledgements

This book results from a long-standing involvement in 14–18 education. It would not have been possible without the generous sharing of experience and material by schools, colleges and individual teachers.

I would like to thank Peter Coleman, Director of Education, Avon and Martin Clarke, Senior Adviser Secondary Education, for their support for my work in the 14–18 field.

I am particularly indebted to Peter March, Principal Careers Adviser, Avon for his constant encouragement and willingness to offer constructive comments throughout. I have also valued the staunch support and searching criticism of Dr Renee Daines, University of Bristol.

The comments and observations of Keith Harrison, Peter Hobbs, Keith Hopkins, David Moon, and Dr Trevor White have been invaluable.

Finally, my thanks are due to my daughter Jane, an unfailing source of help who kept me resolute, and to a number of good friends including Marie Jones and Heather McLean.

Materials and information have also been contributed by the following:

Bedfordshire TVEI Scheme; Cheshire LEA; Kingdown School, Wiltshire; Manpower Services Commission; Derek Jackson, Young Enterprise; Kevin Crompton, Mini-Enterprise in Schools Project; Graham Nutbrown and Sarah Lee, Nailsea School, Avon; PPR (Pupil Personal Recording); Village College, Comberton; Reddish Vale School, Stockport; St Thomas School, Exeter; St Marks School, Bath; Mike Clarke, YTS; Deans Community School; Barbara Thomson, Castleford High School, Wakefield; West Midlands Examination Board; The Industrial Society; Pen Park School, Bristol; Rumney High School, Cardiff; Woolworth; Norton Hill School, Midsomer Norton; Gordon Bell, Cheshire TRIST Programme; Queen Elizabeth School, Corby, Lancashire; Eckington School, Sheffield; Derek White, Marine and Commercial Training; Keith Hopkins, School–Industry Liaison Co-ordinator; David Moon, CPVE Co-ordinator, Avon; Richard Stroud, GCSE Co-ordinator,

Avon; Davenport School, Stockport; Brays Grove School, Harlow; Malcolm Bowring, WJEC Records of Achievement; David Hancox, Oxfordshire LEA; Oxfordshire Examination Syndicate Credit Bank; Brian Whitnell, MSC; Ivor Goddard, Director of CADU, Southern Examining Group; Cherwell School, Oxford; David Wilson, ex-Head of Tong School, Bradford; David Rowley, British Aerospace and UBI.

For my mother

List of abbreviations

ATO	Approved Training Organisation
BTEC	Business and Technician Education Council
CBI	Confederation of British Industry
CDT	Craft, Design and Technology
CGLI	City and Guilds of London Institute
CPVE	Certificate of Pre-Vocational Education
CSCS	Centre for the Study of Comprehensive Schools
CSE	Certificate of Secondary Education
DES	Department of Education and Science
FE	Further Education
FEU	Further Education Unit
GCE	General Certificate of Education
GCSE	General Certificate of Secondary Education
GRIST	Grant Related In-Service Training
HE	Higher Education
HMI	Her Majesty's Inspectorate
INSET	In-service Training
JUPVE	Joint Unit for Pre-Vocational Education
LEA	Local Education Authority
LENS	Local Employer Network Service
MESP	Mini-Enterprise in Schools Project
MSC	Manpower Services Commission
NCVQ	National Council for Vocational Qualifications
NTI	National Training Initiative
NVQ	National Vocational Qualification
RCB	Regional Curriculum Base
ROA	Records of Achievement
RSA	Royal Society for Arts
SCDC	School Curriculum Development Council
SCIP	Schools Curriculum Industry Project
SEC	Secondary Examinations Council
SPACE	Social, Personal and Careers Education
TRIST	TVEI Related In-Service Training
TUC	Trades Union Congress

TVEI	Technical and Vocational Education Initiative
UBI	Understanding British Industry
UI	Understanding Industry
YE	Young Enterprise
YOP	Youth Opportunities Programme
YTS	Youth Training Scheme

Chapter 1

The Technical and Vocational Education Initiative (TVEI)

The Technical and Vocational Education Initiative (TVEI) is a major 14–18 curriculum initiative designed to strengthen provision of technical and vocational education for students of all abilities; it shifts the curricular emphasis towards a more work-oriented approach. It aims not only to stimulate curriculum development, but to introduce new approaches to learning. As TVEI spans the 14–18 age range, it involves collaboration between school and further education.

1.1 Background

TVEI was launched in November 1982 after the Prime Minister invited the Manpower Services Commission to design a new scheme to develop technical and vocational education. This in itself was a complete departure from established practice, and was the first time that a department other than the Department of Education and Science (DES) had been given the right to affect, influence and directly intervene in the education of young people in schools and colleges.

It emerged against a background of rapid growth in structural unemployment and a reservoir of disillusioned young people for whom the diet being offered in schools appeared increasingly irrelevant and inappropriate, if not intrinsically uninteresting. The traditional strictures of 'work hard, pass your exams and you'll get a good job' were no longer true, and viable alternatives were already being sought.

TVEI was introduced to Directors of Education (and it should be remembered that participation was voluntary) as a project which would provide a four year integrated course for students, starting at the age of 14. It would include general, technical and vocational education, including work experience; it would be for students across the ability range; and it would lead to nationally recognised qualifications.

In his letter to all Directors of Education[1] David Young stated: 'Our general objective is to widen and enrich the curriculum in a way that will help young people to prepare for the world of work, and to develop skills and interests, including creative abilities, that will help them to lead a fuller life and to be able to contribute more to the life of the community.' He went on to say: 'Secondly we are in the business of helping students to *learn to learn*' – the now familiar call for the development of transferable skills.

It is in the region of skills aquisition, through experiences which take place in a context outside the straightjacket imposed by academic subjects, that the main enthusiasm and innovative techniques have been developed.

The first 14 pilot schemes in England and Wales began in September 1983 – the time scale demonstrates the flavour of TVEI. Most people involved in the management of educational innovation would have predicted that such a brief lead-in for a project with wide-ranging implications would have been impossible. It was certainly not without its problems, but the very fact that it *did* happen, and young people were involved in a programme of enhanced technical and vocational education a mere ten months after its inception, was a significant achievement.

The first pilots were quickly followed in September 1984 by a further 48 projects in 47 Authorities (43 in England and Wales and 5 in Scotland). Contrary to some speculation, this was not the end of the 'pilot' schemes – a further 12 projects started in September 1985. It was becoming more and more obvious that the Government was investing both cash and commitment to the concept of technical and vocational education, and when all the remaining authorities were invited to submit proposals for 1986, 28 more bids were received. By Setember 1987 virtually all LEAs were involved in some aspect of TVEI. This is a measure of the scale and speed of a massive innovation.

Although the number of students involved was initially small (approximately 39,000 students in 500 schools and colleges by 1985) by the summer of 1986 it had been decided to extend the scheme into a fully fledged curriculum development, before the results of any completed four-year programme could be assessed.

1.2 Aims

The aims of TVEI are:
'In conjunction with LEAs to explore and test ways of organising and managing the education of 14–18 year old people across the ability range so that:
  i. More of them are attracted to seek the qualifications/skills which will be of direct value to them at work and more of them achieve these qualifications and skills.
  ii. They are better equipped to enter the world of employment which will await them.
  iii. They acquire a more direct appreciation of the practical application of the qualifications for which they are working.

iv. They become accustomed to using their skills and knowledge to solve the real-world problems they will meet at work.
v. More emphasis is placed on developing initiative, motivation and enterprise as well as problem-solving skills and other aspects of personal development.
vi. The construction of the bridge from education to work is begun earlier by giving these young people the opportunity to have direct contact and training/planned work experience with a number of local employers in the relevant specialism.
vii. There is close collaboration between local education authorities and industry/commerce/public services etc. so that the curriculum has industry's confidence'[2].

MSC made it clear that they wished these aims to be a major consideration in all programmes, so that the lessons learned could be replicated as quickly as possible. Methods and content should be compatible with the latest developments in skill and vocational training outside school and considerable emphasis should be placed upon monitoring and evaluation.

Emphasis is also placed upon the development of a more vocationally oriented curriculum, providing young people with the opportunity to develop skills which are more closely related to those required in the world of work. For many students this alone is sufficient to add spice to their work, but as *Supporting TVEI*[3] points out, it is not sufficient for the curriculum to be 'dominated by the work ethic'.

Perhaps one of the most far-reaching aims in terms of its effect upon the curriculum is that referring to 'initiative, motivation, enterprise ... problem-solving skills'. These qualities lie at the heart of the TVEI philosophy – it is by encouraging these that youngsters are better prepared to meet the demands of a rapidly changing adult world. It is impossible to acquire skills of initiative and enterprise if pedagogy relies upon teaching serried ranks of individuals by a traditional 'chalk and talk' method. This has led to a re-examination by teachers of what is taking place within their classrooms, and to innovatory, often experimental and generally exciting new approaches to teaching.

There can be little doubt that if the majority of teachers had been opposed in principle to these aims, then TVEI would have died within the first year, but despite reservations, sufficient teachers have become convinced that the aims are worthwhile.

1.3 Structure

1.3.1 The pilot phase

The main structure of TVEI is determined by the Aims and Criteria (see 1.2 and 1.4). These aims and criteria provide a rigid framework, but content and delivery varies. Many schemes adopt a core-plus-option structure.

a. Core

A typical core includes English, mathematics, science, humanities, physical education, careers education and guidance and work experience. Technology and business studies often form part of the core.

The Further Education Unit and School Curriculum Development Committee, in *Supporting TVEI*[4] advocate an identified core for all schemes which would provide breadth and balance, as well as relating to a range of technical and vocational areas.

Their proposed core is based on the following aims:

i. ADAPTABILITY: to develop a flexibility of attitude and ability to learn sufficient to cope with future changes in technology, career and lifestyle.

ii. ROLE TRANSITION: to bring about an informed perspective as to the roles and status of a young person in adult, multicultural society, including the world of work, in order to inform responsible and realistic decision making about future opportunities.

iii PHYSICAL SKILLS: to enable an appropriate development of physical and manipulative skills in both vocational and leisure contexts, and an appreciation of those skills in others.

iv. INTERPERSONAL SKILLS: to bring about an ability to be sensitive to and tolerant of the needs of others, and to develop satisfactory personal relationships.

v. VALUES: to foster a reasoned set of positive social and moral values applicable to issues in contemporary society.

vi. COMMUNICATION/NUMERACY: to develop levels of achievement in language, communication and numeracy skills to meet the basic demands of contemporary society and to provide a foundation appropriate to the acquisition of further skills.

vii. PROBLEM SOLVING: to develop a capacity to approach various kinds of problems methodically and effectively, to undertake courses of action, evaluate them, and modify these actions accordingly.

viii. COPING: to develop the necessary skills for coping with everyday situations together with the ability to collaborate with others and to contribute to their well-being.

ix. SOCIETY: to provide young people with a knowledge of the workings of modern society, and to develop abilities both to cope with it and to contribute to its development.

x. INFORMATION TECHNOLOGY: to provide an introduction to the implications and applications of information technology to society, the individual and to the processes of learning.

xi. LEARNING SKILLS: to develop sufficient competence and confidence in a variety of independent learning situations to maximise individual potential in work and leisure.

xii. HEALTH EDUCATION: to develop an understanding of health and human development sufficient for young people to choose how they can maintain a healthy lifestyle.

xiii. CREATIVITY: to enable young people to become aware of their own creativity and to develop this and their powers of appreciation and critical judgement for vocational, aesthetic and leisure purposes.
xiv. ENVIRONMENT: to foster an appreciation of the physical and technological environment and its relationship with social and scientific issues and principles.
xv. SCIENCE/TECHNOLOGY: to promote an understanding of the nature and discipline of science, and its relationship to technology via the processes of design and principles.

b. Options
A number of new options have been developed as a result of TVEI. These include electronics, biotechnology, creative arts, commercial languages, mass media and electronic music. Additional modules such as agricultural or leisure studies are frequently developed to reflect local career opportunities.

1.3.2   *TVEI extension*

TVEI made the transition from a pilot scheme to a full scale national initiative with the publication of *Working Together – Education and Training*[5], in 1986. A sum of £900 million pounds was allocated over a period of ten years.

The same system of bidding for funds which had been established through TVEI, TRIST and the new DES INSET arrangements is continued. One interesting feature is that money will not be allocated in equal amounts for each year of extension, but will be determined according to the current need.

MSC reviews each LEA's scheme annually. Only those that have completed a three year preparatory programme are eligible. This has repercussions for the Authorities which entered TVEI late. Some were commencing their three year programme at the same time as others were launching TVEI extension. The sum of £900 million indicates a considerably lower level of funding than was available to the pilot schemes.

a. Aims and criteria for extension.
The aims and criteria are broadly the same as those for the pilots; the structure of extension programmes will therefore be governed by the same requirements.

b. Vocational elements
Structure of programmes should ensure that vocational elements:
– keep options open and do not encourage early specialisation
– offer a broad and balanced curriculum
– give students the skills and competencies needed for a technological society
– ease the transition to adulthood
– encourage the application of knowledge, concepts and skills in the real world
– create active learning experiences
– provide alternative teaching strategies throughout the whole curriculum

SCHOOL A: CURRICULUM FOR TVEI STUDENTS AT 14+

Weekly Timetable	
Religious Education Personal & Social Development	10%
Mathematics	20%
English	30%
Physical and Recreational	40%
OPTION BLOCK — Choice of one from Civics Economics Geography History Sociology — OPTION BLOCK	50%
OPTION BLOCK — Choice of one from French German Latin European Studies Italian — OPTION BLOCK	60%
OPTION BLOCK — Choice of one from Physics Chemistry Biology Applied Science General Science — OPTION BLOCK	70%
OPTION BLOCK — Choice of one from Business Studies Engineering Science Technology Agriculture Textile Technology Fabric & Fashion Retail Distribution Secretarial Studies Computer Studies Technical Drawing Craft & Design Child Care Physics Geology — OPTION BLOCK	80%
OPTION BLOCK — Choice of one from Electronics Graphics Control Technology Motor Vehicle Engineering Food Studies & Catering Building Studies Technical Drawing Technology Horticulture Typewriting Computer Studies Craft & Design House-Craft Chemistry Biology — OPTION BLOCK	90%
Information Technology	
Integrating Module Full range of study	100%
ADDITIONAL ELEMENTS IN TVEI PROGRAMMES Work Practice	
Cross-Modular Elements Residential Education	

Fig. 1.1: From *Supporting TVEI* (SCDC/FEU)

SCHOOL C: CURRICULUM FOR TVEI STUDENTS AT 14+
(The Modular Approach)

	WEEKLY TIMETABLE	
'General Education' 65%	English	Language and Literature
	Mathematics	
	Science	One from: Physics, Biology, Physical or General Studies
	Humanities	One from: Geography, History, Understanding Industrial Society
	Design & Technology	One from: Art, CDT, Music, Home Economics, Technology
Technical and Vocation 35%	Modules	(see below)

MODULES

A
- Computing 1
- Conversational French
- Conversational Welsh 1
- Electronics/Microelectronics 1
- Information Systems
- Interview Techniques & Interpersonal Skills
- Mass media
- Typewriting 1

B
- Computing 1
- Electronics/Microelectronics 1
- Electronic music
- Interview Techniques & Interpersonal Skills
- Leisure
- Mass media 1
- Practical office skills 1
- Typewriting 1

Weeks 1-9:   Each student selects and follows one module from Box A and one from Box B.
Weeks 10-18: Each student selects and follows a second module from Box A and Box B.
Week 19:   Assessment of students' attainments.
Weeks 20-28: Each student selects and follows one module from Box C and one from Box D.
Weeks 29-37: Each student selects and follows a second module from Box C and Box D.
Week 38:   Assessment of students' attainments.

C
- Computing 2
- Conversational Spanish
- Electronics/Microelectronics 2
- Government & Society
- Management studies
- Mass media 2
- Photography
- Word processing 1

D
- Business studies 1
- Computing 2
- Electronics/Microelectronics 2
- Interview techniques & interpersonal skills
- Leisure
- Mass media 2
- Technical graphic art 1

Fig. 1.2: From *Supporting TVEI* (SCDC/FEU)

c. **Technical elements**
The technical aspects of the programme's structure should ensure that:
- 'technical' does not mean simply an extension to craft or CDT
- it is a new approach to the APPLICATION of science and technology
- applied science and technology should be part of every student's curriculum
- TVEI should be linked to GCSE
- individualised learning should be encouraged

1.4 TVEI criteria

TVEI criteria for pilot schemes indicated that a variety of approaches would be encouraged; they placed emphasis upon the vocational elements of courses. Students should be encouraged to acquire 'generic or specific skills with a view to employment', albeit within a programme of full-time general, technical and vocational studies. The importance of the TVEI group comprising the whole ability range was stressed.

Of greatest interest to the practising teacher, and those managing either TVEI or an innovation based on similar principles, are the criteria relating to the content of programmes. These state that each project should be made up of one or more sets of full-time programmes with the following characteristics:
  i. Equal opportunities should be available to young people of both sexes and they should normally be educated together on courses within each project. Care should be taken to avoid sex stereotyping.
  ii. They should provide four year curricula, with progression from year to year, designed to prepare the student for particular aspects of employment and for adult life in a society liable to rapid change.
  iii. They should have clear and specific objectives, including the objectives of encouraging initiative, problem-solving abilities, and other aspects of personal development.
  iv. The balance between the general, technical and vocational elements of programmes should vary according to students' individual needs and the stage of the course, but throughout the programme there should be both a general and a technical/vocational element.
  v. The technical and vocational elements should be broadly related to potential employment opportunities within and outside the geographical area for the young people concerned.
  vi. There should be appropriate, planned work experience as an integral part of the programmes from the age of 15 onwards, bearing in mind the provisions of the Education (Work Experience) Act 1973.
  vii. Courses should be capable of being linked effectively with subsequent training/educational opportunities.
  viii. Arrangements should be made for regular assessment and for student

The Technical and Vocational Education Initiative (TVEI)

PROPOSED 14 - 16 CURRICULUM 1987 - 88

	Ten Day Cycle - Four Period Day	Core Area	Core option to be selected in September 1987	Extension option to be selected at Easter 1988 for additional certification	%
(CCC) = Cross-Curriculum Course	1 2 3 4 5	English	English Language GCSE *	English Literature GCSE + Communications GCSE + Drama GCSE + Performing Arts GCSE + (CCC)	
	6 7 8 9	Maths	Maths GCSE * or Foundation Maths Project		
All students are required to study the common core, and make a selection of Option block A or Option block B	10 11 12 13 14 15 16	Science	Integrated Science Double SCISP Certificate GCSE		72.5
	17 18 19 20 21 22 23	Design and Aesthetic Studies	CORE: Art and Design GCSE * OPTIONS: Design and Realisation GCSE * or Technology * of Music GCSE * or Surveying GCSE	Performing Arts GCSE (CCC) +	
	24 25 26	Physical Education	Non Exam or GCSE	Performing Arts GCSE (CCC) +	
Entry to certifications in extension modular courses is not the nesessary objective for all pupils	27 28 29	PSE	PROSPECT MODULAR COURSE - NON EXAM AND PROFILED * (PSE)		
EITHER	30 31 32 33 34 35 36	Integrated Humanities GCSE+ (Manchester Modules)		History GCSE * Geography GCSE * Social GCSE * Religious Studies GCSE *	27.5
	37 38 39 40	Contemporary Languages (French, Spanish, German, Urdu) or - Business Studies GCSE + or - Economics GCSE			
+ New Courses (TVEI) * Enhanced Courses (TVEI) OR	30 31 32 33 34 35 36	Integrated Business Studies + Information Studies Double GCSE: Hampshire Modules			27.5
	37 38 39 40	Contemporary Languages (French, Spanish, German Urdu) Or - Integrated Humantiies + GCSE			

Fig. 1.3: Example of timetable for TVEI extension in a Bedfordshire 11–16 School

and tutors to discuss students' performance/progress. Each student, and his or her parents, should also receive a periodic written assessment, and have an opportunity to discuss this assessment with the relevant project teachers. Good careers and educational counselling will be essential.[6]

In addition to these criteria relating to the content of programmes, others direct that students should be preparing for recognised qualifications, that every student should receive a profile or record of achievement, that every project should be clearly identifiable, and that each four-year project should cater for around 1000 students.

All schemes submitted for TVEI funding had to comply with these criteria, which have been extended without significant alteration to include TVEI extension. The main difference was that *Better Schools*[7] had been published, supporting the aims and criteria of TVEI. LEAs and schools are now encouraged to incorporate the aims and criteria into their curriculum statements.

All LEAs are asked to relate their plans to the Aims and Criteria. In addition, MSC look closely at:
– the LEA organisation for delivery of the TVEI extension programme
– the way in which lessons learned from the pilot phase are to be implemented
– the extent of resource back-up through support centres, data-bases, industry-community support
– policies for equal opportunities and education/industry liaison
– strategies for overcoming teacher shortage in specialist curriculum areas
– inclusion of special needs students

The TVEI unit responsible for the programme continues to review schemes in order to check that they are conforming to their contractual obligations to meet the demands of the Aims and Criteria. This attention to the criteria as a means of ensuring quality control is demonstrated by the fact that over 60% of submissions were rejected in the first year (1987) of TVEI extension.

1.5 Impact of TVEI on institutions and individuals

When the bulk of activity in the pilot schemes took place in a small number of schools and colleges, the impact was considerable. Where a TVEI Centre was established, then the impact on that Centre and on the Authority may have been great, but the effect on individual TVEI schools and colleges was often considerably less.

In one Scottish project, for example, a TVEI Centre served three local schools. Activity in the Centre was intense, yet the impact on school organisation was minimal in comparison with some schemes. TVEI was timetabled for one half day per week and access to TVEI students was restricted to that

The Technical and Vocational Education Initiative (TVEI)

time. In addition to other repercussions, this affected the ability to assess students across the range of their activities, and to provide a comprehensive profile. Staff not involved could, in these circumstances, remain largely unaffected by TVEI.

Despite the lack of effect on organisational issues in this scheme, a very real impact was made in one area. A system whereby TVEI tutors joined regular teachers in the classroom and initiated team teaching had a widespread effect upon teaching styles. This successful strategy was partly accidental, resulting from the Scottish industrial action in which teachers refused to participate in in-service training. It would have been impossible to present teachers with TVEI materials and expect them to adopt new methods of delivery; team teaching was seen as a useful compromise. It proved so successful that it is one of the lessons of TVEI which is to be disseminated nationally.

In contrast, the impact on institutions in the Bradford scheme was considerable. In one school a revolutionary approach to timetabling, facilities for work sampling and residential experience affected everyone.

Hereford TVEI adopted yet another model. A TVEI Centre in Hereford serves ten schools and three colleges. The schools are spread over a wide geographical area which causes massive logistical problems. Arrangements must be made for students to travel from remote areas, and time allocated for travelling to the Centre.

One incidental impact resulting from the bussing of students to a central venue arises from the chance for students to meet young people from other areas. One of the problems of rural deprivation is the shortage of companions of the same age. All of the students interviewed commented on the fact that they enjoyed mixing with new people through TVEI. They also felt that they were lucky to have the opportunity to 'do TVEI, because it is so much more interesting'.

The impact on teachers in the project was reflected in comments such as:

'Things will never be the same again.'
'This is what learning is all about.'
'It's changed my teaching of English completely.'
'Why can't we smash all subject boundaries and build a curriculum around things such as talking and listening, writing, reading, signs and diagrams, numeracy, creating, working in groups etc.'

One feature appreciated by teachers was the provision of residential in-service courses. These usually took place at weekends, but providing they were set in comfortable surroundings, teachers were happy to participate without the necessity of disrupting lessons.

An interim evaluation report[8] acknowledges that the impact of TVEI on institutions is affected by the management style of the scheme. It identifies three main approaches: central control, collaborative control, and diffused control (with each institution developing its own programme). The collaborative model, with groups of teachers working together and with the LEA had the greatest impact and led to the most innovative courses.

TVEI extension should mean that the impact is felt not only in a small number of pilot schools and colleges, but in most of the institutions throughout the country. There is, however, a considerable difference in the scale of funding to support extension. It remains to be seen whether this will affect the impact of the extension phase of TVEI.

1.6 Benefits of TVEI

One of the greatest benefits of TVEI is the opportunity which has been created for introducing substantial changes in the curriculum. It has enabled those with vision to implement changes for which they campaigned prior to TVEI.
Other benefits include:
  i. TVEI has encouraged schools and colleges to provide a more exciting, dynamic experience for young people.
  ii. This has involved a more integrated approach to the curriculum, with cross-subject co-operation.
  iii. The move towards a modular curriculum, with short-term learning objectives and assessments has been fuelled by TVEI.
  iv. More flexible timetabling has become common – the nature of TVEI programmes has led to the abolition of the '40 minute rat race' where students scurried from one lesson to another seven or eight times a day.
  v. Experience-based, participative learning encourages greater autonomy in students.
  vi. The impetus given to pilot schemes by TVEI finance raised morale and enthusiasm amongst participating teachers.
  vii. This enthusiasm is helping to promote the dissemination of TVEI extension.
  viii. INSET for TVEI has helped to up-skill teachers to meet the challenges of a technological society.
  ix. Teachers have found experiential teaching styles stimulating. This has, in turn, affected their teaching in other areas, which is changing the climate in schools.
  x. The mandatory provision of a TVEI profile stressed the importance of new approaches to assessment and profiling.
  xi. In many Authorities the requirement to forge links between schools and further education has led to a long overdue climate of co-operation.

A more detailed account of the effect of changing teaching styles can be found in Chapter 4 (TRIST) which was devoted to in-service training of teachers in line with TVEI principles.

The Technical and Vocational Education Initiative (TVEI) 13

1.7 Drawbacks

Despite the benefits arising from the introduction of TVEI, there are a number of drawbacks; some were evident only in the early days, while others have persisted. Some of the main disadvantages include:

i. Problems arising from the speed of introduction. Schools and colleges were precipitated into programmes for which teachers felt ill-prepared. They were also ill-prepared for the changes in teaching style demanded of them.

ii. Fears about the divisive nature of TVEI were justified in some cases, particularly in those pilots where resources were mainly devoted to the identified TVEI cohort. With the advent of TVEI extension, the problems of divisiveness should be resolved.

iii. Some organisations faced bitterness from teachers who did not work on TVEI programmes, and consequently operated within the same school or college, but with less favourable student-teacher ratios and resources.

iv. TVEI can cause major disruption. One Deputy Head remarked: 'I am on the side of ALL pupils – TVEI is causing chaos for everyone in order to benefit a few.' The extent of the disruption depends upon a variety of factors, not least the enthusiasm of management, and the distribution of resources.

v. INSET was not always of adequate quantity or quality. Even LEAs which gave maximum support and agreed to provide supply cover for staff attending INSET could not solve the problem of teachers' reluctance to leave classes, or that of finding sufficient supply teachers. In one school preparing for its entry into the scheme, up to nineteen teachers were out of the classroom on some days. It is difficult to run an organisation on this basis.

vi. There are still some who question whether the curriculum should be concerned with what they see as a mechanistic training for the labour market.

vii. Some students have expressed the view that TVEI is a 'con' – preparing them for jobs which just are not there. This argument is strengthened by the advent of TVEI extension: if all students are receiving the benefits of a TVEI curriculum, then they cannot claim that they are better prepared for the world of work than their peers.

viii. Some LEAs have lacked commitment to make the scheme a success, leaving it to flounder without senior, identified officers to take decisions and responsibility. This attitude is transmitted to individuals trying to make TVEI work, and the development has become stultified.

1.8 Political rationale

There can have been few people who did not, to some extent, recognise the political overtones in the introduction of TVEI. Reactions varied: there were those (more usually left-wing) councils who refused at all costs to have anything to do with this 'imposition of doctrinaire policies'. Many people shared the views of Shirley Williams when she said:

> 'The DES is powerless ... the Cabinet, impatient to get things done, has used the one weapon to hand, the centrally funded Manpower Services Commission. In consequence the MSC has invaded or taken over very large areas of education and training. It is not accountable to local authorities or even education ministers, and is resented by them.'[9]

Others, whilst possibly regretting the necessity for the involvement of MSC, nevertheless felt that it was a valuable injection of money which would allow the development of policies in which many educationalists already believed.

Furthermore, a substantial body of opinion felt that it was essential that responsibility for implementation should rest firmly in the hands of teachers; that it would be perfectly possible to accept the money and use it to further their own ideas on sound, innovative educational practice (in other words, pick up the money and run!).

Some of the strongest idealogical objections were expressed by those who saw the introduction of TVEI as a complete reversal of the comprehensive ideal, with almost a return to the old system of separating youngsters into 'Technical Schools'. It was seen as inevitably leading to early divisions between academic and vocational courses to the detriment of TVEI students, and to a hardening of divisive barriers largely based upon social class.

In fact, one of the TVEI criteria determines that each cohort should be representative of the whole ability range (and by implication the whole range of social class). Further arguments were put forward by enthusiasts who pointed to the fact that for many students there was no real comprehensive experience in their day-to-day school life, and no alternative to a watered down version of the academic curriculum which was inappropriate and largely irrelevant. TVEI enlarged rather than restricted their choice.

The concerns of practising teachers largely centred on three issues:
i. the question of divisiveness
ii. unease about the intrusion of a political dimension into the curriculum
iii. the morality of identifying and separating groups of young people who would, by the very nature of the exercise, be the recipients of generous resourcing at a time when other sections of the education system were suffering severe financial stringency

This latter point was one which was grasped by the early pioneers, particularly those with a highly developed entrepreneurial skill. They ensured that despite MSC's determination that TVEI students and resources should be separately identified, resources should be available for all students in a pilot school or college. This strategy was adopted in Devon, one of the first pilot LEAs.

This does not, of course, overcome an allied concern about creating 'haves' and 'have nots' – the discrepancy between participating and non-participating institutions.

Those who looked at the broader political implications of TVEI addressed such issues as social control. TVEI, as a state policy implemented through a Government agency outside education, could clearly be described as a means of exerting social control over the lives of young people. There is almost no attempt to camouflage the intention to use the initiative to further Government policy in producing better-trained young workers.

Part of the fallacy of this argument lies in the implication that a better trained workforce will lead to less unemployment. In fact, some of the unkinder critics have suggested that TVEI is nothing but a knee-jerk response to alarming levels of youth unemployment, and is merely the logical conclusion of a movement which began with Callaghan's 'Great Debate' in 1976 (see Chapter 8). On the other hand, those involved in burgeoning courses in pre-vocational education witnessed the ENGAGEMENT of students not known for their motivation. There was an accompanying growth in self-esteem through being able to succeed, and an actual improvement in academic attainment resulting from learning THROUGH integrated courses which were seen as offering relevant experience.

Those who decried the Government pre-occupation with the need for greater liaison with and awareness of the needs of industry ignored the best outcomes of industrial liaison for students (see Chapter 8).

Whilst the early critics of TVEI experienced considerable unease about the political implications of the scheme, there is no denying that for a great many of the school population there was, effectively, no choice. TVEI offered a new way of broadening their horizons and gaining the skills required for coping with modern technology and advanced communications systems which will be needed in the twenty-first century. Rather than TVEI students being discriminated against, it is they who became the privileged class of students; it is this fact which has led to the acceptance of TVEI extension.

1.9 First-hand experience of TVEI: the Bradford TVEI scheme

a. Background

Bradford was successful in being selected as one of the first 14 pilot schemes in the country, commencing in September 1983.

There were, in effect, only two weeks for those devising the programme to produce a workable document. This is another example of the speed of TVEI's implementation. The Bradford proposal developed overtones more in keeping with an adventure than an educational enterprise. A messenger was despatched on the overnight train to London, and arrived with minutes to spare before the deadline.

b. Organisational deadlines
The Bradford scheme built upon links which had already been established between several institutions:
1. Tong Upper School (13–18 Comprehensive: roll 1,410)
2. Yorkshire Martyrs College (Roman Catholic Voluntary Aided: roll 950)
3. Bradford and Ilkeley Community College.

The consortium was aided by the fact that Tong Upper School and Yorkshire Martyrs College share a campus, which eliminated some of the problems that are encountered in schemes with a large geographical spread. Recruitment to the scheme was based upon 250 pupils per year joining in the Fourth Form, on a ratio of 160:90 from the two schools.

The most immediate effect of the resource allocation was the appointment of 28 additional members of staff (16 of whom were appointed to Tong School). An indication of Bradford's commitment can be seen by the fact that these posts were guaranteed as permanent appointments. In addition a Consortium Centre has been built where work on Information Technology, Electronics, CDT, Work Practice, Graphics and Community Studies can be carried out. There is also an Agriculture/Horticulture Centre, where students take responsibility for caring for sheep, cows, pigs and turkeys.

In the Bradford pilot the cohort was restricted to students drawn from the consortium establishments. However, within the establishments, every effort was made to ensure that there was no divisive 'two nations' ethos where an elite group was identified. For the general education component of TVEI all pupils were taught together and the groups were indistinguishable. This, of course, conflicts with the MSC stricture that TVEI students should be identifiable. Benefits from improved equipment, resourcing and staffing are enjoyed by all the students.

c. Curriculum
The injection of TVEI funds was seized upon as an opportunity to inject major changes into the curriculum. Inevitably there was a greater emphasis and wider choice than ever before in technical and vocational courses; new options included electronics, control technology, construction, the modern office, and agriculture and horticulture (MSC advise that vocational elements should reflect employment opportunities in the area).

One new activity which has had an effect both upon students themselves and on staff perceptions of the students as autonomous individuals, is the work practice scheme for the Fourth Year. In this module 25 students in turn took responsibility for organising and running a specific activity within the school. This could entail running a canteen – taking orders, purchasing raw materials, cooking the food, distribution, managing the finance etc. Other activities included reprographics, a repair workshop, electronics, office work, and in their last practice (each student has three placements per year), an enterprise scheme such as jewellery making.

In a more traditional Fourth Year curriculum it is unusual to find this degree of freedom for autonomous action and responsibility available for 14 year old pupils. The Head of Tong School was quite firm in stating that the abuse of such an opportunity is very rare indeed. Residential experience is compulsory and popular.

The opportunity to appoint new staff to augment those already in sympathy with TVEI made the introduction of wholesale innovation easier. The effect of teachers who had a particular interest or area of expertise was infectious.

In the words of the Head, 'perhaps the most significant change is that students are actually DOING more'.

Summary

TVEI has been a major influence for change in the 14–18 curriculum. The design and means of implementing courses has varied widely throughout the country; levels of funding have varied, as has the use which is made of that funding. Some schemes have been more adventurous than others, have broken the mould of traditional timetabling and introduced more integrated courses. TVEI extension sees the dissemination of TVEI practice and philosophy across the whole of the secondary and further education sectors.

What is beyond dispute is that the climate has changed; there is now greater awareness of the need for technology and information technology within the curriculum, of the benefits of links with industry, and on new ways of assessing students.

TVEI has encouraged the development of new courses, new ways of approaching the curriculum, new teaching styles and new ways of helping students to take more responsibility for their own learning.

Notes

1. David Young, Letter written to all LEAs, 1982.
2. TVEI Unit, *Supporting TVEI*, Manpower Services Commission, 1985.
3. See 2.
4. See 2.
5. DES/DofE, *Working Together: education and training*, HMSO, 1986.
6. See 2.
7. HMI, *Better Schools*, HMSO.

8. University of Leeds, *TVEI Curriculum 14–16: an interim evaluation report*, Manpower Services Commission, 1987.
9. Shirley Williams, article in *The Times*, March 25, 1986.

Chapter 2

TVEI-Related In-Service Training (TRIST)

TRIST (TVEI-Related In-Service Training) was a five term in-service training programme funded by Manpower Services Commission (MSC). It was designed for secondary teachers and Further Education lecturers, particularly those teaching students in the 14–18 age range.

Particular emphasis was placed on developing links with industry, on experience-based learning and on helping teachers to prepare students for an increasingly technological society.

2.1 Background

TRIST was officially announced with the publication of *Arrangements for the TVEI-Related In-Service Training Scheme (England and Wales)*[1] in April 1985. Introduction into schools and colleges was intended for September 1985. The short introductory period, which caused difficulties for LEAs, is not necessarily a bad thing – the need to meet deadlines tends to encourage decisive action. In view of some LEA's slow response, MSC could be considered justified in insisting on targets being met.

The basis of TRIST funding, which amounted to a total of £25 million, was contractual. Authorities made a submission, which MSC either accepted, rejected or sought to modify. Funding was allocated on the basis of that contract, and LEA's were required to fulfil the contractual obligations before receiving the next instalment.

It is interesting that TRIST should have been clearly identified as a forerunner of the new Grant-Related INSET (GRIST) which is administered by DES, while TRIST, with its TVEI roots was a Manpower Services Commission initiative.

One area in which TRIST differed significantly from other schemes is that it was not directed primarily at students – in fact the whole thrust was towards the in-service training of teachers, with no pupil involvement. This does not mean, of course, that the ultimate goal was not to alter students' experience of education, but that the means were different.

2.2 Aims

TRIST was specifically designed as a means of providing new or additional INSET. There was to be no approval for LEAs manipulating MSC funds in order to support in-service programmes already underway. As the guidelines to Authorities stated, it was:

> *'an interim, enabling scheme designed to stimulate new and/or additional in-service training and professional development programmes to promote developments ACROSS THE CURRICULUM of the kind envisaged in particular by the principles of TVEI'*[2]

Thus it was clear that the INSET devised should relate to TVEI – even in Authorities where TVEI did not exist. Contrary to expectation, some of the more imaginative schemes originated in LEAs not involved in TVEI.

The very fact that TVEI was so heavily emphasised in TRIST meant that attention was focused on implementing new approaches to INSET, and on encouraging familiarity with cross-curricular issues, experiential learning, and participative, school-focused INSET.

There is no doubt that part of the intention of TRIST was to expand teachers' expertise and their horizons, in the belief that this would have repercussions on students in schools and colleges.

Certain undeclared aims are also detectable: in addition to its role in preparing for the planned extension of TVEI, it is clear that TRIST created a pool of evangelists to preach the TVEI gospel. This helped to reduce resistance to TVEI extension. Allied to, but separate from this is the potential of TRIST as an agent for change. There can have been few initiatives which have touched as many practising teachers as this lavishly funded, short-term, but penetrating initiative.

2.3 Structure

TRIST's structure is less standardised than that of most of the initiatives reviewed in this book. This does not mean that the contracts which were drawn up between MSC and each LEA were not clearly defined. It is more that the nature of in-service delivery and content varied between Authorities. This was recognised and accepted by MSC – it was actually stated that:

> *'The proposals for additional support ...... shall be framed in the context of the in-service training currently undertaken by the Authority'.*[3]

Despite this flexibility there were, however, a number of caveats: only certain areas of training qualified for support, including technology, information technology, micro-electronics, business studies and physical science. Other subjects included: economic awareness, understanding of industry, careers education, assessment and profiling and the changes in vocational courses and qualifications. Equally as important as the content was training concentrating on process, and on new teaching strategies designed to encourage students to think for themselves and to take responsibility for their own learning.

It is these factors, then, which set the structure for TRIST, together with recommendations on the methods of training which should be employed. Methods included full-scale training programmes to up-skill teachers in shortage subjects, in-house work aimed at groups of teachers and lecturers working together, exchanges, both between schools and between school and industry, and LEA-based courses. The underlying theme emphasises the experiential aspects of the training, and the fact that school and FE staff should train alongside each other. (In many Authorities this was the most revolutionary idea of all.)

In practice there were almost as many different structures as there were programmes. They varied from the appointment of a co-ordinator (and often an assistant co-ordinator) who ran a series of courses covering various selected elements from the TRIST guidelines[4], to an Authority which adopted a 'Theme' approach, in which seven themes were identified for INSET. Each theme had a leader and a team of trainers, so that in the region of seventy teachers and lecturers were involved in the delivery of TRIST. In addition to any benefits which may have accrued to the teachers and institutions participating in the programme, the staff development potential for team members is something which should not be overlooked, and which could provide useful lessons for the future.

2.4 Criteria

Whilst LEAs were responsible for administering and planning the TRIST programme, they were required to meet certain criteria, and to ensure that the provision:

'i. is of high quality; to achieve this the necessary ingredients include: the careful identification of training needs by the teacher, the school and the LEA; training based on teachers' current levels of knowledge and skill, and delivered by appropriate methods; the support of the head/principal when new ideas and practices are introduced following training; and the careful evaluation and dissemination of successful developments.

ii. is focused on practice, enabling teachers to build upon existing expertise and to apply the lessons of training in the classroom.

iii. is followed up and translated into effective action at the appropriate level.

iv. offers value for money; administrative arrangements should enable cost-effectiveness to be kept under review.

v. is monitored and evaluated'[5]

Criteria for TRIST were, therefore, concerned with enhancing classroom practice by the provision of INSET which could quickly lead to change. It was also made clear that TRIST programmes should be thoroughly evaluated, and that LEAs were accountable for their expenditure.

2.5 Impact on individuals and organisations

a. Academic versus financial year

One of the major impacts of TRIST was occasioned by the fact that schools and colleges were required to respond to and initiate a major INSET programme in the middle of an academic year. This entailed major disruption. Even when TRIST was underway, MSC appeared not to have recognised the length of preparation time which schools need, or have traditionally expected, in order to plan and implement change.

It is not clear whether the mismatch between the academic year and the MSC's financial year was recognised but disregarded, or whether it was simply not realised that education worked to a different timetable. There is no doubt that TRIST's condensed lead-time, with little chance to adjust organisational factors, had a major impact in many institutions. Conversely, those which were sufficiently flexible to absorb and react to change were those best able to take advantage of TRIST.

The mismatch with the academic year was a factor at the end of TRIST as well as at the beginning. Programmes that were underway have benefited considerably from being allowed to run to the end of the summer term, whereas others came to an abrupt end on 31 March 1987.

b. Withdrawal of teachers from the classroom

The impact on institutions was particularly noticeable in those cases where teachers were used in the delivery of TRIST. The need to organise cover for key members of staff over a prolonged period meant a greater degree of disruption than that required for teachers who may only have attended INSET on a few occasions. Difficulties were increased where the trainer was a senior member of staff as certain tasks cannot be delegated to temporary replacements.

c. Increased staff expertise and confidence

However, the impact was not all negative; the school or college benefited from the trainers' increased experience and confidence. Perceptive Heads recognised this and exploited it to the full, accepting the drawbacks as part of the price paid for intensive staff development. This required foresight and a strong nerve, and it was understandable that some Heads opted for a much lower level of institutional involvement.

d. Supply cover

Perhaps the negative impact on institutions caused by major INSET programmes could be eased by finding a solution to the supply cover problem. If more INSET could take place in the evening and at weekends, this would answer staff development needs whilst minimising disruption to students. There is no overwhelming reason why teachers should not be paid for these extra hours. It would reward committed teachers, have an impact by producing more highly trained staff, re-vitalise the curriculum, and remove the threat to students' schooling.

2.6 Benefits

a. For Heads

For those Head Teachers who recognised the potential of TRIST, and were not threatened by yet one more initiative, TRIST offered the opportunity for development in what had been a largely static period resulting from teachers' industrial action. The wise Head seized this opportunity and used the available INSET to promote development not only of staff – the explicit aim of TRIST – but also the curriculum (which was not part of the TRIST remit).

Many teachers and Heads had long been concerned, quite irrespective of TVEI, with devising a curriculum which was more practical, experience-based and relevant to the needs and interests of young people. In harnessing the power of TRIST and promoting these ideas through the training of staff, Heads found that they could accelerate change.

For many Heads one of the main advantages of TRIST lay in the opportunity to change teachers' attitudes, expectations and classroom practice, and to revitalise the secondary curriculum. In some LEAs the TRIST programme was designed in such a way that it enabled Heads to exert control over the choice and clientele of courses. They also exerted greater influence over the INSET undertaken by their staff, taking into account the needs of the school or college. This was re-inforced by the TRIST emphasis on in-house work.

One interesting feature, which was certainly unanticipated, was the fact that in a time of teacher action, with no meetings and extra-curricular work taking place, many Heads had become isolated from staff. Extensive in-service work, funded by an outside agency providing supply cover for activities within school time, changed this. It legitimated meetings between the Head and staff in a way which had not been possible for some time. A number of Heads were grateful for this avenue of communication.

b. For teachers

TRIST arrived at a time when teachers' morale was at an all-time low. In addition to teachers' action the combination of economic stringency and falling rolls meant that opportunities for change and promotion were becoming ever more difficult. Teachers who took full advantage of TRIST (and the take-up was patchy, varying from those who did not participate in any activity to those who joined every course, conference and working party possible) experienced the chance to re-charge their batteries. They enjoyed the stimulation of sharing ideas and experiences with colleagues from other schools or within their own institutions and picking up new ideas and approaches to refresh their classroom experience. For many it was the first opportunity to consider different teaching strategies, to look at active learning methods and the benefits to be achieved by letting young people take more responsibility for their own learning. For many teachers the benefits lay in purely practical outcomes such as the discovery of teaching materials, methods and contacts to enhance their everyday teaching; others emerged with a determination to change their whole teaching style.

One of the benefits of TRIST valued by virtually all teachers who participated, was the luxury of being given time within the working day to work with colleagues on the curriculum needs of their own institution. To have embarked upon this model alone would have run the risk of TRIST emerging with a set of disparate activities with no overall strategy. Some central LEA direction was clearly necessary in order to avoid anarchy, but the expansion of in-house activities was valued, and will, without doubt, affect the pattern of INSET provision in the future.

c. For institutions

TRIST was, in the most successful cases, an agent for revitalising not only the staff, but the curriculum. Where the opportunity was grasped, there was a more significant change in a short period of time than could have been imagined. In particular, teachers with renewed vigour and commitment played an important part in changing the direction of their institution.

Wiltshire is an example of an LEA which used TRIST as a vehicle to effect change on an Authority-wide basis. Every secondary school was involved in a programme of review and INSET which resulted in the introduction of Records of Achievement. This co-ordinated programme made effective use of the avenues opened up by TRIST, and meant that the impact was felt not only by selected individuals, but by the whole of the LEA's institutions.

2.7 Disadvantages

a. For teachers

For some teachers TRIST posed a threat to existing practice and experience: 'I've taught this way for years – why should I change now?' In a way, the demand for change made them feel that their whole previous professional life was devalued. One teacher involved in a profiling project remarked that she had written perfectly adequate reports for twenty years and saw no reason to change now. What was significant in this case was the fact that a parent, on receiving his child's report complained to the school that the teacher's comments did not reflect what he had expected from a profile.

There is no doubt that for some teachers TRIST was seen as an unacceptable intrusion into their own professional competence and judgement. (The fact that challenge might have been a good thing is immaterial in terms of the individual's perceptions.)

The sheer unfamiliarity of the ideas and methods of delivery was confusing and unsettling for some teachers. Even those who were favourably disposed often found that the additional burdens and demands made by TRIST were heavy. In some cases, particularly for those involved in delivery of the programme, considerable inroads into evenings, weekends and holidays were the price paid for achieving results.

The problem of leaving classes in order to attend INSET grew in importance throughout the project, so that by the end of the time it was clearly a major disadvantage. It was a dilemma for those committed and forward-looking individuals who wanted to take advantage of the chance to develop and up-date their skills, yet felt a commitment to their pupils, who suffered as a result of being left with a succession of supply teachers.

This was a global problem for Heads who were faced with responsibility for ensuring continuity of work across the institution. In some cases, the disenchantment of the pupils manifested itself in unrest within the school. As one teacher put it: 'We are sacrificing this generation of pupils in the interests of those to come in future.'

It was also a logistical problem. TRIST demands reached a stage where supply teachers were virtually unobtainable. Even when they were, the quality of the substitution was, in many cases, unacceptably weak. To the deputy responsible for providing cover, TRIST became a burden involving an ever-increasing number of telephone calls in search of supply teachers.

b. For Heads and Principals

For many Heads the initial reaction was one of confusion. Some adopted an ostrich-like stance where they appeared to think that if they ignored it, it would go away. In many cases these Heads found themselves overtaken by events as INSET adopted a new character. In addition, they found themselves being prompted by staff who were aware of the changes and wanted to take advantage of them.

This was very threatening for some Heads who found the curriculum being steered in a direction with which they were unfamiliar. The number of applications for early retirement increased dramatically during this period; this was not solely due to TRIST, but TRIST was symptomatic of a new climate of change.

The biggest practical problem faced by Heads was undoubtedly the supply cover issue (see above) which was a real and continuing problem – it was splendid to have funding, but for many the issue was: 'First catch your supply teacher.'

c. For institutions

Many of the disadvantages for institutions have already been discussed above: schools and colleges faced disruption and confusion, with staff pulling in opposing directions. This was not universal; where a whole school strategy was evolved it had a strengthening influence.

There were problems associated with timetabling, and with coping with the demands which were made by different TRIST providers.

However, in many cases the full impact of TRIST was not recognised until it was too late to harness its power.

2.8 Political rationale

There are two clearly identifiable strands underlying the political rationale behind TRIST. Firstly there is the reinforcement of the Government's desire to direct educational developments along the lines already outlined in the TVEI chapter – more 'relevant', practical and experiential learning for pupils, geared to the needs of a rapidly changing technological society. Associated with this was the wish to encourage in teachers a more flexible, participative and experience-based approach to teaching and learning.

Whereas TVEI had been introduced as a pilot scheme, to be superseded by an extension programme, TRIST acted as an agent for bringing the philosophy and aims of TVEI to a vastly increased clientele, including Authorities which were not participating in TRIST. Thus it also acted as a 'softening up' process for the imminent TVEI extension. It was a clever strategy, which influenced teachers' receptiveness towards TVEI extension.

The second discernible strand lies in TRIST's relationship to GRIST. The concept of INSET for which bids must be made is such a radical change in established practice that for many who had worked under the old system, it was difficult to accept. TRIST provided a 'trial run': virtually all LEAs in the country were attracted to the carrot of relatively large sums of money which would transform the amount of inset available. They were forced to meet MSC deadlines and criteria for submission, and gained experience of entering into contracts which must be strictly adhered to, albeit within a fairly flexible framework. Although it was directed by a different body from that responsible for GRIST, it was nevertheless part of the overall strategy of central government. The fact that so many TRIST schemes resulted in work being continued under GRIST emphasises the relationship.

TRIST provided saturation exposure to new ideas and teaching strategies, leading to a more willing acceptance of TVEI extension. At the same time it eased the resistance of LEAs to a contract-based, centrally controlled move to the funding of INSET.

2.9 First-hand experience of TRIST: Cheshire TRIST programme

Cheshire's TRIST programme was designed with the very clear intention of changing teaching styles, and developing more experience-based learning.

a. Aims
The aims were:
- To develop more relevant and practical learning strategies
- To extend awareness of the classroom potential of new technology
- To establish/extend school/college liaison and to encourage a more outgoing curriculum in each sector
- To initiate/expand programmes of in-service education in each participating institution

b. Structure
In order to gain maximum impact from the resources available, initial involvement was restricted to twenty schools and colleges. Each institution nominated nine teachers who would become a significant agency for change within their institutions.

Each member of staff was offered eighteen in-service days, divided into four main areas:

i. Cross-curricular issues	– 5 days
ii. INSET relevant to the 9 'areas of experience'	– 5 days
iii. Industrial or educational attachments	– 5 days
iv. Time for dissemination	– 3 days

c. Programme
Whilst all 180 teachers (9 from each of the 20 institutions) could negotiate their own programme, there was a non-negotiable core consisting of three whole days. This core was probably the most influential in changing teaching styles and introducing teachers to new ideas for experiential learning. They were made up of:

Day 1 Communication
This day focused on teaching styles: the methods of communicating with students which teachers were accustomed to using. It called for a searching analysis of individuals' current practice, with the intention of using that information as the basis for change.

The Transactional Analysis model developed by Berne was chosen for this exercise.

Figure 2.1 illustrates a part of one of the exercises in which teachers participated. Figure 2.2 shows the synopsis of teachers' feedback.

PERSONAL BEHAVIOUR QUESTIONNAIRE

Below are some possible school situations, and you are asked to indicate which would be most likely to be your immediate response from those listed. There are no right answers, so it's best to indicate as spontaneously as possible without too much deliberation. You may say – "It depends how I'm feeling", but don't worry – just try to indicate according to how you usually feel.

Please put a ring round the appropriate letter for each situation, and don't go back to a question once you have answered it.

1. You realise that you are going to be a few minutes late for the start of morning school. Your immediate response is to:

    a) Blame the weather/traffic/etc., for delaying you.
    b) Feel anxious about what excuse to give when you arrive.
    c) Quickly think through the priorities for the day.
    d) Say "To hell with it – I've done my best".
    e) Make a quick phone call to ensure that someone looks after your tutor group.
    f) Mentally refine your excuse as you drive to work.

2. As you enter the classroom a pupil compliments you on your new shoes. Your immediate response is to:

    a) Look to return the compliment by saying something nice to the pupil.
    b) Feel pleased that someone has noticed.
    c) Ask yourself why everyone else can't be as pleasant as that pupil
    d) Say "Oh. What was wrong with the last pair ?".
    e) Say "thank you".
    f) Wonder if it is a sincere compliment or if there is an ulterior motive.

3. A pupil has failed to meet the deadline for handing in an important piece of exam coursework. Your immediate response is to:

    a) Say "Don't blame me when you fail the exam".
    b) Think of extenuating circumstances so that you can phone the exam. board.
    c) Worry that you hadn't structured the task sufficiently for the pupil.
    d) Worry about how the Headteacher/Head of dept. will react.
    e) Ask the pupil why the coursework has not been done.
    f) Criticise the pupil for not being prepared to work hard enough.

Fig. 2.1: Extract from Cheshire TRIST programme

4. A pupil leans back on a chair, topples over and bangs his/her head. Your immediate response is to:

   a) Use the incident to press for smaller class sizes.
   b) Think through the proper emergency procedures.
   c) Laugh and say "It serves you right".
   d) Tell the pupil to be more careful in future.
   e) Look around for people to help you.
   f) Rush over to ensure that the pupil is not injured.

5. You have arranged for a visitor to speak to your class. You escort the visitor to the classroom, only to find that it has been left in an untidy state by another group. Your immediate response is to:

   a) Hope that your guest doesn't think that you are responsible for the mess.
   b) Worry that your own class may lose valuable teaching time.
   c) Criticise the colleague you think was responsible.
   d) Seek an alternative classroom.
   e) Make out a case for ancillary helpers.
   f) Feel that it's going to be a bad day.

6. You are congratulated by the Head/Head of Dept. on some work done by the pupils in one of your classes. Your immediate response is to:

   a) Feel pleased that your efforts have met with approval.
   b) Consider whether that particular work merited such praise.
   c) Raise the topic of extra resouces for your subject.
   d) Want the pupils to be given credit too.
   e) Think "It's about time time someone noticed how much I do".
   f) Feel pleased that someone else shares your opinion of a good piece of work.

7. A colleague delays you by not completing your tutor group's reports on time. Your immediate response is to:

   a) Tell them not to worry, and to do them when they can.
   b) Tell them to do the reports as soon as possible as they are inconveniencing you.
   c) Call them a 'wally' and laugh it off.
   d) Decide to embarrass your colleague by telling other members of staff
   e) Ask them what the problem has been.
   f) Feel concerned that they may be overworked.

8. Someone detains you with details of their 'pet' scheme as you are on your way to a lesson. Your immediate response is to:

    a) Interrupt and explain to them that a class is waiting for you.
    b) Escape quickly by expressing great interest and suggesting that they should approach the Head with the scheme.
    c) Resign yourself to listening and arrive late for your lesson.
    d) Ask if there is some other time when you can meet them to discuss it.
    e) Make a quick joke and leave.
    f) Interrupt and tell them that you'll discuss it later.

9. You have something urgent to do and try to make time for yourself by setting some work for your class. A pupil complains that the work is too difficult - without appearing to have even tried it. Your immediate response is to:

    a) Tell them that you will give help only after they have made an effort.
    b) Curse quietly under your breath.
    c) Feel sorry for them and set an easier exercise.
    d) Abandon your plans and start to teach them.
    e) Express great surprise that they are having difficulty in the hope of motivating them to try for a little longer.
    f) Try to find out if there realy is a problem with the work.

10. You go for your break only to find that the coffee has run out. Your immediate response is to:

    a) Think who else in school may be able to lend you some.
    b) Blame someone else for not ordering enough.
    c) Feel it's your own fault for not getting there earlier.
    d) Think of an excuse to visit the school canteen.
    e) Curse under your breath (or out loud).
    f) Realise that other colleagues will want coffee and arrange to get a further supply.

11. A child bumps into you in the corridor. Your immediate response is to:

    a) Tell the pupil off for not looking where they were going.
    b) Discuss with the pupil, the possible dangers of running along corridors.
    c) Apologise and walk on.
    d) Use the incident to get the pupil to carry your books.
    e) Playfully jostle with the pupil before walking on.
    f) Ask the pupil whether or not they have been hurt.

Fig. 2.1 (cont.)

TVEI-Related In-Service Training (TRIST)

12. A pupil arrives at your lesson and reports that they have lost their pen and pencil. Your immediate response is to:

    a) Smile and say, "So what ?"
    b) Feel sorry for him/her and lend one of your own pens.
    c) Think "Why aren't children as careful as we were".
    d) Think "I could make a fortune selling pens - maybe I should buy some stock".
    e) Get them to think where they could have lost them.
    f) Feel upset that your careful lesson preparation has been ruined.

13. Yourself and a colleague have managed to double-book the video for the same lesson. Your immediate response is to:

    a) Worry that it was your mistake.
    b) Jokingly suggest that the two of you fight for it.
    c) Feel sorry for your colleague and let them have the use of it.
    d) Mentally run through alternative lesson plans.
    e) Quickly suggest a reason why you should be given priority.
    f) Blame the school for not having an alternative one available.

14. You are asked by the pupils to organise a disco/trip/etc.. Your immediate response is to:

    a) Tell them you have better things to do with your time.
    b) Feel flattered that they have chosen to ask you.
    c) Say "What a good idea".
    d) Feel sorry for them and agree to do it.
    e) Ask them exactly what they had in mind.
    f) Appear to be enthusiastic whilst thinking of an excuse.

15. A colleague tells you of a controversial proposal that he is about to put to the Head. Your immediate response is to:

    a) Think "Whats in it for me ?".
    b) Tell him not to be so stupid.
    c) Try to please him by agreeing/not-disagreeing with his idea.
    d) Make a joke about his promotion prospects.
    e) Tell him to be careful not to make any enemies among the staff
    f) Ask him how he plans to raise the issue.

SUMMARY OF FEEDBACK FROM DAY ONE ASSIGNMENT

The Assignment:

"Try analysing a lesson in terms of Transactional Analysis, looking at the messages and signals in the environment and lesson style. What does a teacher say and do, similarly, what do pupils say and do? Try to analyse atmosphere, and how discipline is handled".

Which lessons were observed?

- just about every type!
- most subjects
- the whole ability range
- the whole 11 - 19 age range.

Who was asked if they minded being observed teaching?

- mainly trusting friends who were susceptible to flattery!
- not <u>always</u> another TRIST teacher but when the colleague was also involved in TRIST then they watched each others lessons
- a colleague from the same department/another department depending upon time-tabling convenience.

What were the problems in setting it up?

- loss of free periods
- difficulty in arranging to see suitable lessons.

Were there any particularly successful arrangements?

- yes:- (a) School 'A' made time for pairs of teachers to view each others lessons. In some instances non-TRIST teachers were deliberately involved so as to begin the cascade process.

    (b) School 'B' made short video recordings of lessons taught by its TRIST teachers. The teachers then met, watched all the recordings and discussed them as a team.

How were the lessons observed?

- observers sat quietly at the side or back of the classroom
- video recordings were made of lessons

What observations were made?

- classroom arrangements
- words used
- tone of voice used
- body language
- movement within the classroom

How did the pupils react?

- some initial confusion and surprise was noticed but they quickly forgot the presence of the observer. (In one instance the teacher left the room - the pupils subsequent conversation and behaviour indicated that they had totally forgotten they were being observed).

Fig. 2.2: Extract from Cheshire TRIST programme

- Some inhibitions were reported
- in some cases pupils regarded the observer as a resource and drew him into the lesson
- some pupils were very perceptive of their teachers behaviour:-

    (a) one class commented that the teacher had moved between groups more than she normally did

    (b) appreciative comments were made regarding increased levels of practical activities.

What were the conclusions of the analysis?

- ego states are readily observable
- the shifts between ego states occured very quickly
- apart from occasional lapses people held ego states surprisingly constant
- all ego states can be seen but reality is more sophisticated than the model
- the initial ego state of the teacher is often CP or NP - to establish 'proper' relationships
- teachers preferred ego states tend to depend upon their expectations of the group:-

    eg - more CP noticable in lower school or lower ability lessons
      - more A noticable in upper school lessons.

How did people feel about the exercise?

- initially a mixture of apprehension and excitement
- enjoyment of a slightly artificial situation
- scepticism about the model
- an increased self-awareness, particularly in communications with pupils
- finally relief that their professional competence had been demonstrated (even though the exercise stressed <u>analysis</u> not judgement).

In conclusion

The exercise was generally regarded as having been worthwhile. Most teachers expressed interest in the lessons they had observed and welcomed the excuse to exchange techniques, to improve/adapt and learn from it.

It was also seen to promote curiosity in those members of staff other than the nine and so was a useful start to cascading.

Day 2   Learning and teaching styles

Building on the information about course members' teaching styles gained from Day 1, teachers took part in a number of assignments designed to explore alternative teaching styles. The emphasis was on helping teachers to recognise different preferred learning styles, and organising appropriate learning opportunities.

Part of one of the assignments used is reproduced in Figure 2.3.

Day 3   Management of change

Teachers were introduced to alternative models for introducing change into the classroom and the organisation. At the end of the course they were presented with an assignment to be carried out within the context of the TRIST programme. (See Figure 2.4.)

d. Attachments to industry and education

In view of the recurring interest in education/industry liaison throughout all of the 14–18 initiatives, it is helpful to look at one of the other areas making up Cheshire's TRIST provision.

Teachers had the opportunity to participate in a five day attachment either to industry, or to another educational establishment. Whichever option was chosen, the outcome was a broadening of experience which was invaluable in the classroom. Figure 2.5 indicates some of the attachments available in the programme.

e. Dissemination

Three days were set aside for course participants to disseminate their TRIST experience. Although this took place during industrial action, the institutions achieved a high level of participation in the dissemination process – always a problem with in-service training.

Each school or college produced a final report of their dissemination activity. Figure 2.6 reproduces the report of one of the TRIST schools.

By building time for dissemination into the programme, the involvement of other staff was assured, and hopefully laid the foundation for further development work on teaching styles and learning strategies.

Contact: Gordon Bell, TVEI Regional Adviser, TVEI Unit, Room 6, 7th Floor, Cardinal House, St Mary's Parsonage, Manchester M3 2NL.

Summary

TRIST is the only initiative described in this book which was launched with a finite, and relatively short life. This created difficulties, but also created a climate of urgency and purpose.

There is no doubt that TRIST stimulated new enthusiasm in many teachers, and caused LEAs to look carefully at their future INSET provision. After a

TVEI-Related In-Service Training (TRIST)

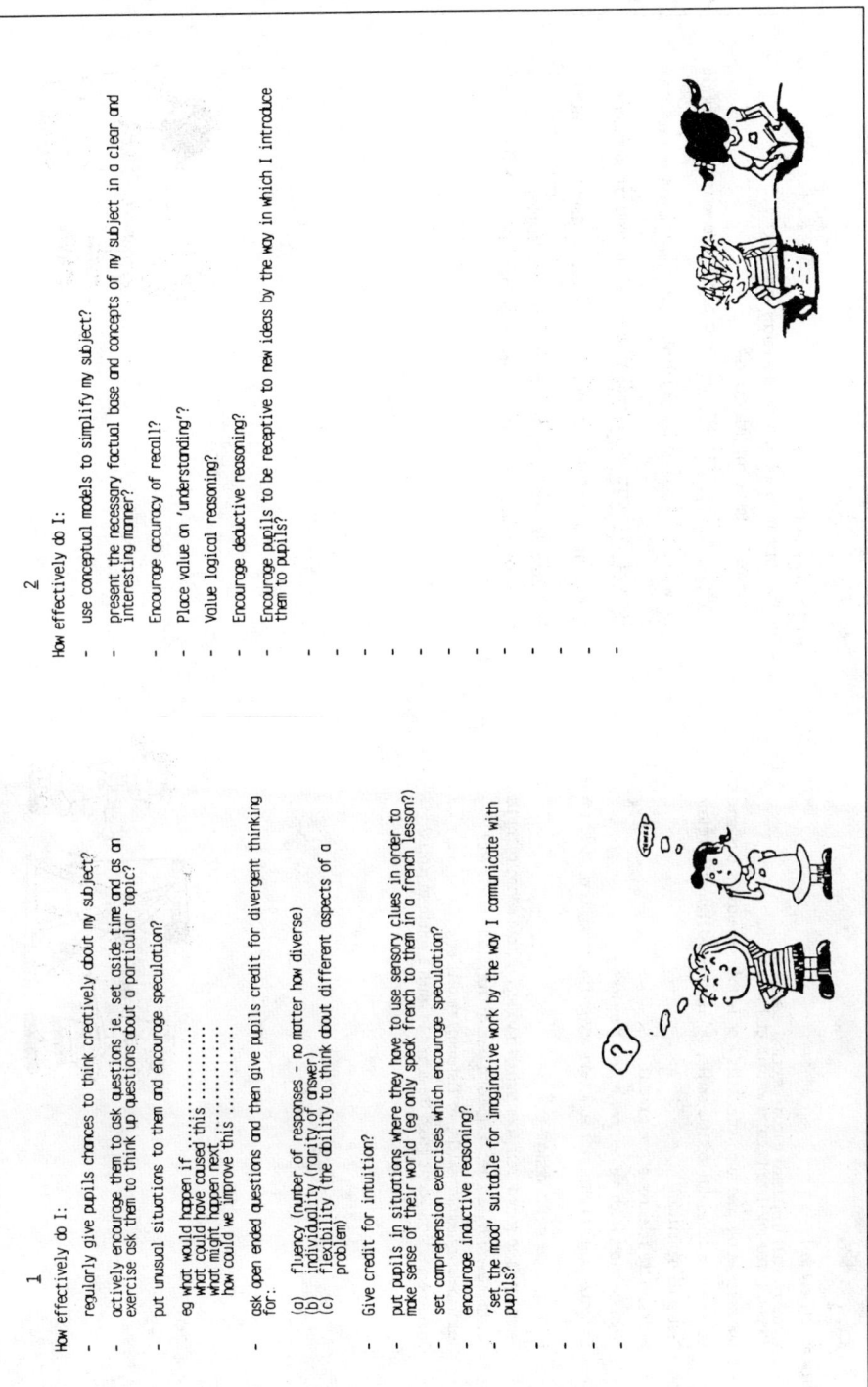

1

How effectively do I:

- regularly give pupils chances to think creatively about my subject?
- actively encourage them to ask questions ie. set aside time and as an exercise ask them to think up questions about a particular topic?
- put unusual situations to them and encourage speculation?

  eg what would happen if ....
  what could have caused this ....
  what might happen next ....
  how could we improve this ....

- ask open ended questions and then give pupils credit for divergent thinking for:

  (a) fluency (number of responses - no matter how diverse)
  (b) individuality (rarity of answer)
  (c) flexibility (the ability to think about different aspects of a problem)

- Give credit for intuition?
- put pupils in situations where they have to use sensory clues in order to make sense of their world (eg only speak french to them in a french lesson?)
- set comprehension exercises which encourage speculation?
- encourage inductive reasoning?
- 'set the mood' suitable for imaginative work by the way I communicate with pupils?

2

How effectively do I:

- use conceptual models to simplify my subject?
- present the necessary factual base and concepts of my subject in a clear and interesting manner?
- Encourage accuracy of recall?
- Place value on 'understanding'?
- Value logical reasoning?
- Encourage deductive reasoning?
- Encourage pupils to be receptive to new ideas by the way in which I introduce them to pupils?

Fig. 2.3: Extract from Cheshire TRIST programme

3

How effectively do I:

- encourage skill acquisition through practical exercises? (physical/speaking/listening/observational etc)
- Use exercises designed to promote skills - or is their development a by-product?
- Use exercises to develop specific skills, ie, is there skill discrimination?
- Test skill acquisition?
- Emphasise the relevance of the content?
- Teach exercises which are designed to test theories?
- Encourage pupils to plan their work (eg essay writing, draughting, field studies etc)?
- Encourage experimental design?
- Teach pupils to record their work through a variety of note making techniques?
- Set comprehension exercises designed to develop analytical skills etc?
- Teach specific learning skills, eg listening, recall, etc.
- Encourage practical work through the manner in which I relate to pupils?

4

How effectively do I:

- allow pupils to follow their own diversions in my work?
- Encourage initiative and independence?
- Encourage skills concepts and knowledge to be used in a variety of situations (ie out of their original context)?
- Allow pupils to make mistakes or follow 'blind alleys' as part of the learning process?
- Force pupils to critically examine and test their concepts and so encourage them to structure their own knowledge?
- Give credit to 'gut' feelings which may be correct but which have no basis in logic?
- Anticipate the resource implications of student led learning?
- Use my own communications skills to encourage initiative in pupils?

Fig. 2.3 (cont.)

ASSIGNMENT DAY 3

We wish to offer two assignments which can be used
to influence individual change, institutional
change.

A INDIVIDUAL ASSIGNMENT

Take any topic within your normal teaching situation which you will be introducing
to a particular group of pupils in the near future. You will find it helpful
to use the model from today to prepare yourself for likely effects from any
planned change.

Reconsider your approach considering not only your introduction of the topic but
also how you will vary your teaching style to cope with the different learning
styles of your pupils/students.

Obviously, you may find it valuable to repeat this throughout the set syllabus
or course planning your method of approach for each occasion.

You may like to ask a colleague to analyse one or more lessons to see how
successful you have been in developing and/or modifying your approach.

B INSTITUTIONAL ASSIGNMENT

Working with your INSET Co-ordinator and other TRIST school/college members,
formulate a proposal for institutional change using the model offered during
Day 3 and the experience you have gained from the individual assignments.

We would like your TRIST school/college Team to produce a paper suitable for
presentation to the senior management of your institution and we would wish
to consider these papers during the Inservice Day for INSET Co-ordinators
which we are planning for later this term.

Fig. 2.4: Extract from Cheshire TRIST programme

INDUSTRIAL ATTACHMENTS ORGANISED BY CHESHIRE TRIST			
DATES	PLACE OF ATTACH. & NO. OF STAFF		TOPIC
July 7-11	ICI, Winnington	(13)	Leading Effective Work Teams
Nov 3-7	UKF	(4)	Looking at the Schools/Industry Interface (Comparison of Learning Styles in School with 1st/2nd Years of Work)
Nov 17-21	ICI, Mond, Runcorn	(10)	Leading Effective Work Teams and Management Training
Nov 24-28	Central Training Unit	(12)	Leadership, Counselling and Work Shadowing
Nov 24-28	Daresbury Lab	(4)	Trainee Observation (To What Degree is School-acquired Body of Knowledge Transferable?)
Dec 1-5	ICI, Alderley Park	(8)	Leading Effective Work Teams and Management Training
Dec 1-5	Rolls Royce	(2)	Trainee Study & Management Comparisons
Jan 19-23	ICI, Winnington	(10)	Leading Effective Work Teams and Management Training
Jan 19-23	Pilkington	(1)	Looking at Apprentice Training
Jan 26-30	La Porte Industries	(2)	Evaluation of Apprentice Training Schemes
Feb 2-6	Halton Training Workshops	(1)	Evaluating MSC YTS Training Schemes
Feb 16-20	British Aerospace	(5)	Looking at Apprentice Training
March 2-5	Learning with Industry	(11)	Four Day Course with Heads/Advisers/ICI/TRIST. "The Management and Leadership of Change"
March 29-April 3	British Nuclear Fuels Ltd.	(5)	Management and Leadership Styles

Fig. 2.5: Extract from Cheshire TRIST programme

CHRISTLETON HIGH SCHOOL

TRIST CASCADE REPORT

After the first three days of common core training, the team meeting felt strongly that we should make moves to involve the rest of the staff is the central issues of TRIST before the impetus was lost in the long break of the Summer holidays. Until this point any 'cascading' had been done in an informal and adhoc way, or with other individual colleages within subject areas. The Team felt that a more organised programme should be launched, so we declared our personality types, learning and teaching styles and paired up with our opposite numbers to complement one another in our presentations. (The pairing was possible as the co-ordinator formed a tenth member of the Team).

The staff was divided into six groups, by our going through a staff list and selecting names of colleagues we felt we could work with. We were inadvertently doing part of the Management of Change exercise. Because of the lesser teaching loads, the senior teacher team member and the deputy head co-ordinator took on two groups. This meant groups of ten staff ie one TRIST team member per four colleagues (4 x 2 + 2). We decided to carry out the cascading in teaching time made available by Upper Sixth and fifth year being examination groups, who had left, which helped us to store up a credit of supply time. So after two planning sessions we covered aspects of Day 1, Transactional Analysis, and the first stages of Day 2 'Learning and Teaching Styles' using many of he group exercises we had experienced on our days of training. The main limitation was the lack of time. One hour to cascade a whole days training. There was some diffidence expressed among team members about their suitability to cascade. Posing as 'expert' in front of ones colleagues, especially before ones senior colleagues, was a little nerve-wracking and daunting. However, the concepts were received enthusiastically and positively by those whom we expected to be cynical, so our confidence was somewhat boosted though our own feeling of credibility still a little in doubt.

At least we felt we had grasped the nettle and involved the <u>whole</u> staff, Head and part-timers alike, in the TRIST training scheme.

On the return to school in September we wanted to use the Inhouse conference method of whole school involvement to tackle the 'Management of Change' topic. A proposed institutional change had been in the pipeline since 18 months previously which had involved a change in the pastoral grouping in the first year from ability bands to mixed ability form groups. This development was abruptly curtailed by industrail action, as meetings and discussion groups had been halted for over a year. As the new scheme would involve a re-consideration of the pupils with Special Educational Needs in School, which had been the topic of our previous Inhouse conference, it seemed an ideal issue to marry to the theory and exercises behind ' Management of Change'. After some planning with Gordon Bell, Bill Harrison and the Senior Team in school we were fortunate enough to book Dr Mike Woods for our actual day who had been one of the providers on the TRIST training day for the Team members. Mike Woods gave a day of his time to help prepare the day with Bill and I, and then came to the school in advance too, in order to place the programme in context. Before the Inhouse conference on the last day

Fig. 2.6: Extract from Cheshire TRIST programme

of the October half term, the team wanted to set the mood and cascade the rest of the 'Learning and Teaching Styles' training day. Once more, we got our 'double acts' together and again, in two hourly sessions, working with the same groups as July, we presented to the rest of the staff 'Learning and Teaching Styles' which completed the run-in and revived interest.

The conference day was a success but followed the 'change psychology' almost exactly moving from shock/elation to retrenchment, but time for consideration and reflection following that day, reports from the six cascading groups and individual questionnaires, have resulted in a balanced and solid view of what the staff think and feel. To consolidate group work the TRIST 'common core' booklets were reproduced as a booklet for all staff. Subsequent training days and industrial attachments remain 'uncascaded', the last days of training have been completed only last week by one team member. The time scale for our institution was too telescoped, especially with rivalry from GCSE which most staff naturally see as a priority. Some supply time will therefore be lost despite strenuous efforts to extend into April our period of cascading which would have allowed us some space to reflect.

However, the Team has not lost time in gathering thoughts. Two whole day team meetings have been devoted to this and to future plans which are listed below. We never envisaged the project lasting eighteen months. We feel the need to continue as a team in the future and to proceed with cascading all the opportunities which TRIST has offered us. The raising of awareness is a responsibility which we feel we share, and the strength of the team in mutual support will ensure that the individual experience will not be lost in the inevitable daily machinations of the institution. There are so many lessons for GRIST in this TRIST project which have only been touched on here. Given more time for consideration this report will become an instrument for implementation, which at its simplest but most important level will improve the already good quality of what we provide in the classroom.

THE FUTURE

1. PRIORITIES

Modular Education
Negotiated Curriculum
Extension of Transactional Analysis
Need for Experimentation
Return to exercises from earlier training days
Cross Curricular approaches
Experiential Learning
Counselling/Listening Skills   )
Professional Review for whole staff   )Underlying themes
Team Building-Status of Individual   )from
Leadership - Decision Making - Involvement)Industrial Attachments
Communication - Shared Responsibility   )
Learning - Working Environment

Fig. 2.6 (cont.)

2. **METHODS OF CASCADING FOR FUTURE USE**

TRIST team intact
Inhouse Conference
Use of Expertise outside Education
Use of 5th - Upper Sixth Teaching
Time after Whitsun
Days 4 and 5 booklets - copy for all staff
Use of Video - a compilation and connected experience - process in classroom
Use of Team Member in Department/Faculty Meetings
Faculty Days ('at homes') - 5 INSET Days?
Identifying areas
Raising Awareness (not opposition) informally by filter system
Emphasis on How (methodology) not What (course content etc well defined already)
Use of TRIST team in current Working Parties in School
Cascading Senior Team (Hierarchy).

3. **CONSIDERING HIDDEN CURRICULUM/AGENDA OF OUR INSTITUTION**

Bells
Standards
Trust
Sixth Form
Assemblies
Supply cover (quality, frequency)
Boy/Girl
Access to information
Guilt - responsibility, being in control, removal of classroom experience

G White
March 1987

prolonged period of teacher action, the opportunity to participate in innovative in-service education was, in the main, greeted with enthusiasm, and led to many changes in schools and colleges.

Teachers who had not been exposed to TVEI were largely convinced that it did not have to mean narrow vocational courses, but could, and should, mean a broad and balanced curriculum.

Those LEAs with coherent, planned programmes appeared to gain most from TRIST – which also drew attention to the importance of flexible and responsive LEA structures, and extended the notion of funding through contracts.

Effects on students varied according to the success of the specific TRIST programme in their area but, overall, considerable progress was made in introducing more young people to practical, experience-based learning.

Notes

1. TRIST Unit, *Arrangements for TVEI-Related In-Service Training Scheme*, MSC, 1985.
2. TRIST Unit, *Guidelines to Authorities* MSC, 1985.
3. See 2.
4. See 2.
5. See 2.

Chapter 3

The Certificate of Pre-vocational Education (CPVE)

The Certificate of Pre-vocational Education is a one year, full-time course of general and pre-vocational education for post-sixteen students in schools and colleges.

3.1 Background

The Certificate of Pre-Vocational Education (CPVE) is a DES initiative which results from pressures which had been increasing since the 'Great Debate' in 1976[1]. It was noticeable that the Government's call for more 'relevant' courses gave credibility to some of the tentative approaches to new teaching styles and content being attempted by a small kernel of teachers, particularly those running pre-vocational education courses. In a number of authorities this extended to Chief Education Officers requesting Head Teachers to devise more vocationally oriented courses (initially for Sixth Form pupils).

Some schools developed their own 'pre-employment' courses whilst others turned to existing courses offered by examination boards; these include City and Guilds, Business and Technician Education Council (BTEC) and the Royal Society of Arts (RSA). At around the same time, the publication of a seminal document on vocationally oriented education added weight and influence to the movement. *A Basis for Choice* (the Mansell Report)[2] advocated an integrated approach to education and training, with courses offering general education through a vocationally biased content. This report was the forerunner not only of the growth in pre-vocational education, but also of developments such as profiling, the negotiated curriculum and experiential learning.

A Basis for Choice[3] was an FEU publication directed primarily at the further education sector. It took a little time for the message to percolate to schools, but with growing awareness of the urgency of providing a more palatable diet for post-sixteen pupils, and with the increasing proliferation of pre-vocational courses, the Government looked seriously at possibilities for a more satisfactory, coherent pattern to post-sixteen' non-'A' level provision.

Coincident with the Mansell Report, the Keohane Report (1979)[4] recommended a single subject approach with some vocational options. This attracted considerable attention but did not gain any substantial following, particularly when its recommendations were compared with the more forward-looking Mansell report.

1980 saw the publication of *Examinations 16–18*[5] which outlined the issues surrounding the development of post-sixteen provision, and sought answers to the question of how one-year courses should be developed.

In 1982 the DES issued a policy statement, *17+ : A New Qualification*[6] which stated that existing qualifications for the post-sixteen, non-'A' level student did not meet the needs of young people. In addition to inadequacies in the curriculum on offer, it was recognised that the bewildering assortment of qualifications served neither student nor employer. A framework encompassing pre-vocational education was proposed which would subsume all existing qualifications, and ensure currency and credibility. The need to consider the relationship with YTS (Chapter 3) and TVEI (Chapter 1) was also identified.

In May 1983 the City and Guilds (CGLI) and the Business and Technician Education Council (BTEC) examination boards were invited by the DES to set up the Joint Board for Pre-vocational Education. Their remit was to develop an over-arching qualification with provision for 17+ students as a priority. September 1985 was the deadline for the first courses. It was decided that it would be most useful to build on existing courses such as BTEC General Award and Technician Studies Courses, the CGLI Foundation and Vocational Preparation (General) 365 Courses, and the Royal Society for Arts (RSA) Vocational Preparation (Clerical and Distribution) and Basic Clerical Procedures.

This was intended to reassure the 'customers' that there would be no sudden break between the existing system (which was still new to many teachers) and the proposed Certificate of Pre-vocational Education (CPVE). In fact, during the pilot year, arrangements were made for students following CGLI and BTEC level one courses to receive certification for CPVE as well.

May 1984 saw the publication of the Consultative Document[7] (known as 'the red book') issued by the Joint Board. This outlined the new proposals. There followed an intensive consultative phase which was completed in August 1984. One problem was that LEAs wishing to pilot CPVE were required to make their bids on the basis of the consultative document. Piloting in 14 LEAs began in September 1984, whilst final details of the framework were not available until early in 1985. It was an interesting experience for teachers and students who had already embarked upon CPVE to discover radical changes in some aspects of their course, whilst details of the profile, a mandatory element in CPVE, were not available until late in the year. Because of late publication of the framework, schools had to adapt considerably during the course.

CPVE was launched nationally in September 1985. It was the first course with national certification designed specifically to cater for students both in schools and colleges, and paved the way to a new concept of education at 16+ whereby young people could choose between the same qualification offered in different institutions, or even in some cases, shared between both school and college.

3.2 Aims

The official aims of CPVE as stated in the 'Blue Book'[8] are that CPVE should:
  i. assist the transition from school to adulthood by further equipping young people with the basic skills, experiences, attitudes, knowledge and personal and social competences required for success in adult working life
 ii. provide individually relevent educational experience which encourages learning and achievement
iii. provide young people with recognition of their attainments through a qualification which embodies national standards
 iv. provide opportunities for progression to continuing education, training and/or work

In some cases the initial aims have been modified or even abandoned. For instance, in the early days of preliminary discussion, not only was it anticipated that young people with a generous clutch of 'O' levels would opt for CPVE, but also that it should form part of the preparation for or progression to 'A' level; this has been slow to materialise.

Whilst the aims listed above are explicit, there are also a number of implicit aims concealed within the framework and criteria for approval of schemes. These include Sir Keith Joseph's (then Secretary of State for Education) call for an educational system which takes into account the principles of 'breadth, relevence, differentiation and balance' (Nottingham, January 1984), and the realistic preparation for an understanding of adult roles in society. These implicit aims are fostered by the inclusion of compulsory work experience as part of every student's programme.

Other aims implicit within CPVE encourage teachers to adopt new strategies and teaching styles: this is reinforced by the requirement for integration of Core and Vocational studies for at least 20% of the time, and for delivery through a team approach. For a course with these parameters to succeed, it is essential that there is a dynamic learning environment. The requirement for regular review and assessment of achievements through formative profiling introduces new procedures for student assessment, putting into practice the ideas of *A Basis for Choice*. These elements of experiential, negotiated learning and student profiling are undoubtedly affecting teaching in other areas of the curriculum.

One way of discovering the implicit, rather than the explicit aims of CPVE lies in the instructions to moderators visiting schools and colleges. Areas identified for particular attention include checking that the overall structure of the course complies with that laid down by the Joint Board; importance is placed upon the degree of integration, the quality and quantity of the work experience offered, and upon progression.

Other factors to which the Joint Board ask moderators to pay attention are the assessment and pre-selection of students, the publicity to which they are exposed, and details of their induction into the CPVE programme. All of this reinforces the concern of those who believe that pre-vocational education should expose young people to a relevant and motivating experience which helps to prepare them for the complex, changing world outside school and college. Few people would dispute this aim of CPVE; perhaps the greatest question centres on whether CPVE is not too little (failing to reach a large proportion of the target group at the upper end of the academic achievement scale) and too late (why should these experiences be restricted to post 16 students?).

3.3 Structure

3.3.1 Course and design

The course offers a one-year, full-time programme occupying between 700 and 900 hours. There must be a balance of Core, Vocational and Additional studies. (But, although institutions must **offer** Additional Studies, it is not mandatory for students to choose them.)

a. Core
The core is made up of:
  Personal and Career Development
  Industrial, Social and Environmental Studies
  Communication
  Social Skills
  Numeracy
  Science and Technology
  Information Technology
  Creative Development
  Practical Skills
  Problem Solving

It was encouraging that the FEU's evaluation of pilot schemes found that teachers had little difficulty in delivering the core. This indicates that many teachers were able to make the transition from subject-based to cross-curricular work. FEU did point out, however, that learning ojectives should not be treated as a syllabus, but should be applied across a range of situations, and selected according to individual student needs.

The Certificate of Pre-vocational Education (CPVE)

b. Vocational

Vocational modules provide the vehicle for the vocational elements of CPVE, and include areas as diverse as ceramics, farm and garden machinery, technical services, business and administrative services and water and gamekeeping.

Vocational modules can be studied at three levels: Introductory; Exploratory; Preparatory.

The intention is to use a vocational focus to enhance the broad base of general education offered in the core. It is designed to increase awareness and to develop flexibility in preparation for the world of work. Some institutions have fallen into the trap of only offering options in which they have a reservoir of expertise. This is understandable, but does mean that students' choices are limited. It woud be better to liaise with neighbouring institutions in order to offer sufficient breadth.

It is counter-productive to offer courses which bear no relation to local employment prospects. Although CPVE is not intended as vocational training leading to guaranteed employment, it undermines the credibility of the course if there is no discernible path for progression to employment or further education.

c. Additional studies

This can be made up of a range of academic, leisure or extension studies. In practice, many students opt for additional examination subjects: they may wish to improve existing qualifications, or to study new areas. Most schools and colleges include leisure activities.

The structure should:
- permit Core and Vocational Studies to continue for the whole duration of the course
- provide a range of Additional studies which must not occupy more than 25% of the total course time
- allow all students the opportunity to experience and improve their attainments in all Core aims
- be designed with vocational studies occupying at least 25% of the time for Core Vocational Studies, and allow students to:
    (i) attempt at least FOUR vocational modules
    (ii) start Vocational Studies with at least ONE Introductory module (unless they have already achieved the purpose of Introductory modules elsewhere)
    (iii) undertake Exploratory modules either before or concurrently with Preparatory modules
- ensure the integration of Core and Vocational Studies for a minimum of 20% of course time
- contain at least 15 days of real or simulated work experience
- be designed to provide opportunities for students to progress into continuing education and/or employment

3.3.2 *Assessment, guidance and counselling*

All courses must:
- have arrangements for initial assessement of students to ensure entry to an appropriate programme
- have arrangements for in-course assessment and review of student achievement, and opportunities for negotiating their programme of study. This will involve the keeping of records through a formative profiling system.

3.3.3 *Staffing, resourcing and staff developments*

All courses must:
- involve a team of teachers whose work will be co-ordinated by a named co-ordinator
- make provision for regular team meetings
- be adequately resourced in terms of staff, equipment and materials
- be supported by a programme of staff development

These headings indicate the priorities identified by the Joint Board[9] which reinforce the need for team planning, integration, profiling and effective careers guidance. Supportive staff development is essential.

3.4 Criteria

3.4.1 *Central requirements*

It is a feature of CPVE that quite stringent criteria must be met before approval of the scheme is granted. One of the reasons for this lies in the desire of the Joint Board to ensure that the spirit of CPVE is honoured. This is important as everyone who completes the course receives the qualification. It is, therefore, a way of accrediting the providing centre rather than examining the individual candidate.

Criteria for approval focus on three key areas: course structure and design; assessment, guidance and counselling; staffing, resourcing and staff development (see 3.3).

3.4.2 *Individual requirements for institutions*

a. Scheme co-ordinator
The first major requirement for any organisation is the identification of a CPVE Co-ordinator, and a CPVE Scheme Management Group. This is a

departure from traditional practice in most schools and colleges. The Co-ordinator has overall responsibility for co-ordinating, implementing and operating the scheme, and for liaison with the Joint Board. In practice this often means encouraging and supporting other members of staff, possibly even providing resources and materials suitable for use on the course. It frequently involves all administrative duties concerned with CPVE and with the organisation of staff development. The success of the scheme, the nature of integration and collaboration depend heavily on the capability of the Co-ordinator as an efficient administrator and as a leader.

b. Scheme management group

The identification of an individual with overall responsibility for delivering the programme was not unusual in earlier pre-vocational courses. What is new in CPVE is the accompanying requirement for a Scheme Management Group. The Management Group is ultimately responsible for the co-ordination of the CPVE scheme within the centre; this applies to single institution schemes where co-ordination consists of ensuring effective liaison between departments, overseeing the nature of integration and the schemes adherence to the framework. It also applies to Consortia schemes where it is necessary to maintain a clear overview of the programme which is delivered on physically separate sites.

The most effective management groups are those which include representatives from outside agencies such as the careers service and employers so that they can contribute to the design and delivery of the programme. In view of the emphasis on careers education and links with the world of work, this seems to be an invaluable extra resource which should be exploited (see chapter 9).

c. Timetabling

CPVE makes demands of the timetabler. The institution must, for instance, take into account the requirement that regular team meetings are timetabled – an excellent means of ensuring integration and a valuable staff development tool, but costly in terms of the hard-pressed institution.

Implicit in assessment and profiling procedures is the requirement for timetabled review sessions. The institution must also adapt timetabling for CPVE to accommodate the longer blocks of time necessary to put the CPVE philosophy of experiential learning into practice.

d. Resources

In addition to the resource implications of the timetabling requirements there is the cost of providing small rooms for student counselling. A CPVE base must also be provided and adequately equipped. This is not an insurmountable obstacle – in one school without any provision, staff and students devoted several weekends to converting and decorating an old storeroom, and begged equipment from local employers. In the present climate of teacher industrial relations it is probably unrealistic to depend unduly on this type of commitment.

e. Teaching styles
A factor which is often overlooked in the debate about in-service training to change teacher attitudes is that there are cost implications in the new styles of delivery. These can include the need for smaller classes, appropriate surroundings and facilities, and opportunities for one-to-one negotiation. This has significant implications for the institution embarking on CPVE. Chalk and talk may have been boring, but it was certainly cheaper!

f. Meeting the criteria
CPVE criteria make demands on the institution which are present from before the onset of the scheme and persist throughout the year. Schools and colleges need to consider:
- how the timetable demonstrates a balance of components
- what learning strategies are to be used to implement the programme
- methods to ensure integration
- organisation of core and vocational studies throughout the year
- sufficient flexibility of vocational options
- the integration and organisation of work experience
- assessment and profiling arrangements
- progression and links with local employers
- details of opportunities for student review

All of these factors, in addition to the key question of staffing, staff development and team meetings have implications for the individual institution above and beyond the national criteria laid down by the Joint Board.

3.5 Impact of CPVE on organisations

The extent of CPVE's initial impact on organisations depended largely on the degree of experience in existing pre-vocational courses. It was less of a culture shock for those schools and colleges which had already taken on board the messages emanating from the initiatives referred to in 3.1. However, this was not necessarily the best preparation for CPVE: new initiatives meriting a bold, fresh approach to timetabling, team teaching and participative learning strategies can often be more successfully introduced in a climate of sweeping change. On the other hand, those schools and colleges which had embarked upon imaginative courses not merely tied to examination syllabuses, had a pool of teachers already willing to consider and implement the principles advocated in CPVE.

a. Teaching methods

There is little doubt that the greatest change called for in CPVE, and the one which had the greatest impact in institutions was a radical change in teaching styles. There was (and is still) a majority of teachers and lecturers for whom teaching means standing at the front of a class and delivering a prepared lesson. This didactic approach goes against the ethos of CPVE, yet it is asking a great deal of teachers who may have been 'successfully' using this method for many years to change their teaching styles in a matter of months.

For those who had already adopted an assignment-based approach to learning, with students working at their own pace, the change was not so drastic. Active Tutorial Work and the movement towards experiential learning has helped, but there is no doubt that for many involved in the pilot programme, and later in the first national programmes, the concept of student-centred learning was completely alien.

b. Timetabling

In purely practical, administrative terms, the spectre of the timetable loomed large in the design of most CPVE schemes. The traditional format of seven or eight separate periods per day is certainly not suitable for effective implementation of CPVE: the CPVE co-ordinator is well advised to make a friend, and if possible a convert, of the timetabler. The curriculum should not be the slave of the timetable. In the schemes where co-operation in design of the curriculum and timetable has been firmly established, a far more coherent programme has resulted.

Many of the most successful schemes adopted a block system of timetabling, with either a four, three, or in the most adventurous, a two period day. This makes the tackling of integrated assignments, of running a mini company, and of organising work experience, a far more practical proposition. Once more, however, it has repercussions on teaching styles. Half-day sessions call for a different approach from 35 minute periods; they demand more in terms of teacher preparation, confidence and flexibility. The outcome has proved challenging and exciting for many teachers, but has also been a worrying and stressful experience for some. The students, too, have had to adjust to a new system of large blocks of time in which they are expected to take responsibility for much of their own education. The transition is often as difficult for them as for the teacher!

One useful strategy adopted by some institutions has been the timetabling of work experience for one day every week. This has the advantage of easing timetabling constraints, and also helps the student by providing links with the real world of work throughout the course. The disadvantage from the student's point of view is a reduction in the 'reality' of the experience through not maintaining a continuous contact with their placement over a two week period.

c. Financial implications

In contrast to the considerable funds poured into TVEI, CPVE was launched, and has continued to run, on virtually a nil budget. No central funds were provided for either materials, capital equipment, the provision of CPVE bases or for additional staffing. However, in most cases there was a generous central provision for in-service training. As a result, many LEAs mounted intensive courses to prepare teachers for the advent of CPVE, and in general the feedback on in-service support has been favourable.

d. In-service training

It is clear from the earlier sections of this chapter that the demands made upon teachers and institutions to rethink their philosophy, practice and organisation was so great that substantial in-service support was an essential prerequisite.

Nationally, the Further Education Unit was given a brief to support staff development through a network of ten Regional Curriculum Bases (RCBs); this was supplemented by the regular publication of CPVE newsletters providing a forum for updating information and regular communication and contacts. In addition to the regional training offered by the RCBs, most LEAs took advantage of the DES funding available for INSET and in many cases supplemented this through the LEA budget.

A typical example of the pattern of provision is illustrated by one Authority which offered 20 day courses for teachers from institutions which had received Joint Board approval. These varied from patterns of one day a week for twenty weeks, to blocks of several consecutive days at intervals. The style and content of this INSET has changed over the period since CPVE was first introduced. In the early days the writing of the submission for Joint Board approval was an overwhelming concern for teachers about to be plunged into leading the initiative within their school or college. Working together in teams to produce this was a legitimate function of INSET. The other major priority was the encouragement of flexible, participative and experiential approaches to delivery of the programme.

Whilst this latter element is still of prime importance, inevitably more and more teachers are coming from institutions which have had experience of running CPVE, and new modules are incorporated into the training. At the forefront of these is the inclusion of industrial placements. If the emphasis in CPVE is upon preparation for the world outside school, upon vocational orientation and upon careers education and counselling, it is an anomaly for the teachers leading the programme to have no first-hand experience, however limited, of work outside the teaching profession. In an ideal world, no teacher of pre-vocational education should be allowed to teach on a course without such experience.

Preparation for teaching on a course which lays stress upon integration and teamwork naturally takes every opportunity to encourage this attitude in its in-service training. This has been the attempt in CPVE training – the course

The Certificate of Pre-vocational Education (CPVE)

which talks about a negotiated curriculum and then proceeds to deliver a pre-determined package quickly loses credibility. The best CPVE INSET has taken this into account and has adopted a negotiated course content, delivered in such a way that participants learn through experience, and work in collaborative teams.

Many teachers who have benefited from the twenty day training have commented that the insight they have gained has had an effect upon their teaching on more traditional courses. This, perhaps, may prove to be one of the most important side-effects of CPVE.

3.6 Benefits

a. For students

Benefits include the chance to enjoy a real alternative to the old, rather sterile diet offered to post-sixteen students, which usually centred on re-taking examinations. Students may still wish to improve their grades in examinations, but they do it as one option in a coherent pre-vocational education programme.

The FEU, in their evaluation of pilot schemes[10] reported that students felt that the freedom and vocational relevance of their courses were a distinct advantage over their previous experience of school. They were particularly motivated by the inclusion of work experience.

Many students participating in CPVE for the first time felt that they benefited from the vocational studies element of the course because of its relevance to their career ambitions, and to preparing them for adult life.

This matches the aims of CPVE and whilst students are not universally complimentary (see 3.7), it does seem that the benefits of providing a relevant curriculum, better able to motivate young people and to prepare them for their role in society, are meeting with a degree of success.

A recurring theme when talking to young people involved in CPVE is that they appreciate being treated like adults. This is encouraging, but it does raise the question of why it is not possible to enable youngsters on other courses to feel the same way.

A common feature of CPVE courses is the noticeable growth in the autonomy of students as they develop confidence and skills to organise and take responsibility for their activities.

b. For teachers

The benefits include the opportunity to experiment and develop new courses that would previously have proved impossible. Despite the fairly prescriptive criteria laid down for acceptance into CPVE, the method and design of the curriculum offers a generous degree of flexibility, which many teachers have found stimulating.

Allied to this, and increasing the feeling of excitement which is often generated by teachers talking about CPVE, is the opportunity to work with colleagues through the provision of CPVE INSET.

Another aspect of staff development is the chance for teachers who may have been in danger of becoming stale to aquire new skills, new insights, and new relationships with students. One teacher close to retirement age said: 'It's the first time I've really had the chance to get to know my pupils as individuals.' On a more prosaic level, many teachers have benefited in career terms by being able to add experience in a new field to their curriculum vitae.

c. For institutions
Benefits often centre around the ability to satisfy what is a clearly expressed need on the part of the clients. Education has to face the realities of market forces when schools and colleges are faced with students who have a choice, particularly when that choice includes a financial incentive as in the case of YTS.

Needs-based provision can focus not only on the benevolent desire to do the best for students, but also upon the needs of the institution to attract customers in times of falling rolls and teacher redeployment.

Other benefits include the effect of new teaching styles which can motivate teachers with a consequent effect upon teaching in other areas of the curriculum.

3.7 Drawbacks

a. For students
Some students find the need to think for themselves is a disadvantage rather than a benefit. They are not ready to give up the security of being told what to do and how to do it. Appropriate guidance and positive experience of succeeding in the course usually helps to overcome these fears.

Students cannot always study the options they choose; there may be a shortage of specialist teachers, or a timetable clash which means that they are disappointed, and possibly disillusioned by CPVE's failure to meet their expectations.

Two year YTS affects students' choice of CPVE. If they opt for one year in the Sixth Form, it means that they forego not only the financial reward offered by YTS, but also half of the training opportunity. This links with another problem facing students: progression from CPVE has always been an issue. It was intended that there should be clear routes of progression from the certificate, but this has not been the experience of many students.

Individualised learning, the key to many successful schemes, is not always without problems for the students. Its success depends heavily on the quality of the teaching. In one school with a Business Studies option, the CPVE group were required to take the same worksheet, and to type it at the same

The Certificate of Pre-vocational Education (CPVE)

time. The teacher then collected them in and marked them. This is not what students are led to believe they will experience in CPVE.

b. For teachers

Treating the students as adults, heralded as one of the great benefits of CPVE, is not a benefit for some teachers. It strikes at the heart of their accustomed teaching style and poses a serious threat. The change in teacher-student relationships is also threatening and while most teachers enjoy the change, some teachers are never able to adjust.

Team teaching, cross-subject collaboration and planning are important parts of CPVE. Some teachers are accustomed to complete autonomy within their classroom, with no 'interference' from outside. The idea of allowing other colleagues into their lessons is unthinkable and challenges the basis of their professional lives.

Many of the problems associated with CPVE are linked with teachers failing to understand what it is about, or with their failing to adapt to the needs of the course.

Almost all of these problems are caused by fear – of the unknown, and of change. The most effective way of overcoming the problems lies in supportive in-service training and experience of the scheme. Problems are rarely as severe in the second year of the programme as they are in the first.

c. For institutions

Management must be flexible and open to new ideas if it is to be able to introduce a worthwhile CPVE scheme. Timetabling, staffing and accommodation make demands upon the organisation. Even the setting up and running of mini-companies as part of the curriculum needs a degree of adaptability which schools and colleges did not used to need.

As CPVE is introduced into more schools and colleges, the question of integration and liaison adds another dimension to the organisational problems. The need for a co-ordinator to oversee the different schemes and courses becomes evident (see Chapter 10).

A new phenomenon facing educational establishments is the exposure to outside observation and evaluation. There has always been the occasional visit from HMI to contend with but, apart from that, Heads and Principals enjoyed considerable freedom. They are now much more directly accountable to agencies outside the LEA.

3.8 Political

It is possible to interpret DES haste to implement a new examination at 16+ as an attempt to combat the threat to DES power and autonomy posed by the intrusion of the Manpower Services Commission and in particular the TVEI scheme. Teachers were faced with sweeping changes emanating from two apparently conflicting sources. TVEI pilots were launched in 1983 (MSC), CPVE pilots in 1984 (DES).

There were, in fact, significant differences between the two: The CPVE framework is based on a one year course leading to a nationally recognised qualification; TVEI is not in itself a qualification, but a curriculum development. TVEI is aimed at the 14–18 year old, and not only at post 16 students. In its early stages it was available only in selected pilot authorities, and only in certain institutions within those Authorities; CPVE was open to all, subject to satisfactory submissions. Most significant was the fact that TVEI was massively funded as a measure of Government determination to effect change and to exert more influence and control over the state education system; CPVE was a Cinderella project in comparison.

Further political influences arose from the continuing change wrought by Callaghan's Ruskin College speech (1976) exhorting schools and colleges to look towards the needs of industry and to prepare young people for the world outside by introducing more 'relevent' experience within schools. With the prevailing need for examination certificates it was inevitable that new curriculum developments should be certificated, and that the logic of a unified, coherent, single examination for seventeen year olds should be advocated. The problem arises when yet again, despite the best intentions of CPVE pioneers, constraints imposed by external certification threaten to dilute some of the more adventurous proposals.

In addition to the battle with MSC, other factors influencing the perceptions of the policy makers included the changing nature of employment. Traditional skills offered by school-leavers were no longer appropriate in a society which was facing large-scale structural unemployment; significantly different forms of employment were open to those who did get a job. The need for a flexible workforce was recognised in the development of a curriculum which laid emphasis on skills rather than on the acquisition of a body of knowledge. Schools in particular were faced with the spectre of falling roles which meant the re-deployment of teachers and reduction in the range of options which could be offered to students. In the face of this threat, many institutions looked upon CPVE as a means of attracting students to spend another year in the Sixth Form. Finally, the new experiential approach to learning which was being developed through many pre-vocational courses was recognised as being a valuable motivator for youngsters who had previously been 'switched off' by schooling.

It would be naive to ignore the fact that although much of the impetus for the development of CPVE stemmed from the genuine desire of committed individuals to provide an educational and vocational experience which was more relevent and exciting, the possiblity of exerting a more direct and central control over the curriculum fitted very closely with other initiatives. The move to a more vocationally oriented curriculum was gathering momentum.

The Certificate of Pre-vocational Education (CPVE)

3.9 First-hand experience of CPVE: Kingdown School, Warminster, Wiltshire

a. Organisation
Kingdown's first CPVE course operated in 1985/6. It is run in conjunction with Trowbridge Technical College and the vocational options are taught by the college staff. The school co-ordinator teaches the whole CPVE group for ten forty-minute periods per week, which strengthens the group identity.

b. Curriculum
The vocational options taken by all students in 1986/7 and 1987/8 were:
i. Technical Services – Information Technology and Microelectronic systems (Some elements of Business and Administrative Services are also included in this option.)
ii. Distribution – Retail and Wholesale
iii. Services to People – Health and Community Care

The majority of students work only as far as the Introductory and Exploratory levels of CPVE. A few students who showed exceptional competence in particular vocational areas achieved Preparatory level. All students took up to two additional subjects at O/CSE, or later GCSE level.

The co-ordinator makes extensive use of visits and project work. Figure 3.1 presents a student's account of one visit to a local garage.

One example of part of a project undertaken for the Retail Distribution Course is illustrated in Figures 3.2 and 3.3.

c. Work experience
All students participate in two weeks of full-time work experience. Placements include banks, supermarkets, information technology, electronics firms and chemists.

Figure 3.4 is an account of the same student's impressions of working in a large supermarket in Warminster. She identifies the requirements for the job as being 'patient, co-operative, pleasant and having plenty of common sense'. She also adds that: 'Remaining pleasant throughout the day can be a bit of a strain.'

This student had gained in confidence and made the most of the opportunity to find out as much as possible about the job. She had a realistic idea of the tasks involved and the qualities needed. This sense of realism is also evident in the work experience diary of a student on placement in a Careers Office.

The relationship which can be built up with local employers is illustrated by extracts from letters sent to the school about students on work experience:

> '*I attach my formal report on Pauline and Natasha following their work experience in this office. As you can see, both displayed keen interest, and although our work is complicated, I think we showed them enough to let them see something of what we do, and the responsibilities connected with the general routine ... we have been glad to give them this opportunity.*'

	Sara Hawkins Sh50 Ms Pugh 30.9.85
	Task:- Visit to Dutton Forshaw
	Aims of: Dutton Forshaw Garage.
	Descriptions / Details.
General impression on arrival.	The garage was clean inside and out. It looked very tidy for a garage.
Pump area	There are four petrol pumps. It's a Shell garage. Oil can also be bought there.
Service area	M.O.T's and Break checks are done here.
Cleaning workshop	The cars are cleaned inside first and then the outside is polished. It's very clean and tidy.
Spares section	There's a unipart for the customers and a spare part for the mechanics. Not very well organised or tidy down there. Public aren't allowed in.
New car compound	The new cars are kept outside, the Police check the compound regularly at night times. There hasn't been any damages yet.
Main showroom	Clean, tidy. There was five cars in the show room, it's said that 12 cars can fit in there, even though I find it unbelievable.
Second hand car area	Most of the cars are checked by the 'AA', this cost £20. There's a two year guarentee on most cars.
Employment	There are 22 people working at the garage, 6 of them are mechanics.
Other points layout of garage.	It's bigger than what I thought, just goes to prove that the front of buildings can be very deceptive.

Fig. 3.1: Account of a student visit, Kingdown School, Wiltshire

Buying petrol here?

Petrol can be bought in litres or gallons. Litres costs 43.3 for 4 star. Gallons costs 196.9 for 4 star. The petrol can be purchased with cash, access, visa, gold card, petrol, dial card and over drive cards.

Free glasses are also offered with certain amounts of petrol bought. There's also a new Vauxhall Astra being offered for a prize.

Buying a new car here?

They sell Austin Rover cars, they have 1 delivery a week. There's a ration 1:1, this means that there is an equal amount of second hand cars being bought as well as new ones. Their cars are guaranteed etc.

Getting your car M.O.T ed.

Cars which are under three years don't have to have an M.O.T. Have cars over three years have to have one every year. The mechanics check for faulty seat belts, brakes, tyres, etc. You can't tax your car unless you've got an M.O.T certificate.

Buying a 2nd hand car here.

All 2nd hand cars are serviced by the AA. This costs the garage about £20.00. There's also a two year guarentee on the cars as well. The garage won't sell cars over four years old or with a 45,000 mileage.

Layout of the forecourt.

There were four petrol pumps, toilets, water and air pumps. There was a shop where you could pay for your petrol and buy other products such as :- oil, polish, sweets, cigarettes etc. You could also join the AA, have photocopying etc. You could also see the showroom and to the left of that the 2nd hand cars.

Task :- How we set about

We done a profile of what we thought about the garage overall. We discussed it in our groups and compared notes. If we missed anything we wrote it down.

Conclusion

I thought the garage was kept tidy and clean, comparing the fact that most people always assume that garages are greasy and filthy etc.

I didn't realise that the garage stretched out so much at the back, it just goes to prove that the front of buildings can be decieving.

__Would you buy a new car here?__

Yes, if I had the money. The people working in the garage seem to know what they're doing. You can guarentee a good service if you have it M.O.Ted there etc.

__Would you buy a second hand car there?__

Yes, because it's got a tu6 year guarentee, it's been serviced by the AA. Of course, they're all fairly new cars. However, I would also like to see the certificate which has proved that the car has been checked.

__Would you work there?__

No, because you don't really get to meet alot of people and it seems abit boring. This type of job doesn't really appeal to me because I'd get very bored quickly.

__Where are there garages in Warminster selling new cars?__

There's Dutton-Forshaw, Bristows, Warren Kings and Boreham Garage.

__Description of problems encountered while on the visit?__

Towards the end of the visit I got a little bit bored because I was trying to make notes and listen to what

Fig. 3.1 (cont.)

Mr. Markley was trying to say. Also, I found it hard to ask questions because a majority of them were hard to explain and that they didn't imdlie with what he saying.

<u>Description of good points</u>
It was very interesting in the long run, I didn't know the garage was that big, well not until we had a fairly detailed tour of the layout. It just goes to prove that the front of buildings can be very decieving.

<u>Improvement of next visit</u>
I think it would a better idea if we asked questions as we are going along, that way everybody can cover most things and it will be even more interesting.

A very good piece of work. You have taken a lot of trouble over this, you have presented it well & have included a lot of very useful information.
Well done.

CERTIFICATE OF PRE-VOCATIONAL EDUCATION

RETAIL DISTRIBUTION

BUYING A SHOP

Preparation must now be made to rent or buy 'your shop'. Accordingly, will you visit the local Estate Agents requesting from them a list of likely properties, informing the agents that whilst you will be conducting a mock purchase or lease arrangement, you would appreciate their fullest co-operation, explaining to them the back-ground to your request.

Your requirements will be centred around the size and location of the property. Other priorities you must be concerned with will be

(a) Rent
(b) Rates
(c) Likely energy costs
(d) Repair to property liability
(e) Length of lease requirement
(f) Toilet facilities etc.

Endeavour to get the agent talking in order to gain the maximum amount of information which will help in your decision to go ahead with your plans.

Following the collection of the property details, proceed to the property, perhaps even taking the key, hopefully being able to inspect the shop, just as though you were "doing it for real".

NB One important aspect when buying/renting a commercial premises must be its location in relation to the likely traffic (your customers) flow.

Perhaps you will find the courage to call upon some local traders to discuss your ideas - after all, they should have all the answers.

Buy a shop or lease it.

Na

A good piece of work.

Fig. 3.2: Part of a CPVE project, Kingdown School, Wiltshire

The Certificate of Pre-vocational Education (CPVE)

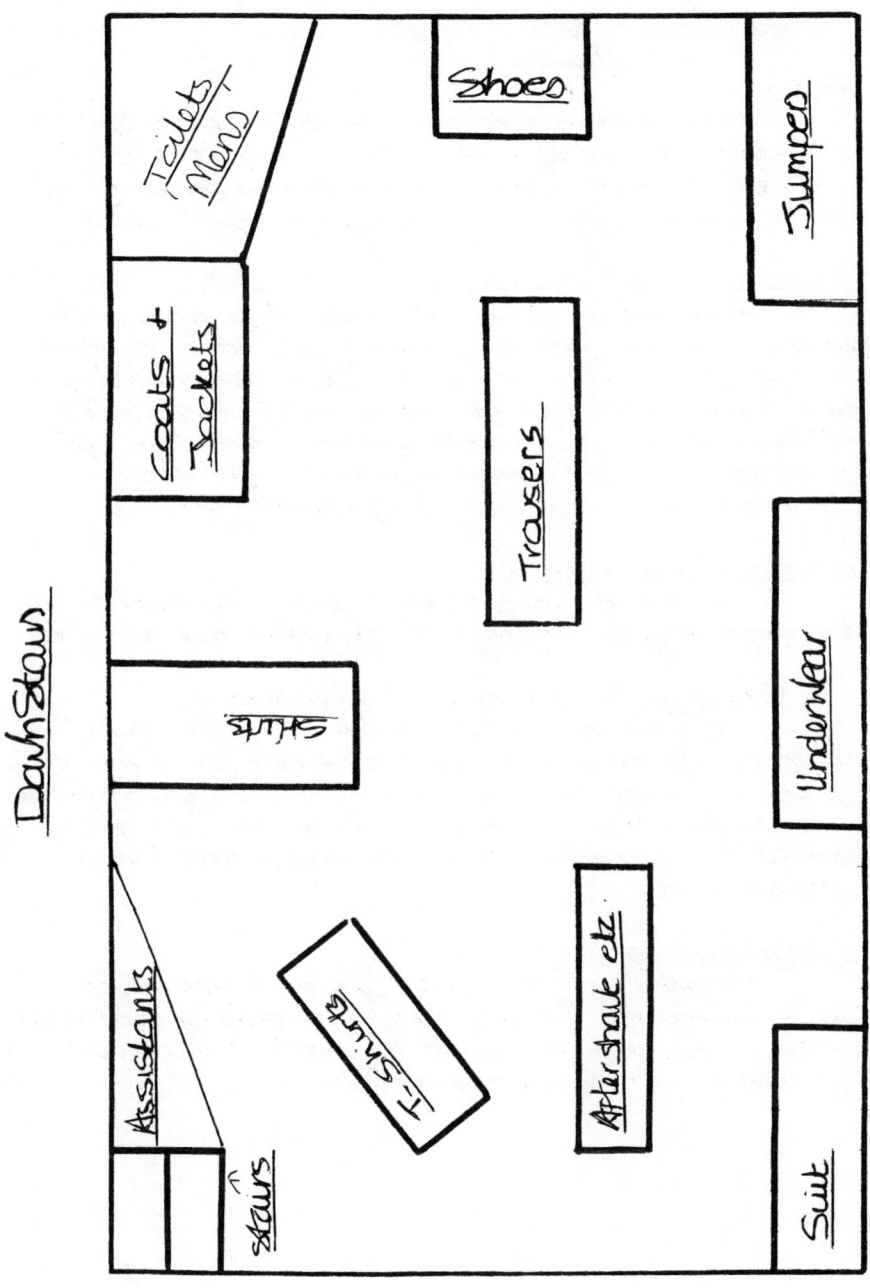

Fig. 3.3: Part of a CPVE project, Kingdown School, Wiltshire

> Sara Hanshaw CbED Mr Pugh
> Safeways.
>
> Uniform:-
> I have a brown overall, I have to wear brown tights and either brown, blue or black shoes. I wear black ones. I also have to wear a name badge which is placed on my top left pocket. I also have to two pens and a watch.
>
> Produce and Meat Departments
> Before I come on the till I have to go around the produce department to check on new stock. The reason for this is that it makes the customer think you have a wide knowledge. Also, some meats from the delicatessen change and go onto the meat department. It's important to do this because if I didn't do it one department would make more money than the other.
>
> Starting or finishing work.
> Whenever you go outside you're supposed to wear something over your overall. It makes it look alot tidier.
>
> Collecting the till and whats inside it
> I have to collect the till from the cash dispenser. The supervisor tells me what till I have to go on. Inside the till there should be a £25 float (unless you're taking over from someone else, it could also mean if that till been used before) There's also a void sheet with a previous 'x' read.
>
> Signing 'on' and 'off'
> Everytime you go on a till you must sign on. If you're leaving the till you must also sign off. Even when you're going for a lunch or tea break. It also applies if nobody else is taking over from you.

Fig. 3.4: Account of work experience in a supermarket, Kingdown School, Wiltshire

Changing the date.

If you don't start work in the morning the date should be changed. However, if you are on a till which hasn't been used in the morning, you have make sure the date is changed.

Void Sheets

If the void sheet hasn't been filled in, you must do it. All you have to do is enter the store number 345, the till number 13 and the date 1.1.86. Then on the back you write your name. Everybody on that till must add their name. To use the void sheet you have to make an error for example: If you put ketchup on the meat department you must put a minus and on the correct department you must put a plus. (It should go on grocery). However, if you overcharge somebody it becomes a little bit difficult. If you over charge somebody under ten pence, all you have to do is put it under the correct department, write it in figures, then in words and finally initial it. If its over you do the same thing but you get somebody higher to sign it. Voids over £1 must be written in words, what went wrong. Its a help if receipts can be kept to help the office people.

Cheques and vouchers.

When doing cheques you have to make sure that the date, cheque card number, signature and serial code are correct. There are five things I have to write on the back of the cheque, the cheque card number, the expirey date, the store number, my signature and finally the till number. Cheques over £50 must be presented with a Driving Licence, Family Allowance or any other form of identification. If this isn't possible, the customer must write their name and address on the back and I have to get somebody higher to sign it. Cheques can not be cashed. Vouches are only excepted if they are in date. Luncheon vouches must only apply to Safeway Food stores Ltd.

Intercom

This is used to contact workers at Safeways instead of shouting out. Here are a few examples 'Customer Service 200, check out 13 please' or 'Grocery Department, Customer Service 600, checkout 13 please.' You can also speak to another person on the checkouts without it going around the store.

Till Check

Every Saturday, a till is taken in to be checked. It's replaced by a £15 float.

Tidying up

All things left behind must be recorded in the book just incase someone comes to claim it. Broken things and soda gas bottles must be placed in the distress trolley. The rubbish bin must be emptied, the desk must be polished and the scales and till must be dusted down. The bags and audit rolls should be left tidy.

How to find out what days you are working.

In each changing room there is a work schedule, it tells you when you're working, what time you start and finish and how many hours you would of worked at the end of the week.

Fig. 3.4. (cont.)

> '*I thought you would like to hear how very successful we feel the two week block placement for Vanessa has been. She has had time to settle into the routine and to develop her own confidence. We have found that this system has worked well with other students in the past and look forward to another fortnight sometime next year.*'

These comments reflect not only on the value of work experience in CPVE, but on the fruitful relationships which can be fostered between schools, colleges and employers. The growth of vocational awareness and personal development of the students is made possible by these important links.

Summary

CPVE created a new climate in colleges and more particularly in schools. It was welcomed by those who had become convinced of the benefits of teaching students through vocational education.

The three components of Core, Vocational and Additional Studies (see 3.3) give structure to what might otherwise lose identity in a general course.

CPVE is now established in most schools and colleges throughout the UK. There have been proposals for its extension to include pre-sixteen students, to part-time two year courses, and as certification for TVEI and YTS. This poses a threat to schools, which have invested time and money in the development of CPVE courses for their Sixth Forms.

While the move towards unification of qualifications advocated by the National Council for Vocational Qualifications (see Chapter 10) is desirable, it appears doubtful whether NCVQ will accredit CPVE as a level one award as part of the new structure. This threatens its survival as a credible, high status course. Jack Mansell, Director of the Further Education Unit has warned that if it is not included in NCVQ it could face extinction[11]. It would be unfortunate if the unique contribution which CPVE can make to the 14–18 curriculum is lost.

STUDENT SELF ASSESSMENT SHEET - TERM I

C.P.V.E. WORK EXPERIENCE DIARY

Name DEAN LAWRIE

Placement CAREERS DEPARTMENT

What went wrong? When typing labels I kept going wrong.

What went well? The whole work experience went very well.

What was difficult?

What was easy? Filing names in alphabetical order and also using different codes.
Getting on with teachers and Mrs. Balzer.
Answering and receiving messages through the telephone

What skills (if any) have improved? Typing

What skills need more practice? If I become an office worker or secretary then typing to a higher standard needs to be returned.

Any other points. The work does get very repetitive like typing and running messages, but being in a small quiet office I sometimes cannot be helped

Signed: Tutor Clare Pugh Student: Deanine
Date : 16.12.85.

Fig. 3.5: Account of work experience in a Careers Office, Kingdown School, Wiltshire

Notes

1. James Callaghan, Speech delivered at Ruskin College, Oxford, 1976.
2. The Further Education Unit, *A Basis for Choice*, FEU, 1978.
3. See 2.
4. Keohane Report, 1979.
5. *Examinations 16–18*, DES, 1980.
6. DES, *17+ A New Qualification* DES, 1982.
7. *CPVE: A Consultative Document*, Joint Board for Pre-vocational Education, May 1984.
8. Joint Board for Pre-vocational Education, *CPVE Framework and Criteria for Approval of Schemes Part A*, Joint Board for Pre-vocational Education, 1985.
9. See 8.
10. *CPVE in Action: a project report*, FEU, 1985.
11. Mark Jackson, '17 plus Exam Threatened with Extinction', *Times Educational Supplement*, 8 August 1987.

Chapter 4

The Youth Training Scheme (YTS)

The Youth Training Scheme (YTS) is a programme offering training to all young people up to the age of eighteen. It consists of structured work-based training, with a minimum of thirteen weeks off-the-job education. In contrast to school-based or college-based post-sixteen provision, trainees are guaranteed a wage, albeit at a lower rate than those in permanent employment.

4.1 Background

The Youth Training Scheme, managed by the Manpower Services Commission (MSC), was launched in 1983, but its origins lie in the Youth Opportunities Programme which ran from 1978–1983.

a. The Youth Opportunities Programme
This was a special employment measure for unemployed under-19 year olds which was introduced and implemented within a characteristically short timespan in 1978. The Youth Opportunities Programme (YOP) offered unemployed youngsters six months' work experience, usually based on employers' premises, in order to bridge the gap between school and work or 'the dole'.

Reactions were mixed: some young people valued the experience they gained; many found permanent employment as a result, particularly in the early years. Many valued the chance to mix in the real working world and to gain not only practical experience, but improved confidence and social skills. However, criticisms included charges that some employers used YOP trainees as a source of 'slave labour' – a charge which was certainly justified in some instances, but which was magnified by media. Schools sometimes saw YOP as a direct threat to their recruitment into the Sixth Form, and a rival to their attempts to provide school-based work experience for their pupils.

YOP cost in the region of £375 million, a significant sum at that time. However, investment in YTS when it arrived was funded at a rate of £775 million.

As it became increasingly obvious that youth unemployment was not simply a temporary phenomenon, the Government took steps to formalise training

The Youth Training Scheme (YTS)

and to develop a structured framework within which initiatives throughout the country would operate.

b. The New Training Initiative (NTI)

In 1981 *A New Training Initiative: a consultative document*[1] was published by the MSC. It received widespread publicity within education and industry. This was followed by *A New Training Initiative: an agenda for action*[2] and was accompanied by the Government White Paper, *A New Training Initiative: a programme for action*.[3]

Thus the New Training Initiative (NTI) was launched with three main objectives:

 i. developing skill training including apprenticeship in such a way as to enable young people entering at different ages and with different educational attainments to acquire agreed standards of skill, appropriate to the jobs available and to provide them with a basis for progression through further learning
 ii. moving towards a position where all young people under the age of eighteen have the opportunity either of continuing in full-time education or of entering a period of planned work experience combined with work-related training and education
 iii. opening up widespread opportunities for adults, whether employed, unemployed, or returning to work, to acquire, increase or up-date their skills and knowledge during the course of their working lives

c. The Youth Training Scheme

The new YTS scheme contained a number of features which differed from the old Youth Opportunities Programme, including:

 i. structured, work-based training (employers could no longer justify using a young person to undertake the same routine task throughout the placement)
 ii. a minimum of 13 weeks off-the-job training (often provided at a College of Further Education)
 iii. broad-based foundation training
 iv. introduction to new technology, a definite, declared emphasis on the movement away from simply occupying the trainee and towards the development of skills and competencies
 v. the development of training in areas which had no history of training before the advent of YTS
 vi. an innovative approach to training trainers through the network of Accredited Training Centres

In the early days, one of the criticisms of YTS lay in the lack of skilled trainers to undertake the work. MSC sought to overcome this difficulty by providing appropriate training.

d. Two-year YTS

It is already clear that developments in this sector rarely remain static: the next stage was the introduction of a two-year YTS programme.

Discussions started in 1985 with the publication of the White Paper, *Education and Training for Young People*[4] which advocated:
- the development of a pool of better-qualified entrants into the labour market
- a two-year programme for sixteen year olds and a one-year programme for seventeen year olds (this has a number of implications for schools and for those offering CPVE)
- emphasis on employer-based schemes
- a launch in April 1986
- progression to vocational qualification

In contrast with YOP which was launched as a temporary measure to alleviate a specific crisis, this scheme emphasised a permanent new approach to training a young workforce.

4.2 Aims

The original aim of one-year YTS was to provide a training opportunity for school leavers. The advent of two-year YTS saw the development of more clearly defined aims which can be summarised as:
  i. the opportunity for proper training to be made available to more young people
 ii. the provision of a more broad-based education and training programme developing a wider range of competencies
iii. the provision of training leading to appropriate and recognised qualifications
 iv. the development of better qualified young entrants into the labour market

The aim associated with the personal and social development of young people and the acquisition of new skills is a genuine concern of the majority of those involved in the delivery of YTS, whether employers, other managing agents, YTS personnel or off-the-job trainers.

The need to provide young workers with a 'passport to performance'[5] is an aim emphasised by Manpower Services Commission.

YTS also aims to create a pool of more highly trained young workers. Such a pool of young people who have experienced high quality training is seen as being closely related to economic success in the international marketplace.[6]

4.3 Structure

4.3.1 One-year YTS

This was based upon a one-year training opportunity with a minimum of thirteen weeks off-the-job training which usually took place in Further Education colleges. Attempts by schools to provide this element were rejected by MSC.

4.3.2 Two-year YTS

The two-year scheme introduced in 1986 faced the criticisms and problems encountered in the earlier scheme. A more structured framework was devised with prescribed criteria which providers had to meet before approval for a scheme was granted.

The structure of two-year YTS consists of four main elements:
- inputs
- training processes
- outcomes
- certification

a. Inputs

Planned work experience and on-the-job training forms the backbone of the majority of two-year YTS programmes. It offers young people the chance to acquire and practice skills in a working environment alongside adult workers. 'Real' work is most usually the hallmark of the scheme, with a commitment to provide proper, planned and varied training.

Off-the-job training and education must occupy twenty weeks over the two-year period. There is no rigid prescription about the distribution of this part of the programme, although there is an expectation that the original format of thirteen weeks in the first year should be adhered to where possible.

Where young people join the scheme at seventeen, they are entitled to seven weeks off-the-job training. The MSC defines this element as 'a planned and directed programme of learning which takes place outside the day-to-day pressures of a job and away from the normal workplace'.

b. Training processes

As in the original YTS programmes, great emphasis is placed on well-planned induction and initial assessment. It is interesting that in 1987 a greater emphasis on this induction process was introduced into CPVE (Chapter 3). One of the discrepancies relating to profiling, which gained support through YTS, is that YTS turned its back on assessments made of youngsters in school. The justification for this was that the individual should be given a chance to wipe the slate clean, but it did tend to undermine the work of those trying to enhance young peoples' self-esteem by providing them with a package of 'can-do' assessments to take with them into work or training.

There are signs that this policy is being re-assessed in the light of the growing demand for progression and rationalisation of accreditation, particularly through the work of the National Council for Vocational Qualifications (NCVQ).

A second emphasis in training is the requirement for participative learning; it is difficult to refute the argument that learning by taking part, whether in academic or practical activities, is a most effective way of learning. It is a theme which recurs in most of the other developments explored in this book, but which gained prominence through the pioneering efforts of YTS.

A pillar of YTS has always been, and still is, that students have a right to continuous assessment. This is discussed in greater detail in 5.5.2, but it was partly through the medium of YTS that the profiling movement gained recognition. Associated with this requirement for continuous assessment is the need for a built-in process of guidance and regular review. It is upon these four precepts of induction and initial assessment, participative learning, continuous assessment and guidance, and review that the training processes in the YTS framework are based.

c. Outcomes

The outcomes sought by managers of YTS are:
i. competence to perform satisfactorily in a job
ii. the acquisition of a range of basic core skills which are transferable, and will enable the trainee to progress into a variety of different occupations

This second outcome is one of the most difficult for trainers and trainees to achieve.

There is no guarantee of permanent employment for young people leaving YTS, but it is at least hoped that individuals gain the personal resources with which to cope with life.

d. Certification

From the earliest days, the YTS structure incorporated a plan to provide trainees with a nationally recognised form of certification. The emphasis is on vocational qualifications which will indicate competence, and should be issued by a body with national credibility.

There should also be opportunity for progression, which is becoming a major issue. The establishment of the NCVQ should have an important bearing on this aspect of certification, and on the development of universally recognised accreditation.

Another aspect of accreditation lies in the development of national Records of Achievement (Chapter 6), which has much in common with the YTS profile and Certificate.

4.4 Criteria

MSC has paid particular attention to improving the quality of YTS provision. One of the major criticisms of early schemes was the patchy nature of the quality of provision. Some Managing Agents went to great lengths to ensure that trainees received high quality experience and appropriate guidance. Others could justifiably be accused of exploiting young people as a source of cheap labour, with little genuine concern for their training needs.

4.4.1 *Approved Training Organisations (ATOs)*

This preoccupation with quality led to the establishment in April 1987 of 'Approved Training Organisations' (ATOs). All subsequent YTS programmes were to be delivered through these ATOs, which entered into contractual obligations with the Manpower Services Commission.

Organisations wishing to become Approved Training Organisations had to satisfy MSC on their ability to deliver under ten main headings:
- arrangement of a two-year training programme
- previous record in training
- resources
- competence of staff
- premises and equipment
- assessment of trainees
- effective programme review
- positive commitment to equal opportunities
- positive commitment to health and safety
- financial viability

There was some leeway in that prospective ATOs that did not receive full approval in April 1987 were given an opportunity to reapply for April 1988, but regulations stated that those not reaching full status by that date were not to be issued with further contracts.

This can be seen as making real efforts, reinforced by teeth which were previously lacking, to ensure a fairer deal for trainees.

4.4.2 *Individual requirements*

a. Health and safety

It is the task of the ATOs to ensure that all health and safety requirements are satisfied in premises where trainees will be working. Regular equipment checks are also required (there have been tragic accidents involving YTS trainees and MSC are clearly concerned that safety procedures should be strictly enforced).

b. Assessment

Trainees are entitled to regular, systematic assessment of both on-the-job and off-the-job training.

These assessments are based upon competence objectives: when the objectives are achieved, they must be recorded in the Record of Achievement (see Figures 4.1, 4.2 and 4.3).

Trainees must be involved in making the assessments, and encouraged in self-assessment. The importance of assessment in contributing to YTS certificates which have credibility, and can contribute to vocational qualifications is stressed.

c. Regular review

Representatives of all the main groups involved – ATOs, managing agents, employers – should meet regularly to review the training programme, evaluate current practice and plan future developments. This is an effective way of keeping the importance of meeting criteria on the agenda, and for sharing good practice.

d. Equal opportunities

Organisations must demonstrate that they have a positive commitment to equal opportunities and must provide evidence that trainees really are experiencing equality of opportunity.

e. Financial viability

Organisations must demonstrate that they have financial resources to enable them to fulfil their part of the contract. For young people to benefit from proper, systematic training, it is essential that the firm is still in operation over the period of the contract. It is not difficult to imagine firms that are in financial difficulties seeing YTS trainees as a cost-effective means of bolstering the workforce. Trainees must be protected from this type of exploitation.

4.5 Impact on individuals and organisations

a. On organisations

The impact for schools and colleges is very different. For schools, which are not able to participate directly in YTS, impact lies in the necessity to advise students on appropriate YTS schemes, to be aware of the changing nature of YTS training, and to be a source of advice and guidance for fifth and sixth formers.

The other main impact of YTS on schools lies in its relationship as a competitor for the recruitment of 16+ students. Competition is strengthened by the proposal to use CPVE as one of the forms of accreditation for YTS. This means that students will be able to obtain the same qualification as that offered to them in school, whilst attracting a salary at the same time. Until a

ACHIEVEMENT RECORD

MODULE : 6 ORAL COMMUNICATION

TRAINEE'S NAME :

STANDARD TASK TITLE.	REF.NO.	SUCCESS OBSERVED : - TRAINEE'S INITIAL/DATE.						FINAL STANDARD ACHIEVED : - SUPERVISOR'S SIGNATURE/DATE.
Make telephone call	6.5.A							
Checking switchboard equipment	6.6							
Carry out answering machine procedures	6.6.A							
Carry out routine checks on switch-board equipment	6.6.B							
Receiving a telephone call	6.7							
Receive telephone call	6.7.A							
Making a telephone call (on extension to manual switchboard)	6.8							
Make telephone call - Extension on a manual switchboard	6.8.A							

Fig. 4.1: Extract from a YTS profile

SUPERVISOR'S ASSESSMENT FORM

	CORE SKILLS	GOOD PROGRESS/WEAK AREAS
NUMBER	1. Operating with numbers	Says she finds figure work hard
	2. Interpreting numerical and related information	Grasped new filing system quickly.
	3. Estimating	Underestimates length at some tasks.
	4. Measuring and marking out	N/A
	5. Recognise cost and value	Has learned to economise on phone.
COMMUNICATION	6. Finding out information and interpreting instructions	Good — especially in direct personal contact
	7. Providing information	Written work could improve — spelling!
	8. Working with people	Shows initiative in offering help
PROBLEM SOLVING	9. Planning: determining and revising courses of action	Not always successful in choosing
	10. Decision making: choosing between alternatives	easiest/quickest way to do job.
	11. Monitoring: keeping track of progress and checking	Checks her work conscientiously.
PRACTICAL	12. Planning for a practical activity	Works in organised, tidy manner.
	13. Carrying out a practical activity	Has learned how to lift safely.
	14. Finishing off a practical activity	Must remember to turn machines off!

SKILL TRANSFER — Comment on trainee's ability to

1. Adapt skills learned previously to this placement? — Quickly adapted to this section's filing system.
2. Work things out for him/herself? — Good — see comments on WP programme

Fig. 4.2: Extract from a YTS profile

The Youth Training Scheme (YTS)

CERTIFICATE

PART 3

Trainee's Name . . . . LISA JONES . . . .

ACHIEVEMENT IN THE FOUR YTS OUTCOMES

1 Competence in a range of Occupational Skills

Achieved competence in reception duties in a variety of offices. Achieved competence in word processing, using 2 different systems. Acquired basic office organisation skills, including filing, reprographics, handling mail and using telephone.

2 Competence in a range of Transferable Core Skills

NUMBER
Checked numerical data and statistics. Compared costs and recognized value in making travel arrangements.

COMMUNICATION
Provided information to the public. Noticed the needs of colleagues and responded accordingly. Dealt appropriately with complaints from the public. Worked in a team with colleagues.

COMPUTER AND INFORMATION TECHNOLOGY
Carried out procedures for starting up, loading and running word processing programmes.

PROBLEM SOLVING
Planned itinerary for official meetings. Dealt with difficult members of the public on reception. Decided which benefit category clients belonged to.

PRACTICAL SKILLS
Able to operate keyboard equipment. Able to carry out health and safety checks. Well organised and tidy.

3 Ability to transfer skills and knowledge to new situations

Taught herself to operate new word processing programme having previously learned another. Social and communication skills improved in range of reception duties often involving difficult clients.
Applied knowledge of filing systems to various different offices.
Applied data presentation skills learnt at college to work place.

4 Personal Effectiveness

Showed initiative in volunteering help.
Developed friendly, relaxed relationships with colleagues and supervisors.
Dealt successfully with difficult clients.
Mature and responsible for a 17 year old.

A B Croft
....
Managing Agent's Signature

Fig. 4.3: Part of a YTS summative profile

standard allowance is paid to 16–18 year olds, regardless of their chosen course, this will continue to be a point of contention between schools and YTS schemes.

MSC proposes placing a teacher with experience of YTS into every secondary school in an attempt to overcome the suspicion of teachers. In exchange, it is expected that teachers will be able to influence the educational quality of YTS.[7]

Colleges of Further Education, which are encouraged to participate in YTS as off-the-job providers, are in a different situation. Initially, they were totally unprepared for the influx of students, many of whom had lower academic qualifications than those to which they were accustomed, and many of whom were reluctant customers. However, adjustments were made and new staff recruited within a short period; FE now works in close collaboration with YTS.

The impact on the institutions was significant and, for many staff, unwelcome. However, pragmatists welcomed a new source of revenue and idealists have welcomed the opportunity to introduce more adventurous teaching methods.

b. On individuals

YTS has had a great impact on the lives of young people: post-sixteen options have been significantly altered. Where students faced the alternatives of work, further education, school or unemployment, alternatives have been expanded to include a two-year (or, in the case of seventeen year olds, a one-year) training and employment opportunity.

This not only means the chance to receive training whilst earning a wage but, almost more important, removes the feeling of uselessness and inadequacy felt by students unable to find a job on leaving school or college. This in turn has an impact on attitudes further down the school.

YTS also offers the individual a new route to employment: trainees are not infrequently offered permanent employment as a result of their placement. In an increasing number of industries, permanent employees are registered for YTS training.

4.6 Benefits

Despite initial suspicion, there is no doubt that YTS has substantial benefits to offer both individuals and participating organisations.

a. For individuals
  i. For the first time, students are offered a real alternative to unemployment.
  ii. This generates a sense of purpose. Pre-YTS it was common for school-leavers without employment to drift into a state of lethargy where they

The Youth Training Scheme (YTS)

saw no purpose in getting up in the morning and lost motivation for job-seeking.
iii. There is an opportunity to experience life in the world of work, to mix with adults and gain first-hand knowledge of the pressures, constraints and rewards of work, whilst still in a partially protected and supervised environment.
iv. Within this environment young people have the chance to develop skills, which means that they have more to offer when seeking employment.
v. In addition to these work-related skills, trainees have the chance to continue with the education that many rejected whilst still in school, and a chance to gain credible qualifications.
vi. These qualifications can be the gateway to progression to more advanced qualifications. (This is more an aspiration than a reality, but is a target which should be met through the National Council for Vocational Qualifications.)
vii. YTS offers the added attraction of payment during training.
viii. For many young people, YTS is a route to full-time employment.

b. For organisations
i. Companies assist in the creation of a pool of more highly skilled workers which they have the first opportunity to recruit.
ii. On-the-job training means that trainees' skills are developed in line with local employment needs – opportunities in the Vale of Evesham differ from those on Clydeside.
iii. Cash incentives, in the form of grants paid to employers, subsidise the cost of training new personnel.
iv. The problem of employees leaving after an initial investment in induction is reduced – employees are likely to have a more realistic understanding of the nature of the work.
v. A YTS programme can be a more effective way of selecting staff than reliance on traditional examination qualifications.
vi. With the refinement of new assessment procedures, including the issuing of a profile stating what the candidate CAN do, recruitment from other YTS programmes is made easier.
vii. Companies have the opportunity to make a contribution to the community in which they are based by helping young people to a better start in life.
viii. Colleges and other off-the-job providers gain a new source of revenue, which they have exploited fully.

4.7 Drawbacks

A number of disadvantages offset the benefits outlined above; YTS originally faced fierce criticism which has now subsided to a large extent. However, charges are levelled that YTS has many unresolved problems, particularly from the standpoint of the trainee.

a. For individuals
  i. There is still a 'status' problem. Although it is less common, some school-leavers will not accept YTS because of the stigma of failure with which it is sometimes associated.
  ii. It is not seen as a 'proper' job.
  iii. The quality of training is still patchy – unlucky individuals can experience poor, restricted training, which makes them less marketable than peers who experience high quality training.
  iv. Some employers' attitudes to off-the-job training lacks commitment. There is inadequate guidance and interest in what may seem an unproductive activity.
  v. Low salary levels encourage the 'slave labour' label.
  vi. Trainees are still sometimes exploited by unscrupulous employers who view them as a source of cheap labour.
  vii. Despite efforts to improve progression routes, there is still no real progression into Higher Education and even the opportunity for vocational qualification is variable.
  viii. The prospect of full-time employment at the end of training is uncertain; the trainee lives with this uncertainty throughout the two years of training.

b. For institutions
Institutions choose to become part of YTS. They can therefore be expected to have a realistic idea of the demands and problems which can occur and either accept them, or take steps to prevent them. Nevertheless, certain disadvantages are associated with YTS for the organisations:
  i. In the case of Further Education Colleges, off-the-job provision entails major changes in the curriculum, in methods of teaching and in personnel needed to staff the courses. Many teachers are unable to accommodate the changing clientele.
  ii. Unfilled vacancies remain a source of concern for employers, who cater for a specific number of placements which may not be filled. This is costly and disruptive. One example is that of a construction company in Bournemouth[8] which could not fill more than nine of sixty seven vacancies. This was despite the fact that a salary of £50 per week was offered, in comparison with the current YTS rate of £27.50, with every trainee guaranteed a job at the end of two years.

The Youth Training Scheme (YTS)

iii. New controls on finance for YTS mean that payment is only made to employers for the number of trainees in post, and not for any vacant placements. This results in an uncertain cash flow for companies that may need to operate within strict limits for financial planning.
iv. A substantial commitment to training is involved which means that permanent staff must be detailed to supervise trainees.
v. There can be difficulty in integrating older, permanent staff and the new recruits.
vi. It can be an uncomfortable new experience for both on-the-job and off-the-job providers to be subjected to external inspection and evaluation.

4.8 Political rationale

It has been argued that the Government's swift introduction of a Youth Opportunities Programme and Youth Training Scheme owed more to expediency than to any deep-rooted desire to enhance the training opportunities of the young. YOP was a reflex response to an alarming increase in youth unemployment. The magnitude of this problem can be illustrated by the figures from one area which is not noted for its high unemployment rate.

In 1974 employment vacancies notified to the Careers Service stood at 2,500, whilst there were 250 young unemployed. Just three years later, in 1977, these figures had exactly reversed. There were 250 vacancies, with 2,500 young unemployed seeking employment. The extent of this upheaval took careers officers, teachers and employers unawares. There was an expectation amongst young people that providing they worked at school and gained a reasonable report, they would have a job. In fact, the norm in this area was that sixteen-year-old leavers could choose from a number of offers. The contrast left many people in the education service feeling impotent to help their school leavers.

No doubt there was a degree of altruism in the Government's intervention in the provision of alternatives to the dole; there was also an element of expediency. Publicity given to the plight of the young unemployed did little to foster confidence in the Government.

There were also widespread fears of disaffection and unrest amongst an unoccupied band of young people with little upon which to expend their energy. They were disillusioned by the reality of unemployment, without hope for the future and without resources. There is a strong case in favour of the argument that it was fear of civil unrest which prompted the initial crisis initiatives. These initiatives provided the first evidence of the effectiveness of direct Government intervention, which led to more sweeping interventionist strategies such as TVEI.

The political implications have since become more complicated; they include elements such as the desire to create a better-trained, flexible workforce in order to help the country to become more competitive in the international marketplace. Forecasts that it would mean the effective raising of the school-leaving age to eighteen have been proved correct. In contrast with the last statutory raising of the school-leaving age (to sixteen) this has been accomplished almost painlessly. What is certain is that sixteen-year-old unemployment is no longer a factor. Careers offices which until relatively recently were preoccupied with helping sixteen- and seventeen-year-olds to get jobs now find that their work has been re-defined. The Government has removed the problem of youth unemployment from the political arena.

A further political factor is the extent to which direct Government control is now being exercised in areas which previously enjoyed comparative autonomy. This extends through the whole school curriculum into the post-school arena.

It can be argued that this is an attempt to extend the degree of social control which can be exercised by Government, breeding a quiescent youth, socialised into accepting their place in society. Schemes such as YTS are also accused of producing technocratic factory fodder.

The contrasting argument presents Government as a benevolent and concerned institution bent only on helping young people to make the most of themselves, to develop their skills and to enable them to reach their full potential in order to lead full and rewarding lives. There is no doubt that YTS is the result of an interventionist strategy: perhaps the verdict on whether it is benevolent or sinister depends on whether one is a dispassionate observer or potentially unemployed at the age of sixteen.

4.9 First-hand experience of YTS: Marine and Commercial Training Company

The Marine and Commercial Training Company is an Approved Training Organisation situated in Lowestoft. It was previously associated with the Anglia Marine Group Training Association which provided training for employees of the boat-building yards.

With the increase of fibreglass boats, and a reduction in the need for traditional boat-building skills, the training association was taken over by a private, professional training company.

a. Background information
The company began training for YTS in 1983. It takes trainees from Scotland to Kent. This is an unusual feature of YTS provision, and reflects the specialist nature of the training provided.

b. Scope of YTS training
Around one hundred trainees are registered with the company at any one time. Training mainly centres on boatbuilding, marine operations, sailmaking

The Youth Training Scheme (YTS)

and other skills associated with boats, although they do run a clerical training course.

c. Pattern of training

Two-year YTS trainees have three blocks of off-the-job training in the first year. The fact that they have to travel from all over the country means that they have to live in lodgings. In both years of their training, they return to a company near their homes for practical, on-the-job training in between blocks with Marine Training.

Year 1: Two week block
This first session is devoted to induction, health and safety regulations, first aid, and computer studies.

Three week block
The first part of this block of training consists of revision of their computer studies work in preparation for an RSA examination in computer studies

This is followed by general boatyard skills: splicing, knots, construction methods, hull shapes. Trainees also study a glass fibre and reinforced plastic module.

Seven week block
This is an intensive, basic craft skills module. Subjects covered include: joinery, technical drawing, timber technology, adhesives. They also study marine engineering: fitting, small metal fabrication (eg pumps, brake housings).

Year 2: Four week block
In this block trainees concentrate for the first two weeks on joinery, scarf joints, deck beam exercises, knees etc. They also have formica exercises where they learn bonding, shaping, cutting.

Finally, they have an individual project, such as making a wall unit or a mahogany table, which enables them to use the skills they have aquired.

For the last two weeks they gain practical experience of fitting out small dinghies.

Four week block
For this session trainees have a project connected with bigger boats. Depending on what boats are in for repair, this might include clinker repair, plywood repair, fitting out a larger hull, cold-moulded dinghies.

d. Benefits
i. Students benefit from a first-class, professional training which reinforces their practical experience.

ii. They can build up credits from the modules of study to gain certification through the British Marine Industries Federation and City and Guilds Skills Building Module Certificate.
iii. Prospects of full-time employment are excellent: for trainees who complete the scheme, 97% are offered full-time employment.

e. Drawbacks
i. For some trainees, having to live away from home is a difficult experience.
ii. From the training agencies viewpoint, this is an expensive course to fund. Materials are particularly expensive.
iii. Because of the specialised nature of the training it is not easy to gain a place on such a scheme.

f. In conclusion
This account illustrates the diversity of experience open to young people, and the high quality of training provided by the best training organisations.

For further information about this scheme contact:
Derek White
Marine and Commercial Training
Marine House
Harbour Road
Oulton Broad
Lowestoft
Suffolk NR 32 3LZ

Summary

A major consequence of YTS is the effective raising of the school leaving (or work entry) age to eighteen. Whilst young people are still faced with conflicting options at sixteen the inevitability of unemployment has been removed. Some feel that it has been removed for cynical, political and exploitive motives[9]. Supporters of YTS point to the removal of the stigma of unemployment previously facing fifth formers in schools. It would be unfortunate if hints that YTS might become compulsory materialise; it would undermine much of the benefit which students gain from YTS, and would create problems for employers faced with reluctant recruits.

The pattern of recruitment into full-time employment has been altered, with erosion of the apprenticeship system and its replacement by entry through YTS. There is, however, evidence to suggest that the methods of recruitment have not changed. Applicants for 'premium' YTS placements still face rigorous selection tests, accompanied by rigid examination requirements.

YTS initially involved schools very little; its immediate impact was upon Further Education colleges, that were called upon to change the courses provided, to operate throughout the year, and to adapt teaching styles. New approaches to assessment and profiling have been reinforced by their adoption in YTS.

One feature of YTS has been the growth in entrepreneurial private training agencies competing to provide off-the-job training.

The speed of initial introduction of YTS, and the ad hoc nature of its growth led to variations in the quality of schemes. Tighter controls and greater emphasis on quality should result in fewer unsatisfactory schemes.

Finn suggests that the government is:

'*using unemployment and the mechanism of training schemes to secure a permanent change in the skills and attitudes of the British working class*'[10]

Whilst this may be partly true, it is worth considering the bleak future facing many sixteen year olds before the introduction of YTS. At the very least they are now provided with a chance to learn new skills and to receive a wage, however small. Perhaps most importantly, it offers them the opportunity to retain individual dignity and to hope, rather than to despair, even before they have started their adult lives.

Notes

1. Manpower Services Commission, *A New Training Initiative: a consultative document*, MSC, 1981.
2. *A New Training Initiative: an agenda for action*, 1981
3. Department of Employment, *A New Training Initiative: A programme for action*, HMSO, Cmnd 8455, 1981.
4. *Education and Training for Young People*, 1985.
5. Bryan Nicholson, *YTS News No. 27*, MSC, 1986.
6. See 5.
7. Jeremy Sutcliffe, 'Move to have YTS Expert in Every School', *Times Educational Supplement*, 24 September, 1987.
8. *The Times*, 'Only 9 Apply for 67 Youth Jobs', *The Times*, 21 August 1987.
9. Finn D., *Training without Jobs*, Macmillan, 1987.
10. See 9.

Chapter 5

The General Certificate of Secondary Education (GCSE)

The General Certificate of Secondary Education (GCSE) is a single system examination which replaces GCE 'O' Level and CSE examinations. Responsibility for the introduction of GCSE lies with the Secondary Examinations Council (SEC).

5.1 Background

Introduction of the new examination was announced on 20 June 1984, and was implemented with what appears to be undue haste: the first courses began in 1986. The impression of a shot-gun marriage is, however, misleading.

There is a long history of debate and recommendation leading up to the establishment of a single system of examining at sixteen plus. As long ago as 1943 the Norwood Report[1] referred to the desirability of making the examination of young peoples' attainments an internal matter, based upon assessments carried out within schools.

A further dimension was added with the publication of the Beloe Report[2] in 1958 which presaged the introduction of CSE examinations. CSE was designed to offer certification to a wider clientele than the 20% catered for by GCE. However, even at this stage the dangers inherent in a two-tier examination system were recognised:

'... teachers may be faced with difficult choices in deciding which pupils should take which examinations ...'

While the CSE examination was still in its infancy, *Examining at 16+*[3] highlighted a movement towards a common examining system:

'There are now two separate systems of examining the educational attainment of pupils aged about sixteen. Yet the distribution of attainment is continuous.'

Despite the advantages that many teachers felt were offered by CSE in terms of greater teacher involvement in assessment and setting of syllabuses, there was already a move towards its abolition.

The General Certificate of Secondary Education (GCSE)

Peter Clare[4] identifies the first public reference to a common examining system as that found in the Schools Council's resolution on 7 July 1970 which states that:

> '... there should be a single examination system at the age of 16+ and that this should be under the Schools Council.'

A Schools Council Working Party was established to pursue this idea, and joint GCE and CSE examinations were piloted in 1974/5. Following proposals from the Schools Council, the Waddell Report[5] published in 1978 gave advance notice of some of the features of any new common examination. The report suggests the possibility of having differentiated papers, where it would be possible to 'choose between alternative papers or tests set at different levels of difficulty'. It also states that all grades should be awarded on a single scale, and should bear a common title.

In addition to these elements, Waddell drew attention to the need for greater teacher involvement in the assessment of students, and significantly to the need for National Criteria.

A flurry of activity followed the publication of this report, and a common examination seemed inevitable. It was followed, however, by growing lethergy.

This situation changed dramatically in June 1984 with the then Secretary of State, Sir Keith Joseph's proposals for the introduction of GCSE. The time-scale identified for implementation seemed to many to be impossibly short. It seemed likely that the Government would bow to pressure to postpone the introduction (and many would still claim that it would have been better for students and teachers if this had happened). However, Sir Keith was adamant and the old GCE and CSE examinations were replaced by the GCSE in the summer of 1988.

5.2 Aims

The main aims of GCSE are:

a. Acknowledgement of success

Every pupil should be given the chance to demonstrate what he or she 'knows, understands and can do'. This is the GCSE password, yet it should not be disregarded simply because it has become a cliché. Perhaps one of the most significant differences between this and previous examinations, is that a serious attempt is made to measure and give credit for what students CAN do, rather than to highlight what they can not.

One way in which this is translated into practice is that in designing syllabuses, the approach centres upon questions such as: 'What is it reasonable to expect the average pupil to achieve in this task?' This level is then established as a G Grade and the baseline for further assessment, so that higher level activities and attainments attract higher grades. This contrasts with the old basis for examination which identified the top level of performance, and removed marks according to the individual's failure to meet this target.

In a very real sense, therefore, the GCSE seeks to reward achievement rather than to penalise shortcomings.

b. The move towards criterion referenced assessment
A second aim of GCSE is to facilitate a move from the overtly norm-referenced nature of examination assessment, where grades are governed more by the candidate's performance in relation to other candidates than to a fixed standard of performance. A criterion-referenced approach is advocated, where standards are established, and it is the candidate's ability to meet those standards which is measured, not ability in comparison with peers. This would be more evident if Grade Criteria were fully developed, but it is still influencing the assessment procedures of teachers and examiners.

c. Greater emphasis on coursework
The inclusion of a compulsory element of coursework allows work done under realistic conditions to count towards the assessment, rather than depending solely upon the candidate's ability to perform under stressful conditions.

d. Common syllabuses
The introduction of nationally approved syllabuses reflects the aim of ensuring comparability across the country, and of enabling students to move schools and areas without being penalised. In practice it appears that the problem is not solved; variations in coursework requirements alone make it difficult for students to change schools in the middle of their course.

e. Practical, problem-solving approaches
The growth in importance of oral work, of communication skills across the curriculum, and the need for information and skills to be relevant to the candidate's life outside school reflects the aim of GCSE to equip young people with practical, problem-solving skills.

5.3 Structure

Central characteristics of GCE's structure include:
  i. Amalgamation of the existing seven GCE, eleven CSE and one joint GCE and CSE Boards to form five groups of Boards:
  Welsh Joint Education Committee (WJEC)
  Northern Examining Association (NEA)
  Midland Examining Group (MEG)
  London and East Anglia Group (LEAG)
  Southern Examining Group (SEG)
  ii. All GCSE syllabuses must conform to National Criteria. This is probably

The General Certificate of Secondary Education (GCSE)

the most significant change and is intended to ensure uniformity throughout the country.

iii. Differentiation: all GCSE examinations must contain differentiated papers, or differentiated questions within the same papers. This question of differentiation caused confusion in the early days. Briefly, candidates of different abilities are tested by differentiated papers, differentiated questions, differentiated tasks or differentiation by outcome.

iv. GCSE syllabuses and assessment procedures are scrutinised by the Secondary Examinations Council (SEC) in order to ensure that they conform to National Criteria. This is a massive task which has caused backlogs and delays.

v. Grades are awarded on a single scale: A to G. An approximate guide to the comparability of these grades with the old GCE and CSE Grades can be represented as:

O Level	GCSE	CSE
A	A	
B	B	1
C	C	
D	D	2
E	E	3
	F	4
	G	5

vi. Standards must be no less exacting than those required under the previous system.

vii. Assessment is not restricted to external examination. Approximately 20% of total marks are allocated for coursework, although this varies between subjects. Coursework assessment is subject to external moderation. The main feature of this element is that the student's whole future is not determined by the standard of performance on one single day.

Two further features of the structure of GCSE that were stipulated at the outset, but that now seem subject to increasing delay and possibly removal are:

viii. Grade Criteria. It was initially envisaged that the development of Grade Criteria to facilitate criterion referenced testing within subjects, should be in operation from an early stage. At the time of writing, a realistic estimate for their introduction is now the mid-90s. Despite the difficulties, SEC are investing considerable time and manpower in an attempt to conquer some of the complexities which have emerged.

ix. Distinction Certificates. This idea, for rewarding candidates performing consistently well in a number of subject areas, is one which looks less likely to be implemented. It met with opposition on the grounds of its elitist connotations and now appears to occupy a low priority.

5.4 Criteria

5.4.1 Central requirements

The central requirements for GCSE are determined by the published National Criteria, which consist of General Criteria, to which every examination syllabus must conform, and Subject Specific Criteria, which govern content of certain subject syllabuses.

It is more relevant to consider General Criteria in this chapter. Details of subject specific criteria are readily available for teachers with an interest in a particular curriculum area.[6]

General Criteria govern not only the published subject criteria, but also provide the yardstick against which all new syllabuses and submissions for courses seeking GCSE certification must be measured. They set out the principles which govern all examinations and syllabuses, and establish ground rules for the conduct of examinations.

In particular, the regulations for subjects seeking approval require that every syllabus shall specify:

i. A title – giving a clear indication of the nature of the subject; GCSE aims to cut down on the proliferation of examination titles by offering broad overall headings.
ii. Aims – the educational aims of the course to be followed must be spelt out clearly.
iii. Content and skills – syllabuses must include a sufficient body of knowledge and require a sufficient range of skills to be demonstrated.
iv. Assessment scheme – this section is particularly detailed, and emphasises the necessity to assess according to the principle of 'fitness for purpose'. The relationship between the educational aims and objectives of the course must be reflected in the nature of the assessment procedures adopted. The importance of subject validity and reliability (does the assessment measure what it sets out to measure, and can it be accurately reproduced in a number of other contexts?) is stressed. Other issues, such as the duration of examining time demanded of young people, and the appropriate combination of teacher assessed and examination board assessed components are indicated.
v. General Critieria also determine prohibited combinations of subjects (usually as a result of overlap), presentations and format, freedom from political, racial or sexual bias, clarity of language, and the relationship of the syllabus to other areas of studies.

Full details of the General and Subject Criteria can be found in *GCSE: The National Criteria* (HMSO 1985).

5.4.2 Individual requirements

This section figures less prominently than in other initiatives. With the identification of national criteria, and nationally approved syllabuses, the scope for individually identified requirements is largely eliminated.

The 'no options' generalisation is tempered to some extent by the opportunity for schools to opt for locally devised Mode 2 or Mode 3 syllabuses, though these must still conform to the subject specific national criteria, or to the General Criteria.

5.5 Impact on individuals and organisations

GCSE has had a major impact on organisations, on teachers and on students. The impact can be divided into three main areas:
– curriculum (and learning styles)
– resources
– INSET

a. Curriculum

There is increasing emphasis on coursework, with an associated move away from the importance of memory, recall and orderly presentation towards a more practically based examination, with a greater emphasis on process skills. This does not, however, mean that the necessity for courses to contain a significant body of knowledge is denied.

The shift towards a criterion-referenced approach to assessment has also meant a major change of emphasis for many teachers. Although there will be some delay in arriving at the full introduction of grade criteria, a move away from norm-referencing, which was already detectable, is gathering strength.

Impact on the institutions has extended beyond the fourth and fifth year in which GCSE is taking place. Schools have found that it is impractical and undesirable to adopt different teaching and learning strategies in the lower school, so GCSE methodology and increased emphasis on problem-solving approaches have found their way into the lower school curriculum in a very short space of time.

It is interesting that such is the radical nature of the change demanded of teachers that in one subject, (Mathematics), compulsory coursework as a method of assessment is not required until 1991.

b. Resources

The consensus of opinion among teachers and managers in education is that GCSE was an enormously expensive innovation, with resource implications which were not fully recognised by the Government. Despite the initial anxiety, teachers were largely trying to do the best for their pupils. However, they felt increasingly frustrated by the inability to acquire even the basic essentials for their courses.

The Government argues that generous sums of money were pumped into GCSE and doubtless that is true, but many still felt that it was inadequate. Without doubt, the introduction of GCSE had major financial implications for institutions. This issue will be explored more fully in 5.7, but many teachers felt that resources were simply not adequate for the purchase of new books, practical apparatus and to support the cost of field studies.

c. INSET

Probably the biggest single impact upon both institution and individual brought about by GCSE is that caused by INSET. There was an urgent need for adequate training to bring teachers up to date with the new examination and to give them the skills and confidence necessary to transmit these new approaches to their pupils. However, the effect of taking large numbers of teachers out of schools for training had a serious effect upon the organisation and the day-to-day life of the school. Coinciding as it did with TRIST (Chapter 4), which was also taking teachers out of school, classrooms were denuded. This affected the quality and quantity of what pupils were experiencing within the classroom.

The impact was also felt in those institutions which provided teachers to carry out the training – they were losing key figures for substantial periods of time, although it could be argued that they were reaping the benefit of developing very knowledgeable individuals within their own institutions.

Problems associated with the training will be discussed in more detail in 5.7, but they centred around finding a sufficient and consistently good supply of trainers. Many teachers felt cheated by the inadequacy of the INSET to which they were exposed and voiced their criticisms strongly.

GCSE is the single innovation which has had an impact upon virtually every teacher in the Secondary system (maintained and independent); there can be few who have escaped its influence. For some the impact was traumatic, calling for a change in 'tried and tested' teaching styles and curricula; for others it was an opportunity to put into practice an approach which was more in line with their beliefs about the nature of learning.

5.6 Benefits

i. One of the main benefits associated with GCSE lies in its function as a catalyst in changing teaching methods, the expectations of learning strategies for young people, and the approach to assessment. This is particularly true when it is taken in conjunction with other initiatives such as TVEI, which seeks to promote a more experience-based, problem-solving approach to education. One result of this should be the development of a

The General Certificate of Secondary Education (GCSE)

workforce which is more independent, and better prepared for life after school.
ii. A benefit which many students welcome is the chance to gain credit for work over a period of time, rather than the 'all or nothing' approach of the sudden death examination.
iii. Increasing emphasis on oral and practical work results in pupils who are more articulate, and able to communicate with adults and others. This is a real factor in determining the results of job interviews, for example.
iv. The elimination of duplicated administrative procedures for public examinations is one benefit which does not attract attention, but which means that senior teachers can use their time more productively.
v. Avoiding the division of students into two categories as early as the third year has significant benefits for the organisation of the school, for the morale and self-image of many students, and arguably for the attainment level of pupils who are not already locked into a self-fulfilling prophecy by seeing themselves as second-class students.

5.7 Drawbacks

Many of the disadvantages associated with GCSE relate to its introductory period, and have already been referred to earlier.
i. One of the main problems lies in the fact that so many new, radical changes were being thrust upon teachers at the same time, and at the same time as they were still trying to deliver the old examination systems to existing pupils. Whilst it is true that TVEI, Records of Achievement and GCSE can work to make a more cohesive approach to education, they can also serve to make the beleaguered teacher, struggling to accommodate all these changes, feel more threatened than ever. It should also be remembered that the introduction of GCSE came at the height of teachers' industrial action and the climate did not lead to a welcome for new or extra work. Many teachers boycotted GCSE training during the action.
ii. Under-resourcing of a major shift in the infrastructure of the examination system is one of the major problems. Although the DES announced that it was providing some £70 per pupil to support introduction of GCSE, this included costs of INSET and other capital costs which were invisible to teachers. Teachers were interested in the amount of additional money they had for purchasing books and equipment: this amounted to approximately £27 per pupil, which was woefully inadequate.
iii. The short lead-in time allowed for GCSE caused protests from the teachers' unions. They clamoured for an extended preparatory phase, and all the indications were that they would succeed. However, Sir Keith Joseph remained adamant that the first courses would commence in September 1986. It may be that the problems associated with GCSE

could have been overcome more easily if teachers and examination boards had been allowed a more realistic preparatory phase.

iv. Part of the problem connected with the short lead time was the fact that a number of aspects had not been thought through properly. One example of this lies in the assessment of students. It is admirable to talk in general terms about new approaches to assessment, but classroom teachers were faced with the dilemma of exactly HOW they assessed particular sections of work. There were additional problems associated with the fact that they were now required to indicate exactly how they allocated marks for each section, and had to be able to justify those marks. All of this imposed an additional burden upon teachers, who found it hard to deliver in the time available.

v. The question of time to assess students is a recurring problem. For example, in Science the teacher has to observe individual pupils carrying out an experiment, then mark that practical work according to a set of criteria. Teachers are presented with a daunting task which stretches their professional expertise to the limits.

vi. From the point of view of both teacher and student, the demands created by the increase in coursework and oral work can cause serious problems. Not least is the potential for overloading pupils with coursework requirements which might occur in several subjects at the same time.

vii. Students who were amongst the last taking the dual examination system were penalised by the diversion of teachers' attention and time through INSET. Those embarking upon GCSE courses suffered from the experimental nature of their experience, which caused concern to many parents. Quite apart from this, early entrants for GCSE did not experience assessment by Grade Criteria, whilst those participating after the mid 90s presumably will.

viii. A potentially serious disadvantage lies in the requirement for differentiated papers and questions. If great care is not exercised, we could find ourselves back in exactly the same situation of sorting students into categories and predicting their future chance of success just as the old system of GCE and CSE did.

ix. The proposal to redesign syllabuses in line with a national curriculum adds a new dimension to the problems facing teachers.

5.8 Political rationale

One motive for removing a two-tier examination system is allied to the move to do away with a two-tier school system, with grammar and secondary modern schools. The drive for equality of opportunity for all pupils can be detected in both movements.

The division of examinations into GCE, targeted at the top 20% of the academic achievement range marries neatly with the proportion of able youngsters creamed off by the old grammar schools, whilst CSE, aimed at the next 40% of the cohort, offered a solution to the strongly growing demand for certification from the pupils, teachers and parents of the Secondary Modern School. Of course the figures were rarely so tidily allocated – the overlap was far less distinct, and was made still more confusing by the fact that more pupils sat for public examinations than had been anticipated.

The move towards the introduction of comprehensive education in the 60s and 70s highlighted the disparity of the dual system and the undesirable nature of categorising students, not now by separate school systems, but by separate certification procedures.

It was, therefore, logical that the same sociological pressures which had influenced comprehensive education, should be brought to bear on the examination system within the new schools.

Paradoxically, a reason for promoting GCSE came from a Government which supported an independent education sector through the Assisted Places Scheme and campaigned for GCSE as a means of 'improving standards'. Thus GCSE was an initiative which satisfied the philosophy of both the left and the right wings of politics and education, and as such attracted a powerful lobby in support of its introduction.

A further influence upon the speed of introduction could also have been the threat posed by the strengthening Records of Achievement movement. During 1983, when profiling was rapidly gaining in popularity, the DES was sensitive to the climate of opinion. In some of the most influential examination boards, it was being freely admitted that work towards a common examination at 16 plus lacked impetus, whilst the excitement lay in the development of new profiling initiatives.

The cynical observer might argue that GCSE offered the perfect opportunity for the Government to take a proactive role in determining the curriculum on a national scale.

To sum up, motives were probably a mixture of idealism, self-preservation and expediency.

5.9 First-hand experiences of GCSE: Nailsea School, Avon

With the advent of GCSE, the Head of English seized the opportunity to influence examination in English at sixteen plus by putting forward proposals for a 100% coursework syllabus. Together with another Avon teacher, he devised a syllabus which sought to test young people's grasp and command of English in a way which would not only maintain, but improve standards set under GCE and CSE. At the same time, students would have the opportunity to explore the use of language in a creative manner and to improve communication skills. What was surprising to the two originators of the scheme was the extent to which it was embraced by other schools. Following a meeting called to explain the proposal to colleagues in other establishments, fifty of the sixty-two Avon secondary schools now subscribed to what is known as the 'Avon Consortium Syllabus', which is validated by the Southern Examining Group (SEG).

a. Content

The GCSE Certificate is awarded to pupils without any external examination component. Work which the student undertakes throughout the two year period of the course is taken into account in the overall assessment. A final folder contains ten pieces of work (though major exercises count as the equivalent of two separate contributions). The writing which takes place reflects a variety of styles and purposes, but the main change from the old examination system is the flexibility which is given to teachers and students. This is reflected in the opportunity for drafting, for preparatory work, and for a variety of situations in which the work is carried out, maybe at home, in groups, or as a result of discussions etc. An interesting development is the inclusion of some English literature within the English GCSE. As a result, pupils not taking English literature at GCSE level will still have exposure to some literature. Some of the work must be carried out in 'controlled' situations, under the supervision of the teacher, but this is still far removed from the old, single examination.

The final folder of ten pieces of work is the result of selection by teacher and student.

Oral work plays an important part in the course, and includes talk, role play, group discussions and telephone conversations.

b. Assessment

Assessment takes place as work is completed; these assessments are the subject of internal moderation by teachers within the school, external moderation by groups of teachers from other schools, and finally moderation by the Examination Board.

Each piece of work is accompanied by what the pupils call a 'top sheet' (see Figure 5.1) and includes a section of self-assessment by the pupil.

The student must include evidence of study of some aspect of media, one piece based on a complete text, such as a novel, two pieces written under controlled conditions, two pieces illustrating comprehension, and two pieces showing a range of different kinds of writing. In addition, three different assessments of oral work are included.

c. Teachers' and students' reactions

Teachers at Nailsea were clearly committed to this new approach to teaching and examining English. Comments included observations on the increasing

NAILSEA SCHOOL ENGLISH FACULTY
ENGLISH / ENGLISH LITERATURE COURSEWORK

Name: James Greengrass Date: 10/9/87
Candidate number: _____ Year: (4th) 5th 6th

Title of Unit: Ludwig — fear from the past

Type of writing: Collage text
Approx number of words: 200   Redrafted? YES / ~~NO~~
Texts/stimulus/preparation for writing: None

Conditions under which unit was written: Controlled in Classroom for one double lesson

Controlled? YES / ~~NO~~

Self assessment/student's comments: I liked this and enjoyed writing it. I hope I've given a sense of fear.

Teacher's comments (content, style, appropriateness): Yes you did. I thought this was excellent — the sections of writing were very well done, as I liked the way you incorporated the fragments of other texts without needing to make an obvious

Mechanics: or straightforward story. Does this owe something to the Detective Novel work we did? I like the way in which you

Advice: make writing (manuscript) itself become the mystery. It makes me wish there was a whole novel to follow! Have you come across The Name of the Rose by Umberto Eco?

Grade: (A) B C D E F G U   Moderated grade _____

R.3011/

Fig. 5.1: GCSE Assignment assessment sheet, Nailsea School

emphasis on meaning and understanding, on the welcome flexibility in the means of demonstrating competence, and in the teaching methodology. They noted the additional demands made of teachers who are marking and examining. It is necessary to really read, and to work at the assessment. It is certainly not possible to assess on the basis of qualitative impressions. They did recognise, however, that not every teacher would be able to cope with the demands made of them with this approach; the flexibility inherent in the syllabus reflects a corresponding flexibility demanded of teachers.

In response to questions about the maintenance of standards, teachers were in no doubt that standards were definitely higher under this system. Assessment standards are monitored carefully and checked using sophisticated procedures.

Pupils appeared to enjoy their work and were motivated by the fact that what they were doing in the classroom really counted in their final certification. It was interesting, though, to realise that they were not able to make any real comparison between this method of working and the old system because, for them, what appears revolutionary was the norm.

An example of the type of coursework developed by one teacher can be seen in the following extract. A question from the 1987 English 'O' Level examination paper (see Figure 5.2) is included for comparison.

In the words of the teacher:

> '*In this piece of work, which is a collage text, students showed their awareness of different uses of language and image by cutting up, editing and ordering material which they had been given.*
>
> *They were presented with a number of photographs of people and places, and a number of extracts from writing with a wide range of purposes and styles. They were then invited to incorporate these into a piece of writing of their own, by cutting out and pasting up whatever they had selected. They were not asked to write explanations of what they thought the pieces of writing or image were. Instead, their interpretations of each fragment was implicit in the way they had chosen to incorporate it.*
>
> *Materials included: a timetable; a piece of news journalism; instructions for assembling a vacuum cleaner; a medieval manuscript; diagrams; a handwritten message; part of a poem; part of a play; part of a letter.*
>
> *The exercise enabled students to experiment with the presentation and layout of their work, and to look at how visual format (table, diagram, type, print, handwriting, for instance) influences the nature of a written message, and the way a reader is likely to interpret it.*
>
> *The pieces of work they produced took various overall forms, including letters, poems, narratives and puzzles. Often they became stories or accounts explicitly about writing:*

The General Certificate of Secondary Education (GCSE)

"*I cut this out of the bible.*"
"*He'd found the file on the doorstep. Just the references to the abbey and one other thing, a sentence from a modern book* ..."

Students also added more layers of their own by experimenting with their own writing to produce a number of different styles or ways of presenting words.'

Section A

1. A large sum of money has been donated to your school or college. Give the differing views of a student, a teacher and a parent on how it should best be spent.

Fig. 5.2: GCE 'O' level question 1987

Summary

GCSE is still in a state of flux. Proposals for the disbanding of SEC, and its substitution by the School Assessment and Examination Council, caused additional problems at a time when it appeared that early difficulties were receding. However, it seems clear that several new trends in the Secondary experience can be attributed to the advent of GCSE.
  i. There is a lessening of the importance attached to content and increasing emphasis on process, understanding, and the development of skills.
 ii. Assessment philosophy has shifted to accommodate the 'know, understand and can do' theme of GCSE.
iii. Bottom up, rather than top down assessment is gaining credence. GCSE attempts to identify the foundation level of a student's achievement and build up to higher levels. This contrasts with the old system of setting a standard and deducting marks for failure to achieve it.
 iv. A greater emphasis on practical approaches to learning and problem solving is already evident.
  v. Problems associated with accelerated introduction, under-resourcing and demands for change in teaching styles have resulted in some teachers becoming frustrated and disillusioned.
 vi. Despite this, it seems that both young people and teachers are enjoying their work for GCSE. It remains to be seen whether the initial difficulties can be overcome in such a way that the potential benefits of GCSE can be fully realised.

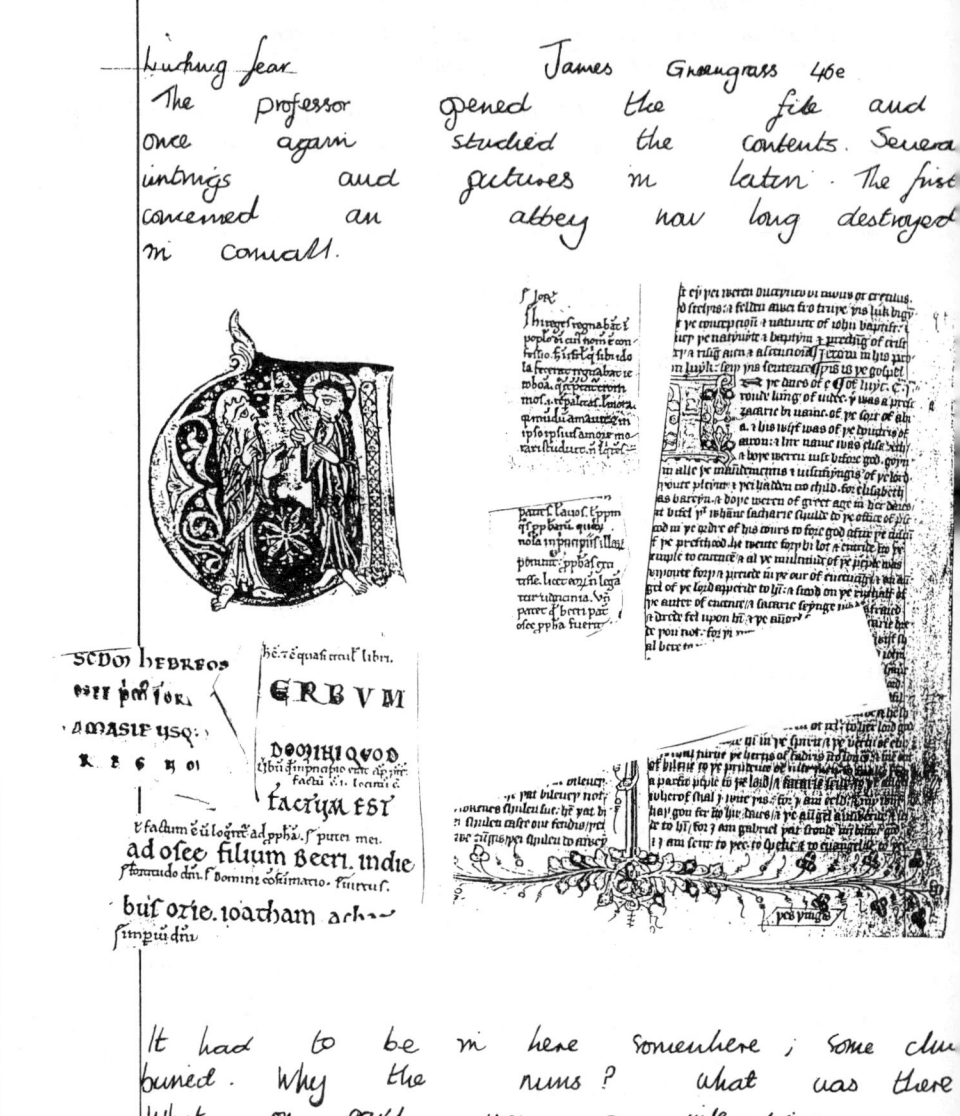

Fig. 5.3: Students' collage work GCSE English, Nailsea School

on the floor not daring to use the bed feeling that it made him too vulnerable. He'd found the file on the doorstep. Just the references to the abbey and one other thing. A sentence from a modern book

```
And the rotten rose is ript from the wall.
```

The day afterwards he started to notice that he wasn't alone. There were noises outside his door, shufflings from next door. When he'd come back from shopping he found that someone had tried to force his door.

He grew afraid, fear hung like a shadow over him. But why? Why him.

Notes

1. The Norwood Report, 1943
2. Secondary Schools Examinations Committee, *Secondary Schools Examinations other than GCE (Beloe Report)*, HMSO, 1960.
3. *Examinations at 16+*, HMSO, 1966.
4. *GCSE Inservice Training Programme Supplementary Materials*, SEG, 1985.
5. *Schools Examinations – report of the steering committee to consider proposals for replacing the General Certificate of Education Ordinary Level and Certificate of Secondary Education examinations by a common system of examining. The Waddell Report*, HMSO, 1978.
6. *GCSE: The National Criteria*, HMSO, 1985.

Chapter 6

Profiles and records of achievement

Profiles, or records of achievement, record the whole range of students' achievements and experiences, including practical skills, attitudes, personal achievements, personal qualities and academic attainment. The student is involved in the formation of the record. This has not only a summative function, providing an end statement on a student's overall achievement and performance (which may be at the end of a piece of work, a year, or a school career), but, more significantly, it is part of the continuing learning process whereby the pupil and teacher jointly review progress with the aim of improving motivation, personal development and future attainment.

6.1 Background

Until the late 1970s, references to 'profiles' were rare. The interest which has developed since that time has its origins mainly in a grass roots movement founded by practising teachers.

This was reinforced by the involvement of a number of national bodies, principally the FEU (*A Basis for Choice*[1]) and the Schools Council. A number of examination boards concerned with pre-vocational education such as City and Guilds of London Institute (CGLI) and the Royal Society of Arts (RSA) also developed profiles designed to fit their particular courses. Post 16, the MSC's Youth Training Scheme introduced a profile to certificate the YTS programme.

The main thrust certainly came from teachers working in the classroom. By the early 1980s individual school or college profiling schemes were proliferating and a number of examination boards (usually in partnership with one or more LEAs) had entered the arena. These included the Oxford Delegacy of Local Examinations (Oxford Certificate of Educational Achievement [OCEA]), the South Western Examination Board (South Western Profile Assessment Research Project [SWPARP]) and the Northern Examining Association (Northern Partnership for Records of Achievement [NPRA]).

In 1984 the DES published what could well prove to be a seminal document with its *Records of Achievement: a statement of policy*[2]. This called for arrangements to be made by 1990 for all sixteen-year-old students to receive records of achievement. A number of pilot schemes were set up and the information gathered formed the basis of national guidelines, published in 1988.

6.2 Aims

The aims of profiles and records of achievement have moved away from the original concerns which prompted teachers – namely dissatisfaction with public examinations, and the provision of more comprehensive information for employers and other users[3]. Greater emphasis is placed on the process, which encourages students to take responsibility for their own learning by participating in assessment, and by engaging in regular dialogue with teachers about their progress.

The DES outlines the purposes and aims as being:
 i. Recognition of achievement. Records and recording systems should recognise, acknowledge and give credit for what pupils have achieved and experienced, not just in terms of results in public examinations but in other ways as well. They should do justice to pupils' own efforts and to the efforts of teachers, parents, ratepayers and taxpayers to give them a good education.
 ii. Motivation and personal development. They should contribute to pupils' personal development and progress by improving their motivation, providing encouragement and increasing their awareness of strengths, weaknesses and opportunities.
 iii. Curriculum and organisation. The recording process should help schools to identify the all round potential of their pupils and to consider how well their curriculum, teaching and organisation enable pupils to develop the general, practical and social skills which are to be recorded.
 iv. A document of record. Young people leaving school or college should take with them a short, summary document of record which is recognised and valued by employers and institutions of further and higher education. This should provide a more rounded picture of candidates for jobs or courses than can be provided by a list of examination results, thus helping potential users to decide how candidates could best be employed, or for which jobs, training schemes or courses they are likely to be suitable[4].

This concentration on the formative process gives added weight to the argument that the principal aims of records of achievement place assessment at the heart of the learning process, strengthen the relationship to the curriculum, and replace the traditional recording and reporting systems.

The overall aim must be to improve the quality of students' learning, to improve the quality of relationships and dialogue between student and teacher, and to give the student a fairer, fuller and more rounded picture to take away at the end of eleven years of compulsory schooling.

6.3 Structure

The structure of individual records of achievement varies considerably, though the differences are far less obvious now than they were in the early 1980s. Most summative records fall in line with the recommendation[5] that they should contain:
i. information, other than academic success, which throws light on personal achievements and characteristics
ii. evidence of attainment in academic subjects and practical skills, including any graded results in public examinations

This can be presented in a number of ways, but one useful model separates the components into four main sections:

a. Personal achievements

This section plays an important part in the formative process, enhancing students' self-esteem and self-confidence by helping them to recognise that many of their activities and interests are worthwhile and worth recording.

It is, however, of little value to simply record lists of experiences without associated tutorial involvement and guidance. The mechanics of recording vary widely, and range from schemes where the student keeps a regular diary (not generally popular with students who resist the feeling of compulsion associated with a diary), a log-book system which is completed every two to four weeks, or a relatively 'free' process whereby students make entries as they wish.

The type of activities which are commonly entered in this section include:
work experience
community service
part-time jobs
spare-time interests or hobbies
service to other people
service to the school or college
sporting activities
clubs[6]

Some important questions:
i. What experiences should be included?
ii. Should entries be verified or contributed to by an adult?
iii. How should this information be presented?
iv. How can recording best be organised – by a diary system, log book, separate sheet?
v. How often should achievements be recorded?
vi. Should external awards and certificates be included?
(See Figures 6.1 and 6.2.)

STOCKPORT RECORD OF ACHIEVEMENT

PUPIL'S NAME LYNNE BENNETT.

PUPIL'S PERSONAL RECORD

My main interest is playing the tenor horn which I have been doing for four years. I spend a lot of my time making my own clothes which works out to be cheaper. I am a member of a Young Enterprise Company where we make toys and switches for handicapped children. Which we entered Young Engineer for Britain 1985 and reached the national finals held in Wembley Conference centre. To relax I enjoy listening to pop music, but I rarely have time for this because I am out nearly every night of the week with the band. I spend a lot of my time making clothes, both knitting and sewing. I make them for myself, family and friends and I used to knit for a shop. I had a morning paperround for 3 years but had to give it up because it proved too much, having to get up at 6·30 every morning. With my paperround wages I saved up to buy myself a tenor horn which costs £200. I now babysit for a little boy who is 3, and sometimes a girl and boy aged 7 and 9.

I am very active with the brass band which my dad runs, I am very ambitious. I am fairly timid but try to make an effort to avoid obstructing others. I am not determined to always get my own way. I was head girl at primary school. I am very respectful of people who respect me.

My appearance to me is quite important. I am very reliable and try to keep my word.

PUPIL'S SIGNATURE L. Bennett

The statement on this sheet has been written by the pupil, who was given a series of suggestions as to the kind of entry which might be of interest to others.

The entries have been discussed with the pupil, but there has been no alteration to presentation or grammar unless the pupil specifically asked for help or advice.

PUP

Fig. 6.1: Personal recording, Davenport School, Stockport

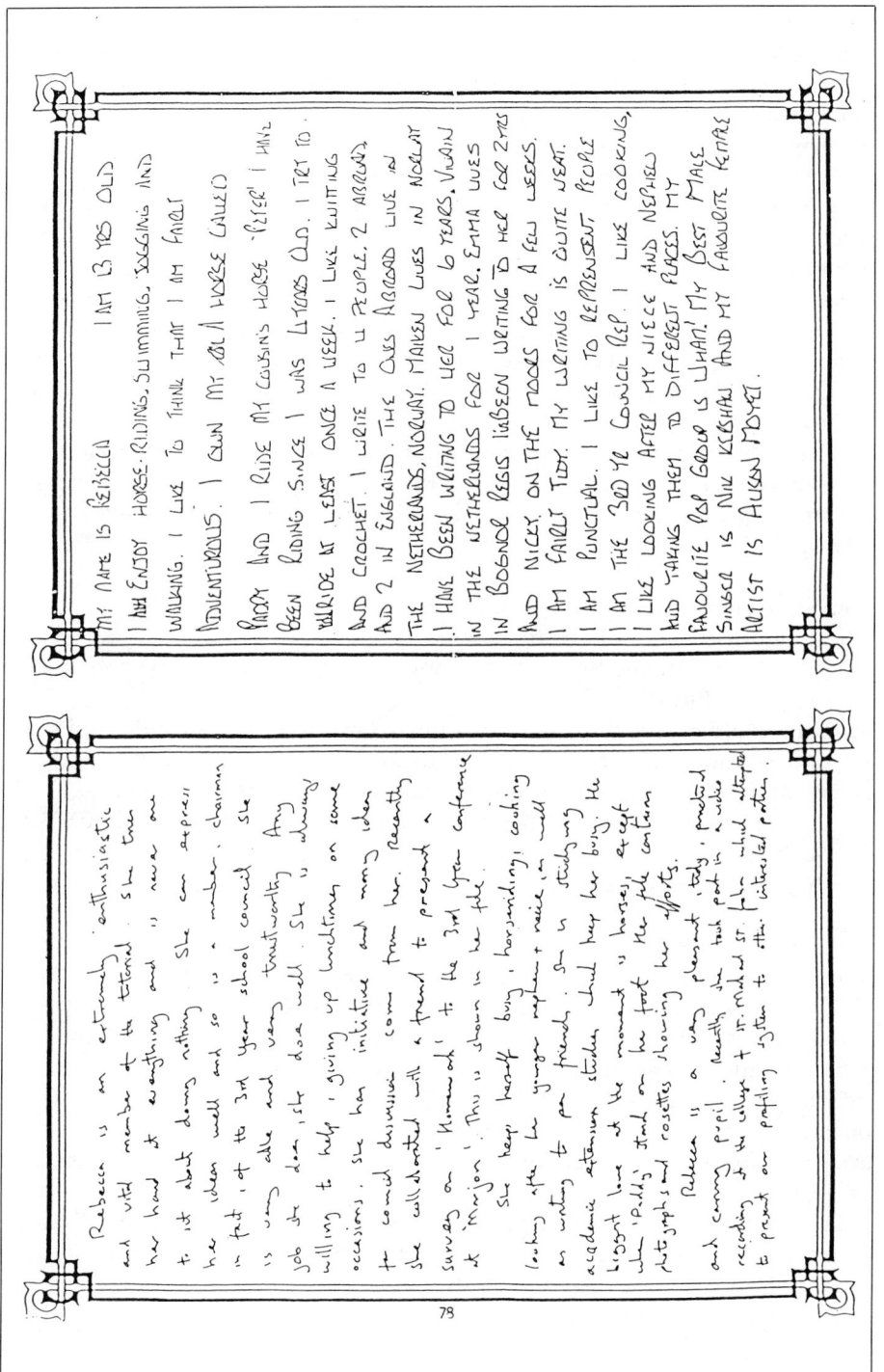

Fig. 6.2: Extract from PPR Tutor's Handbook

b. Personal qualities

The inclusion of comments and assessments of students' personal characteristics causes considerably more controversy than personal achievements. Some people feel that this element represents an unwarranted intrusion into the privacy of the individual, and that it is subject to bias and subjectivity.

Nevertheless, for many students this may be the one area in which they have outstanding attributes; they would be penalised if they were unable to receive credit for, or draw attention to, aspects of their personality which help to bolster their own self-esteem and improve the picture which they can present to employers. The converse argument can also be put forward.

Therefore, despite the dangers, the inclusion of personal qualities as a separate section is recommended, but with stringent safeguards attached to the nature of the qualities included and the method by which they are assessed, recorded and reported.

Giving the student control over entries to this section, seeking contributions from more than one teacher, and providing illustrative, supportive evidence are some ways of mitigating the difficulties whilst still doing justice to the student.

Some questions to ask when planning this section:
 i. What qualities should be included?
 ii. To what extent should evidence supporting assessment of personal qualities be included?
 iii. How could personal qualities be assessed in practice – during lesson time, tutorial time, extra-curricular activities?
 iv. What number of qualities should teachers be expected to assess?
 v. Is it necessary for both teacher and student to comment on EVERY quality?
 (See Figures 6.3 and 6.4.)

c. Cross-curricular skills

The recording of cross-curricular skills encourages teachers and employers to look at the whole person, rather than at their performance within separate subject areas. This is central to the philosophy of profiling and records of achievement. In practice, it is an area which has caused teachers considerable difficulty. It demands flexibility to enable the student to develop skills which operate across the curriculum, and to assess those skills across subject boundaries. Notable exceptions are to be found in prevocational courses and the best of TVEI.

Despite the difficulties, it is worth persisting. It is in this area that the effects of records of achievement upon the curriculum can be most clearly seen. If these skills are to be assessed, then the curriculum must be modified in order to accommodate them.

Profiles and records of achievement

HOW I SEE MYSELF

NAME: _____   _____   Tutor Group: **5HA**

Date Completed: _____

	Student's Comment	Quality	Teacher's Comment
1	I am always in school dress. And neat and tidy in the way I look.	Appearance	Mrs P. Cookson — She always looks neat and tidy. *Signature*
2	I am Reliable in and out of school.	Reliability	I have never found Rhona to be anything other than reliable. *Signature*
3	I am an honest person, If someone has lost something I will try to find the owner.	Honesty	Rhona is totally honest & trustworthy person. She is maturing into a wonderful young lady. *Signature*
4	When I am the leader of a group people do listen to me, and take my advice, If I need help I will ask for it.	Leadership	Rhona has a strong dominant personality and is more often than not organizing those around her. She does listen to advice. *Signature*
5	I am quite flexible and when my mind has to be changed I will make the right decision.	Adaptability Flexibility	Certainly an acceptable sort; shows initiative but always willing to respond to collected suggestions. *Signature*

Fig. 6.3: Personal qualities, Brays Gore School, Harlow

- Personal Qualities -

In this section of your Record of Achievement, you have the chance to create a picture of the kind of person you feel you are. Everyone is a special person, with different interests, enthusiasms and ideas: it is these which make you unique, an individual quite unlike anyone else.

To help you start thinking about how you want to describe yourself, you will find a list of different qualities which people have. Under each heading, there are some questions to ask yourself, and examples of the kinds of activities or views we think of when we use a word such as 'co-operative' or 'caring'.

Start by making notes in the blank spaces on your OUTLINES sheets beside each of the qualities. All sorts of information is useful here - activities you enjoy, things you believe are important in your life, the way you try to treat other people, issues you care about. All of this information helps to build up a unique picture of you - as you think you are.

When you start to make your notes and think about what you want to say, there is one thing, above all, which is important. Being honest. Nobody is perfect and probably none of us would much like a person who was! Our friend like us in spite of our funny habits, and sometimes because of them. But one thing you need to remember about this part of your Record, is that it gives you the chance to write down the good news and the bad news: the person you are, and a bit about the person you'd like to be.

After you've worked for a while on your outline, you'll have the chance to explain your ideas to your group tutor, who may be able to help you add bits you hadn't thought about before. You will have the chance to meet with your tutor on your own several times in the coming year. When you go to see your tutor, he or she will encourage you to talk about the things you're interested in at the moment and help you build up the written picture of yourself that you want to include in your Record of Achievement.

Try to include some aims to work towards - you may want to become a better listener, or the opposite - better at speaking up for yourself in a group. Becoming more clear in your own mind about what you're good at and what you find difficult is half the battle towards becoming more confident. It's a step towards being able to use your personal strengths to achieve what you want from life.

Above all, have fun working through the various sections. Try to bring yourself to life on the page, to draw a portrait which is a good likeness. After all, there's nobody quite like you, anywhere!

.... a self-portrait -

Fig. 6.4: Personal qualities, Comberton Village College

Determined....

Being determined can be shown in lots of ways. You may be the kind of person who likes to see a job through to the end, even if, at times, it's hard to keep enthusiastic about it. Do you ever find you give up when the going gets difficult, or do you battle on and ask for help if you need to get something right? What sorts of situations encourage you to be determined - sporting activities, schoolwork, tasks you're doing in your free time? Do you ever suspect that you can be a bit stubborn and determined to have your own way? Can you think of an example of something you succeeded with in the end that you feel proud of because you know you had to work hard to get it?

Taking Responsibility....

Try to think of as many examples as you can here of ways in which you show you can be trusted to be responsible. You may be trusted to take responsibility for other people - younger members of your family or other people's children is a great responsibility and sign of trust. Perhaps you've been given responsibility for organising events such as trips or parties, fund-raising events. If you have a part-time job, what do your employers expect you to be responsible for - money, equipment, property? Do you have responsibilities at home? Remember that noting down examples of what you do is really important in this section.

Caring....

What do you care about? Do you feel you are sympathetic to other people's problems and try to understand how they feel about things? Can you understand or at least put up with, people whose ideas are different from yours? Do you find time to help others in your family, or through voluntary work perhaps with children or old people? Would you offer to help even if there was no 'reward' in it for you, just because you wanted to? Have you ever been involved in events designed to raise money for people not as lucky as yourself? Do you think you're good at listening to friends' problems and offering help and support when they're down?

Enthuastic....

What do you get enthusiastic about? Music, sports, drama, making things, collecting things? Are you the kind of person who likes being busy and involved in activities all of the time? Sometimes? Would you describe yourself as lively or energetic? Perhaps you are, like most people, enthusiastic about some things and not others. Try to make a list of enthusiasms.

Reflective....

This means simply thinking things over, enjoying solo pursuits such as reading, listening to music or playing an instrument, perhaps just cycling along on your own, thinking things over. Do you feel that spending some time on your own is important to you? Perhaps you are the kind of person who prefers other people's company to your own - how much do you enjoy being by yourself? If it is important to you to be alone sometimes, can you explain why?

Co-operative....

Being co-operative means that you are able to work with others. There are many ways of describing this quality - being helpful enjoying joining in with others, trying hard not to prevent others from doing what they want. Do you find it hard to turn down a request for help, to say 'no' to people? Perhaps you sometimes wish you could say no more often! It could be that you co-operate because you and others will gain in the long run, or it could just be because you prefer doing things in which you work together as a team.

Careful....

Carefulness can be seen in lots of different ways. Taking care of possessions is one example - so is taking care over decisions you make. Do you think things out and weigh them up before making decisions? Do you avoid taking risks, or do you think that being cautious is boring? You might feel you are careful about everything you do, or only about things you feel to be important. Possibly you feel you are too cautious at times - equally you might will wish you were better at looking after clothes, books or possessions!

Fig. 6.4 (cont.)

Reliable....

This has to do with whether others can rely on you to do your best for them. Do you feel you always try to keep your word, do what you feel you ought? Are you the sort of person who never leaves a task unfinished, or tries not to be late? If you're a 'sometimes' person when you think about these questions (we all are!), in what kinds of situation do you feel people can rely on you? Do you feel that other people could depend on you to keep your word and trust you if they needed to?

Image....

What kind of image do you think people have of you? Is your style of dress casual, smart, a mixture? What sort of situations do you think call for care over your appearance? If someone saw you for the first time, what kind of person do you think they would take you to be from your appearance? Equally important, what sort of personality do you think other people would describe you as having? Quiet, shy, cheerful, easy-going, lively? There are lots of ways to describe people - what words do you think others would use about you? Most important of all, do you you think that the image others have of you is the same as your own? In what ways do you think people might have a wrong impression of you? How would you like to be described?

The next step....

Now that you've finished your outline for the portrait, try to think about some of the things about yourself you'd like to change a bit, or improve on. You can't do much about the shape of your nose, or the colour of your eyes, but there are probably aspects of you that with a bit of work, could become stronger. Choose just one area of your portrait at present that you're going to try and develop.

Write yourself a target to aim for. The next time you review your statement and discuss it with your tutor, you can look back on what you aimed for and see how much progress you've made. As we said at the beginning, nobody's perfect, thank goodness, but we can all become a little bit more so, with care and practice!

Some important questions:
i. What skills should be included?
HMI[7] suggests:
Communication
Numerical
Observational and visual
Imagination
Organisational and study
Physical and practical
Social
Problem-solving
Creative
   Is this list too long, or are there other skills which should be added?
ii. Should all of the skills identified be assessed by all teachers? If not, what is it reasonable to expect teachers to assess?
iii. What is the best way of recording skills assessments?
iv. How should students be involved in their own assessments?
(See Figures 6.5 and 6.6.)

d. Subject attainment

It may seem difficult to imagine today, but there were many who argued against the inclusion of academic attainment in a profile or ROA as recently as the early 80s. It is hard to sustain that argument; the work which students undertake in subjects or courses forms a major part of their experience within education. The whole credibility of the record is undermined if full academic assessments are not included.

One of the most exciting consequences of the influence of records of achievement on academic assessment is to be found within those schools, colleges and LEAs which have recognised the fact that students must play an important part in academic assessment as well as in the 'soft', area of personal achievements and qualities.

This affords not only the opportunity, but the expectation that learning objectives will be set and shared with students so that they understand what they will be attempting to master in the next period of work. At the end of that time they, as well as the teacher, will assess how far they have managed to meet those objectives. This not only helps students to understand what their learning programme is about, and to become involved in assessing their own progress, but it strengthens the diagnostic function of assessment by making strengths and weaknesses far more readily identifiable.

The move towards this approach to assessment is supported by the increase in self-assessment encouraged under GCSE, so that the two schemes are complementary, rather than conflicting.
(See Figure 6.7.)

Profiles and records of achievement

Some important questions:
  i. How can the format for this section be designed to reflect both student and teacher input?
 ii. Should the setting of subject objectives be undertaken by individual teachers, or should it be a departmental decision?
iii. What procedures can be established to ensure that students can contribute to their own assessments?
 iv. How can assessments made under this scheme be used to replace the old reports to parents?
  v. How can the information gathered during the formative process best be transferred to the summative record of achievement?
(See Figure 6.8.)

e. Summative record of achievement

Early profiling developments emphasised the importance of institutions being able to devise profiles which arose solely from their own curricular experience and reflected the values of the school or college. It soon became clear however that in order for records of achievement to gain credibility on a national scale, it would be necessary to impose some degree of uniformity. There is a continuing tension between the desire for a 'home-grown' version, and a recognisable document valued by users and capable of transfer from one part of the country to another.

Whilst the importance of records of achievement which grow from the curriculum is undeniable, it was common for the term to be applied to widely differing documents: some were dossiers up to one inch thick, others were a folded A3 sheet. Clearly there was a need for a degree of rationalisation.

DES guidelines indicate that the summative ROA should provide a brief and clear synopsis of the student's attainments in all of the areas outlined above. This may be presented in a folder which gives students the opportunity to include evidence of examination results (although this will be added at a later date, as results are not available at the time ROAs are presented) and other evidence of work or awards of which the individual may be proud.

The idea of national guidelines setting parameters within which records must be developed, but which leave room for flexibility in the internal processes leading up to the final record, offers a sensible compromise.

Practice varies in different parts of the country, but whether the final record of achievement is to be designed by the individual school or college, whether it is an LEA initiative, or whether it emerges from a consortium made up of examination boards and LEAs, the questions which need to be asked include:
  i. What format should be adopted?
 ii. Are the four categories of personal achievement, personal qualities, cross-curricular skills and subject attainment appropriate for inclusion in the summative document?

REDDISH VALE SCHOOL
RECORD OF ACHIEVEMENT
SUBJECT ASSESSMENT

NAME: _____ TUTOR GROUP: _____

SUBJECT: ___PHYSICS___ COLUMN: ____ TEACHER: _____

GENERAL SKILLS	NEEDS IMPROVEMENT	STRENGTH	COMMENT/EXAMPLE OF WHERE SKILL HAS BEEN USED
COMMUNICATION – ORAL			
COMMUNICATION – WRITTEN			
WORKING IN A GROUP			
WORKING INDEPENDENTLY			
PLANNING			
USING RESOURCES			
FOLLOWING INSTRUCTIONS			
SUBJECT SKILLS			
PRESENTS EXPERIMENTAL RESULTS IN TABLES/ GRAPHS OR CHARTS			
DESIGN AN EXPERIMENT TO SOLVE A PROBLEM			
DRAW CONCLUSIONS FROM EXPERIMENTAL EVIDENCE			

Further Comments:

Subject teacher: _____ Student: _____

Fig. 6.5: Subject assessment, Reddish Vale School, Stockport

```
SECTION 09:   PROBLEM-SOLVING ABILITIES

Question:
                    How does the student react to familiar
                    and unfamiliar situations and what
                    ability is shown in adopting a
                    systematic approach to problem-solving?

Category - Familiar Situations

01  +   prefers to work in familiar situations.

02  +   works confidently in known situations.

03  +   achieves success when carrying out familiar tasks.

Category - Unfamiliar Situations

04  +   responds confidently in unfamiliar situations.

05  +   responds instinctively to unfamiliar situations.

06  +   takes up new challenges enthusiastically.

07  +   tackles new situations with forethought.

Category - Systematic Approach to Problem Solving

08  +   is able to work through the various stages in a
systematic approach to problem-solving.

09  +   can help with identifying several courses of action
and make valid choices.

10  +   has shown creative thought when seeking possible
solutions to challenging problems.

11  +   enjoys taking part in group problem-solving
assignments and frequently plays a leading role.

12  +   is capable of deciding what needs to be done in
investigatory and practical situations.

13  +   is skilled at assessing the extent to which the work
done meets the identified objectives.
```

Fig. 6.6: St Thomas School, Exeter

St. Mark's School Art Department Assessment Years 1 - 3

NAME / CLASS / PROJECT	Observation and Recording	Imaginative response	Problem solving	Organisation	Investigation	Technical ability	CONTROL OF VISUAL ELEMENTS											Co-operation	Effort
							Line	Shape	Tone	Pattern	Texture	Proportion	Colour	Composition	Structure	Form	Space		

COMMENTS		GRADE
TERM 1		
TERM 2		
TERM 3		

Fig. 6.7: Subject profile developed for GCSE, St Marks School, Bath

DESCRIPTION OF WORK	MATERIALS USED

SELF ASSESSMENT Please answer the questions fully.

What did you enjoy most about this unit of work? Why?

Was there anything you disliked or found difficult about it?

How much effort did you make?

Are you pleased with your work? Can you say why?

Could you have improved it?

What have you learned from this unit?

Did you do enough research?

St. Mark's School Art Department Assessment Years 1 – 3

NAME / CLASS / PROJECT	Observation and Recording	Imaginative response	Problem solving	Organisation	Investigation	Technical ability	CONTROL OF VISUAL ELEMENTS											Co-operation	Effort
							Line	Shape	Tone	Pattern	Texture	Proportion	Colour	Composition	Structure	Form	Space		

COMMENTS		GRADE
TERM 1		
TERM 2		
TERM 3		

Fig. 6.7 (cont.)

Profiles and records of achievement

PROJECT	What did you enjoy most this term? Which was your best piece of work? Was there anything you disliked or found difficult? Could you have improved anything? Could you have worked harder? What have you learned this term? Was your behaviour good?	MEDIA USED
TERM 1		
TERM 2		
TERM 3		
EXTRA CURRICULA ACTIVITY		

CERTIFICATE

DEANS COMMUNITY HIGH SCHOOL

This is to certify that _____
has attained

LEVEL 6
IN
CHEMISTRY

by showing proficiency in the following areas:

Ability to write balanced chemical equations such as $3Cu + 8Msq^+ + 2NO_{3(sq)} \rightarrow 2NO_{(g)} + 4H_2O_{(d)} + 3Cu^{2+}_{(ea)}$.

Ability to perform chemical calculations using the data in chemical equations. These involve formula weights, the male and the concept of concentration.

A knowledge of the order of activity and electrode potential of metals and ability to relate these to displacement, redox, and corrosion and electrolysis phenomena.

A working knowledge of the pH scale of acidity. Perform neutralisation and precipitation experiments, following their progress by conductivity measurements. Ability to prepare graphs and extract information from them.

Knowledge of some sulphur chemistry incorporating preparation and properties of sulphur dioxide and sulphuric acid. Ability to contrast the properties of the concentrated and dilute acid.

Knowledge of some nitrogen chemistry incorporating the manufacture and oxidation of ammonia, preparation and properties of nitric acid and the nitrogen cycle and nitrogenous fertilisers.

DATE:

Signed: _____ Head of Lower/Middle School.

_____ Head.

Fig. 6.8: Subject contribution for Summative Record of Achievement, Deans Community School

Profiles and records of achievement

iii. How can the work carried out in the formative process best be translated onto the summative document?
iv. How can users best be included in, and informed of, developments in records of achievement?
v. Is it appropriate to comment on attendance and punctuality? If so, how should this be represented?

One of the most pressing issues associated with the summative record of achievement is that of validation and accreditation, in order that the final product will have credibility and status.

6.4 Criteria for records of achievement

There are certain features which are essential if the outcome is to be a genuine profiling process and not merely a cosmetic version of the old reporting system.
i. All students should be included regardless of ability – this applies equally to pupils in special schools and to academic high fliers.
ii. The record of achievement should operate throughout the student's secondary career and carry on into further education. (It is interesting that, increasingly, the advantages of including primary pupils are being recognised.)
iii. The ownership of the final record should rest firmly with the student whose permission must be given before it can be reproduced for use in references.
iv. The student should be actively involved in all stages of preparation of and contribution to the record of achievement.
v. It should be recognised that profiling and the recording of achievement are integral to the learning process, and are inextricably linked with the curriculum and with the assessment and reporting policies of the institution.
vi. Parents, employers and other users should be involved in the planning and development of the record of achievement.
vii. The record is a statement of the student's achievements to date, and not an instrument for predicting future potential. (This does, however, make it difficult for Careers Officers to offer appropriate guidance.)

(See Figures 6.9 and 6.10.)

6.5 Impact on individuals and organisations

Records of achievement inevitably make a major impact on organisations – if they do not, then they are merely pale imitations of what should happen. However, the word impact is not necessarily synonymous with 'difficult'. Many schools have found that the impact of profiling and ROA has been one of revitalising both work and relationships.

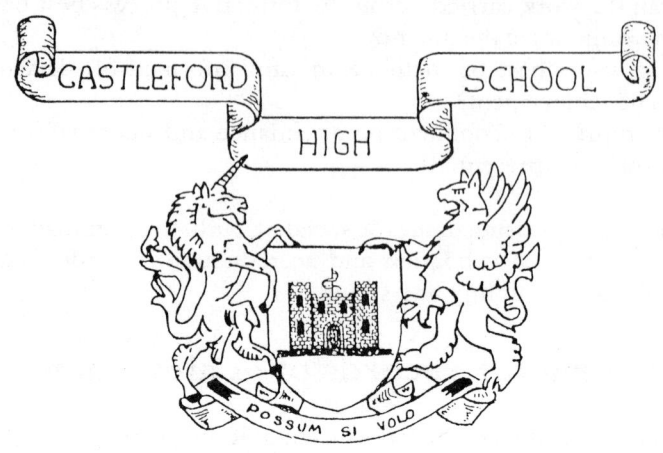

SIXTH FORM 1986

PROFILE COURSE
SPONSORED BY MARKS & SPENCER PLC

A STATEMENT OF ACHIEVEMENT FOR

_____ Chris Seage _____

Fig. 6.9: Summative Record of Achievement, Castleford High School, Wakefield

CHRIS SEAGE

Introduction

Throughout his school career Chris has consistently shown good sense and commitment. His passage through the sixth form has seen a continuing growth of maturity and skills.

Chris has, on a number of occasions, shown the capacity to organize and lead colleagues as well as contributing to group activity in a less directive role: he has often acted as the voice of common sense when others have been less realistic. However, Chris has not always found the role of leader easy but is mastering the subtleties and clearly progress is being made. Chris completes the course with a substantial list of personal achievements to his credit and I have thoroughly enjoyed working with him.

Group Meetings, Consultations, Counselling

Chris responded quickly to the changed requirements the course places upon students. Following a brief spell as group secretary he was elected to the position he clearly wanted - group chairperson. His early self assessment record reflects a desire to lead and within six weeks was organising the staff sixth form disco. The role of chairperson proved to be a difficult one, especially as he got little help from some colleagues but his capacity to express views, respond to situations quickly and organise the activities of others ensured a well prepared disco.

Unfortunately the event was not the success we had hoped for and Chris in particular, took longer than most to recover lost confidence. For some time afterwards his commitment to activities wavered and he relinquished the job of chairperson. Through the 'benches project' Chris once again found his niche and completed the course more skilled in the art of leadership and with the confidence to express and sustain views that had an influence on the opinions of those around him.

Business Management

Tuck Shop Chris has been fully involved in the running of a school tuck shop. His experiences include the purchase and handling of stock from outsider suppliers, cashing up and security. Chris has always fulfilled his commitment to this activity and taken an active role in decision making. Where money is concerned he has been particularly diligent and trustworthy.

Fast Foods Not the most confident of students in the Domestic Science area, Chris has nevertheless been involved in the preparation and selling of baked potatoes and hot dogs. His self assessment record reflects his awareness of these activities as valuable group building exercises and the development of his own organizational capacities.

Christmas Cakes Chris, along with another student, produced Christmas cakes for their own consumption. The member of staff involved commented on the good results the students had achieved and commended them for their capacity to solve problems with little or no help.

Wine Making Chris wasted no time in getting this project started and had lager fermenting before others had even purchased their kits! Wine production was taken at a more leisurely pace. The whole group acquiring a more thorough theoretical preparation before participating in its production.

Painting and Decorating A small group of which Chris was a member, planned the redesign and decoration of a classroom. The activity included preliminary survey, discussion, costing. Unfortunately, the capital was not available to see the project through to a practical completion.

Staff – Sixth Form, Halloween Disco/Buffet As already noted Chris took a leading role in this event which included: costing, production of tickets, food preparation, art work and preparation of the venue for the evening. Chris took on the crucial role of team leader and was personally responsible for much of the high quality decorations present on the evening.

In all these activities Chris has shown his capacities for organisation and a concise way in dealing with problems.

Community Projects

A group of six students undertook the construction of playground seating for the pupils of Smawthorne First School. The project was initiated in November and completed by Easter. Chris was involved in the following:

Planning... preliminary meeting with client, outlining a brief, appraising clients needs, drafting of sketches, deciding upon the most suitable design.

Materials.. purchase of materials – sand, cement, wood, collection of materials from Selby, planing of wood to size, co-ordination of material delivery on site.

Construction marking out of site, laying foundations, modification of plans, use of tools – trowel, spirit level, plumbline, mixing cement, bricklaying.

Organisation coping with kids, working on Sundays, use of staff room, liaison with staff, managing of colleagues, meeting deadlines, contact with local press, appraising the finished product.

Chris led the team during the early stages of the project producing an initial design and organising others. Some of his colleagues however reacted adversely to his 'style' of leadership and opted for an alternative design which was just as well as Chris encountered considerable difficulties in turning sketches to formal plans. He continued to work and co-operate with his colleagues despite his obvious disappointment.

During the construction phase Chris once again came to the fore and played an invaluable role in sharing his considerable construction skills with the team. He had learnt from his early attempts and was now able to instruct without alienating his colleagues.

His construction work was impressive in quality and earned a commendation from Professor Cowan, a university lecturer and construction engineer. Chris's contribution at this stage was crucial as other team members had only limited brick laying skills. The eventual success of the project relied heavily upon his contribution.

He was justifiably proud of the completed benches and especially during the construction stage showed a care for detail and a level of brick laying skill that a professional would be satisfied with.

The whole group earned the praise of both schools, and the L.E.A. and were featured in the local press. (see appendices 1 & 2)

Fig. 6.9 (cont.)

English Studies

Chris has made steady progress in all language areas. He has proved to be a confident speaker with the ability to clearly state and defend a point of view. He interacts well with both adults and colleagues and is always willing and co-operative.

Computer Studies

As part of his Science for Life studies Chris has become involved in developing his existing keyboard skills. He is familiar with computer hardware and has had practice in entering, retrieving and altering data for the school bank. Chris has been entered for an R.S.A. computer literacy qualification which he should acquire in due course.

Media Studies

Chris has played an important role in the production of a video which depicts elements of the Profile Course. He has quickly acquired the technical skills required to assemble, work and control the camera and has been introduced to the idea of using a storyboard for planning. Throughout the year his competence has increased becoming more critical of the product and as a consequence, his work has become more serious and determined. He has proved to be most adept at solving practical problems and is able to convey this understanding in a concise way. Chris has proved to be

> "very enthusiastic and a good motivator of others. Confident, articulate and willing to try out new ideas."

R.S.A. Visit

During this final term the group had to organise and entertain two visitors from the Royal Society of Arts. Chris was fully involved in all elements of this. He showed a lot of confidence in preparing the meal and interacted well with colleagues. He spoke with obvious pride when questioned by Professors Tomlinson and Cavan about the Bench Project. His self assessment diary reflects his commitment to the day, an awareness of the reasons why some elements didn't quite go as planned and his perception of the value of such encounters.

SIGNED..Student

SIGNED......Roy Vaughan...................Tutor

The West Midlands Examinations Board

Form WMRA 1/L

Record of Achievement

LIST OF UNIT OUTCOMES

Scheme Title: Art and Design

Reference: SA/AD/2

Number of units in scheme: 10

Unit Reference	Unit Title	Unit Stage
FA4	Introduction to Ceramics	4

Unit Outcomes:

Knowledge

The student can:

1 identify different forms of clay.

2 describe the working techniques of different clays.

3 describe some different kiln techniques.

4 explain alternative decoration and finishes for ceramics.

Skills

The student can:

5 prepare clays for use.

6 use techniques appropriate to the clay.

7 make ceramic sculptures and vessels.

8 prepare a design for an artefact.

Experiences

The student has:

9 extensive experience of working with a variety of clays.

10 used a potter's wheel.

11 used a kiln.

12 discussed the design and manufacture of ceramics with a professional.

[Turn over

Fig. 6.10: Summative Record of Achievement, West Midlands Examination Board

Profiles and records of achievement

Introduction

The West Midlands Examinations Board Record of Achievement provides a record of positive achievements, personal and academic, for the student named on the outside front cover. The document has been prepared in partnership between the student, teachers and The West Midlands Examinations Board.

This record may contain one or both of the following sections:-

    a   **Section I** is a Personal Record of Achievement and it is in two parts as follows:

        (i) Part A is completed under 7 headings.

        (ii) Part B is optional. It may add to the information in Part A, reflect a Centre's own personal record practices or record achievements beyond those gained in full-time education.

    b   **Section II** is a Certificate of Achievement that records and details academic achievements.

The wallet in the document may contain additional certificates, documents and papers relating to other aspects of the student's achievements.

A full explanation of the aims, objectives, formative processes and administrative procedures, which have culminated in the preparation of this document, is given in the 'Guide to The West Midlands Examinations Board Record of Achievement' — Form WMRA 2. The Guide, together with further exemplar material, may be purchased from The West Midlands Examinations Board at the address given below.

The West Midlands Examinations Board
Norfolk House,
Smallbrook Queensway
BIRMINGHAM B5 4NJ
021-643 2081

The West Midlands Examinations Board
Record of Achievement

Form WMRA 1/A

SECTION I
The Personal Record
FOR
Roger A Jones

PART A

The following statements have been prepared by the student in consultation with a teacher. They record positive achievements which have been attained during the period of secondary education. The statements may be entered in the student's handwriting or in type.

1 **Personal Interests, Experiences and Achievements**

I did work experience at Asda Stores, Sandall. The work I did was very interesting. Most of my interests are outside school. I enjoy going to the roller-disco and auto-grass racing. I have won two trophies for second places. Auto-grass racing is like stock-car racing. I drive a mini-clubman with a roll-cage and special safety belts. We race Saturdays and Sundays. I am a scout and have done a Cycling Proficiency Test and passed a St. John's Ambulance Examination on first Aid. I had a prize in the third form for progress.

2 **Attendance and Punctuality**

I go to school everyday and I get there on time if the Bus is on time.

3 **School, College and Community Service**

Looking after the old folk at Sandall Old Peoples Home. Taking some of them to the dentist. Collected money for Battle of Britain week. Baby sitting for friends.

Fig. 6.10 (cont.)

4   **Personal Qualities**

I get on well with others at school. I am responsible for keeping the money for the school tuck-shop. I am always there. I have learnt to deal with other people and I try to be polite.

5   **Communication Skills**

I like to talk to the teachers and I enjoy talking to other people.

6   **Ability to cooperate with others**

I work in the school tuck-shop. I have learnt to work with other children, some I didn't use to like.

7   **Practical and Athletic Skills**

I'm very good at woodwork, but I have done well at swimming and cricket.

This record was prepared in consultation between a teacher and the student on 17th May 1985

Signature of student R. A. Jones
Signature of teacher Y R Bartholomew

The West Midlands Examinations Board
Form WMRA 1/B

Record of Achievement

SECTION I
The Personal Record
FOR

Roger A Jones

PART B

This second part of the Personal Record is optional. It may be used by Centres/students to add to the information given in Part A, to reflect a Centre's own personal record practices or to record achievements beyond those gained in full-time education. The statements may be entered in the student's handwriting or in type. Alternatively, the teacher may use Part B to record positive statements of achievement about the student.

Roger did well in his work experience with us at Asda Superstore. He got on well with the permanent employees. We would consider him for a vacancy should one arise.

B Smith
Recruitment Manager
Asda Superstores

Roger interviewed well for his work experience placement and gained very complimentary remarks from the Recruitment Manager.

His social skills have developed well both in terms of co-operating with others, and in terms of oral communication with his fellow students and members of staff. He speaks with confidence and he has a good range of vocabulary. He is very gregarious and popular.

Roger is very actively involved with auto-grass racing. It has enabled him to develop into a confident young man whose reliability in relation to school work has improved. He is able to organise his work efficiently and his presentation is of a consistently good standard. Because of his keen interest in auto-grass racing, and the demands that it places upon him, in addition to his home-work, Roger has had little time to become involved in the extra curricula life of the school. This has not prevented him from leaving school with a number of educational and personal successes to his name. We wish him well for the future.

This record was prepared on **15th May 1985**   Signature of student *R. A. Jones*

Each statement, which refers to achievements beyond those gained in full-time education, may be supported by the signature of someone who can authoritatively confirm the achievement.

Signature of teacher *M. D. Kempson*

Fig. 6.10 (cont.)

Profiles and records of achievement 135

> Form WMRA 1/L
>
> *The West Midlands Examinations Board*
> *Record of Achievement*
>
> LIST OF UNIT OUTCOMES
>
> **Scheme Title:** Mathematics   **Reference:** WAR/MA/1
>
> **Number of units in scheme:** 10
>
> | Unit Reference | Unit Title | Unit Stage |
> |---|---|---|
> | MA2 | Mathematics | 2 |
>
> **Unit Outcomes:**
>
> Knowledge
>
> The student can:
>
> 1 distinguish between income and expenditure.
>
> 2 explain how accounts are used in commercial organisations.
>
> 3 explain the reasons for supporting account entries with credit and debit vouchers.
>
> 4 prepare two alternative forms of account sheet.
>
> 5 explain the basic principles and reasons for audits of accounts.
>
> Skills
>
> The student can:
>
> 6 complete a range of forms and statements which relate to the personal financial affairs of a young adult.
>
> 7 maintain a simple account sheet.
>
> 8 maintain credit and debit vouchers in relation to an account.
>
> 9 balance and audit a simple account.
>
> 10 use the basic rules of arithmetic as they relate to money.
>
> 11 estimate simple money calculations mentally.
>
> 12 use a calculator to undertake elementary calculations relating to personal finance.
>
> 13 explain three of the charges which are made by banks for maintaining a personal account.
>
> Experiences
>
> The student has:
>
> 14 maintained an account in a simulated commercial environment.
>
> 15 visited a bank and experienced the daily routine of a bank counter clerk.
>
> 16 handled and completed a range of forms and statements relating to the personal finances of a young adult.
>
> Concepts
>
> The student can:
>
> 13 describe the underlying features of design which are capable of practical realisation.
>
> 14 identify design faults.

It has already been stated that records of achievement have implications for the curriculum, for assessment, and for recording and reporting. This means that all of these procedures must be exposed to review and to a searching examination of existing practice. Ideally the three areas should be considered together, but for the sake of expediency they are separated:

a. Curriculum

Perhaps the most profound influence on the curriculum has been in the inclusion of skills, attitudes and achievements that have not previously been assessed. The immediate effect is to cause teachers to re-examine the curriculum in order to be sure that what students are being assessed upon is actually provided. Profiling prompts teachers to look afresh at what they teach and how they are teaching it. This has repercussions on teaching styles throughout the school.

The growth of developments in the modular curriculum has implications for the recording of achievement. Another element which highlights the close correlation between profiling and the curriculum is the new emphasis on cross-curricular skills which has been referred to earlier. If these skills are to be assessed, then opportunity must be created for them to be developed.

Profiling should develop from the curriculum; in addition to any national curriculum or Local Authority curriculum statement, many schools and colleges engage in regular curriculum review. In some cases modification of what is taught and how it is taught arises from the issues that have been raised for staff by the introduction of profiling. In other cases, the curriculum review precedes the development of the profiling system. Regardless of the order in which this happens, it is essential that questions are asked early on about the nature of the learning opportunities available to students.

b. Records of achievement and assessment

The introduction of records of achievement offers an ideal opportunity to undertake a thorough review of the assessment policy within the school or college. Some schools which have given 100% commitment to the introduction of profiling have then found that because there is no agreed school policy on assessment, there is a real barrier to reaping the full benefits.

Some of the key questions which it is useful to ask when undertaking a review of this kind include:
  i. What do we want students to learn and gain from what we are teaching?
  ii. What, out of all that they learn, do we want to assess?
  iii. Why do we want to assess that particular aspect?
  iv. How are the assessments to be carried out in practice?
  v. Is there a common assessment policy throughout the department/school/college?
  vi. How are we going to record the assessments which are made?
  vii. How can we ensure that students take an active part in their own assessments?

Profiles and records of achievement 137

These are merely some of the questions which might be addressed, but each one of them carries a number of associated questions. For instance, why conduct assessment? Is the purpose of assessment primarily:

for pupils?	(for diagnosis, for guidance, for motivation)
for teachers?	(for feedback on class performance, for curricular guidance, for curricular evaluation)
for parents, employers?	(monitoring performance/curriculum control, provision of information selection/allocation of life – chances)

c. Records of achievement and reporting

One of the great beauties of a formative profiling system operating throughout the organisation lies in the fact that a structured, comprehensive method of acquiring information about students is already in place. It is unnecessary to duplicate the work entailed in gathering this information by continuing with traditional reporting systems. Profiles should provide fuller, more reliable information for students, parents, further and higher education, employers and the Careers Service.

A strategy for accommodating the time involved in assessing more systematically, and engaging in regular dialogue with students, is to replace existing reporting procedures with profile reporting. This needs a clear recording and reporting policy, which is compatible with that of assessment and records of achievement. For some teachers, a review of reporting procedures is a very effective introduction to ROA; it highlights the amount of time which is devoted to report writing which is often bland and uninformative.

One effect which the new approach has had on many schools is to cause them to adopt completely new reporting systems, perhaps including a breakdown of the skills to be assessed in each subject (see Figure 6.11). The response of parents to this increased level of information has been extremely favourable. It is impossible for a school or college to introduce a record of achievement without it affecting the reporting system.

One way of managing the impact on the institution is offered in the model[9] which suggests four steps towards implementation:

1. Consultation – with staff, parents, pupils
2. Identification of priorities
3. Re-organisation – either on a major (eg re-structuring the timetable) or a minor level, in addition to the practical necessity. This reassures staff that steps are being taken to ease their task.
4. In-service training – this is the key to developing staff skilled in assessment and review of students. It can be the route to overcoming many of the problems discussed in 6.8.

Whichever strategy is chosen for the introduction of records of achievement, the outcome will be significantly more effective if it is the result of whole school or college involvement, and if all staff (and students) have been able to contribute to the planning process.

Name			Form	Course		Date	
Subject		Typewriting		Teacher			
Skills/Achievements				Very Good	Good	Satis-factory	Not yet Satis-factory
Can display paragraphs in blocked, indented and hanging form							
Centre horizontally and vertically							
Interpret and display effectively manuscript work							
Display main headings, sub-headings and shoulder headings							
Divide words satisfactorily at line-ends							
Detect and correct errors in an acceptable form							
Display Memoranda							
Take clean carbon copies							

Fig. 6.11: New report influenced by records of achievement, Pen Park School, Bristol

6.6 Benefits

   i. Better relationships between students and teachers.
  ii. Improved levels of student motivation.
 iii. Enhanced self-image and self-esteem.
  iv. Provision of better information for students, parents, users.
   v. More effective evaluation of courses and progress.
  vi. Integration of curriculum, assessment and reporting.
 vii. Reinforcement of pastoral work in school or college.
viii. Production of a better leaving record.

6.7 Drawbacks

   i. Leads to an uncomfortable disruption of the status quo.
  ii. Fear of change and additional demands made on staff.
 iii. Creates extra work.
  iv. Presents organisations with additional administration burdens.
   v. Intrusion into students' privacy.
  vi. Leads to the socialising of students into acceptance of their place in life.
 vii. Creates a danger of over-assessment.
viii. Students are more likely to be penalised if they have poor teachers.
  ix. Additional time required.

6.8 Political Rationale

In contrast with some of the other developments described in this book, there is no clear political motive discernible in the initial introduction of profiles. Influence was exerted by the FEU by its championing of profiles as a better way to assess achievements. This was in line with their promotion of more integrated courses based on experiential learning, but there is little evidence at this stage of any centralised direction.

It was not long, however, before profiling was identified as a central feature of assessment procedures for the CPVE, largely as a result of the influence of *A Basis for Choice*[8]. It also became a mandatory part of TVEI schemes, reflecting growing Government interest in new ways of developing and assessing technical and vocational skills.

There was still a danger, at this stage, that profiling would become an activity reserved for only a section of the school population, more particularly students on pre-vocational courses, or those unlikely to achieve a high degree of success in public examinations. The view of those involved in the birth and growth of profiling and records of achievement was that if the concept had any merit, then it was of equal value for all students, and should operate across the board.

The Government was not slow to recognise the strength of the commitment of those involved, and to take steps to assume control of a movement which threatened to develop an independent life. The publication of *Records of Achievement: a statement of policy*[9], outlined DES thinking and future plans, and drew together the main strands of records of achievement.

It has been argued that the hasty announcement and introduction of GCSE had more than a little to do with DES disquiet at the prospect of huge areas of the curriculum and assessment of students being devolved into the hands of teachers and LEAs; decisive steps were taken to counteract the threat.

6.9 First-hand experience of records of achievement: Rumney High School, Cardiff

a. Background
Rumney High School, with almost one thousand pupils on roll, is situated in a mixed urban/suburban catchment area. The school is part of the DES/Welsh Office pilot schemes (see 6.1). The thirty-one schools throughout Wales taking part in the scheme were required to conform to certain criteria[10]. For the purposes of the pilot project, profiling started in the Fourth Year, extended to the Fifth Year, and in 1987 embraced the First, Second and Third years. The onset of the teachers' industrial action, which coincided with the start of the pilot project, had an effect on the strategies needed to introduce records of achievement into the school.

b. Introduction of records of achievement
 i. In the absence of staff meetings, the school co-ordinator (who is also the deputy head) met with every head of department and every year tutor individually to outline the aims of the project.
 ii. All heads of department were asked to consider with their subject staff what they were teaching, and how they were assessing students' work. They were then asked to devise a method of profiling for their department which met the criteria.
 iii. Pastoral heads were asked to consider how the work they were already doing could be developed, and how they could make time for individual interviews with students.
 iv. The school co-ordinator made opportunities for staff in-service training throughout the project, even when this meant sessions with individuals.

Profiles and records of achievement 141

c. Subject profiles
  i. Every subject area developed a list of comments.
  ii. Comments are intended to cater for the whole ability range, including special needs students (see Figure 6.12).
  iii. Each student is given a list of subject objectives and a list of possible profile statements.
  iv. Teachers assess students during lessons; students are involved in their own assessments and a joint decision reached. (The co-ordinator noted that although there was not universal student involvement in the first year, it had been extensive in some departments and was being emphasised in the second year of the scheme.)
  v. Assessments are fed into a computer, which produces a printed copy for each student's folder (see Figure 6.13).
  vi. Some departments, such as modern languages, already integrate teaching, assessment, GCSE and records of achievement into one coherent process.

d. The pastoral team
  i. The pastoral team developed a list of comments which they wished to form the basis of the personal qualities section.
  ii. Assistant tutors were allocated to each form in the Fourth Year. This enabled tutors to withdraw students for individual interviews. In the Fifth Year this cover was provided by senior members of staff.
  iii. Profiling has been introduced into the lower school, starting with the personal qualities and personal achievements sections.
  iv. It has also been extended to the feeder primary schools.
  v. Every student has the list of personal and social qualities (which are also included in subject profiles).
  vi. Teachers and students make separate assessments, which then form the basis for discussion in the individual interview.
  vii. Each student has a Personal Achievement form (Figure 6.14). They are accompanied by verification slips for adults other than teachers to complete where appropriate (Figure 6.15).

e. The summative document
The school adopted an exhaustive (and exhausting!) process of review and collation as part of their commitment to be fair to every student.

A panel comprising the form tutor, year tutor, assistant year tutor, head of upper school and school co-ordinator reviewed all the assessments for every student in the Fifth Year.

A personal statement written by the student is incorporated into the summative document (Figure 6.16).

The presentation ceremony for records and achievement attracted a large attendance of both students and parents.

MATHEMATICS

Can comprehend whole numbers.
Can add whole numbers.
Can subtract whole numbers.
Can multiply whole numbers.
Can divide whole numbers by a number up to 10.
Can analyse simple problems and apply appropriate arithmetical operation.
Can add decimals.
Can subtract decimals.
Can use a calculator for simple arithmetical processes.
Can apply simple arithmetical processes to money.
Can tell the time using a 12 hour clock.
Can tell the time using a 24 hour clock.
Can use a ruler to measure accurately.
Can interpret a timetable based on a 12 hour clock.
Can interpret a timetable based on a 24 hour clock.
Within their own ability can work with enthusiasm.
Can recognise a sensible answer to a problem.
Knows relevant quantities for weights.
Knows relevant measures for distances.
Can interpret a simple block graph.
Has a good understanding of the rules of number.
Can perform a simple arithmetic mentally.
Can perform everyday money calculations.
Can handle fractions met in everyday life.
Can handle decimals met in everyday life.
Can work with 12 and 24 hour clocks.
Understands and can apply simple percentages.
Understands the common systems of measurement.
Can measure and draw accurately using mathematical instruments.
Can draw and use a scale drawing.
Can use a calculator to perform simple calculations.
Can use a calculator to perform complex calculations.
Can estimate and can select an appropriate degree of accuracy.
Can calculate area and perimeter of simple figures.
Can calculate volumes of simple solids.
Can calculate areas and volumes of composite figures.
Understands money transactions such as wages and taxes.
Understands and can calculate averages.
Can interpret graphs and diagrams.
Can read information presented as a table.
Can interpret and present data in tabular and graphical form.
Can use simple trigonometrical ratios and can apply Pythagoras.
Can select and apply a range of trigonometrical techniques.
Can interpret simple algebraic symbols.
Can interpret transform and solve simple algebraic equations.
Can apply a range of algebraic techniques in problem solving.
Can solve simple geometric problems in triangles and quadrilaterals.
Can solve simple problems in a range of geometric shapes.
Can select and apply appropriate geometric techniques.
Can recognise a sensible answer to a problem.
Has good powers of retention.
Can analyse simple problems and apply appropriate techniques.
Can apply combinations of mathematical techniques to problems.

Fig. 6.12: Mathematics comment bank, Rumney High School, Cardiff

Profiles and records of achievement

Name : $$$$$$ $$$$$$$$

MATHEMATICS

Has a good understanding of the rules of number.

Can perform simple arithmetic mentally.

Can perform everyday money calculations.

Can handle fractions met in everyday life.

Can handle decimals met in everyday life.

Can work with 12 and 24 hour clocks.

Understands and can apply simple percentages.

Can use a calculator to perform simple calculations.

Can use a calculator to perform complex calculations.

Can calculate area and perimeter of simple figures.

Can calculate volumes of simple solids.

Understands and can calculate averages.

Can interpret and present data in tabular and graphical form.

Can use simple trigonometrical ratios and can apply Pythagoras.

Can select and apply a range of trigonometrical techniques.

Can interpret simple algebraic symbols.

Can interpret transform and solve simple algebraic equations.

Can solve simple problems in a range of geometric shapes.

Can select and apply appropriate geometric techniques.

Can analyse simple problems and apply appropriate techniques.

Fig. 6.13: Mathematics Record of Achievement, Rumney High School, Cardiff

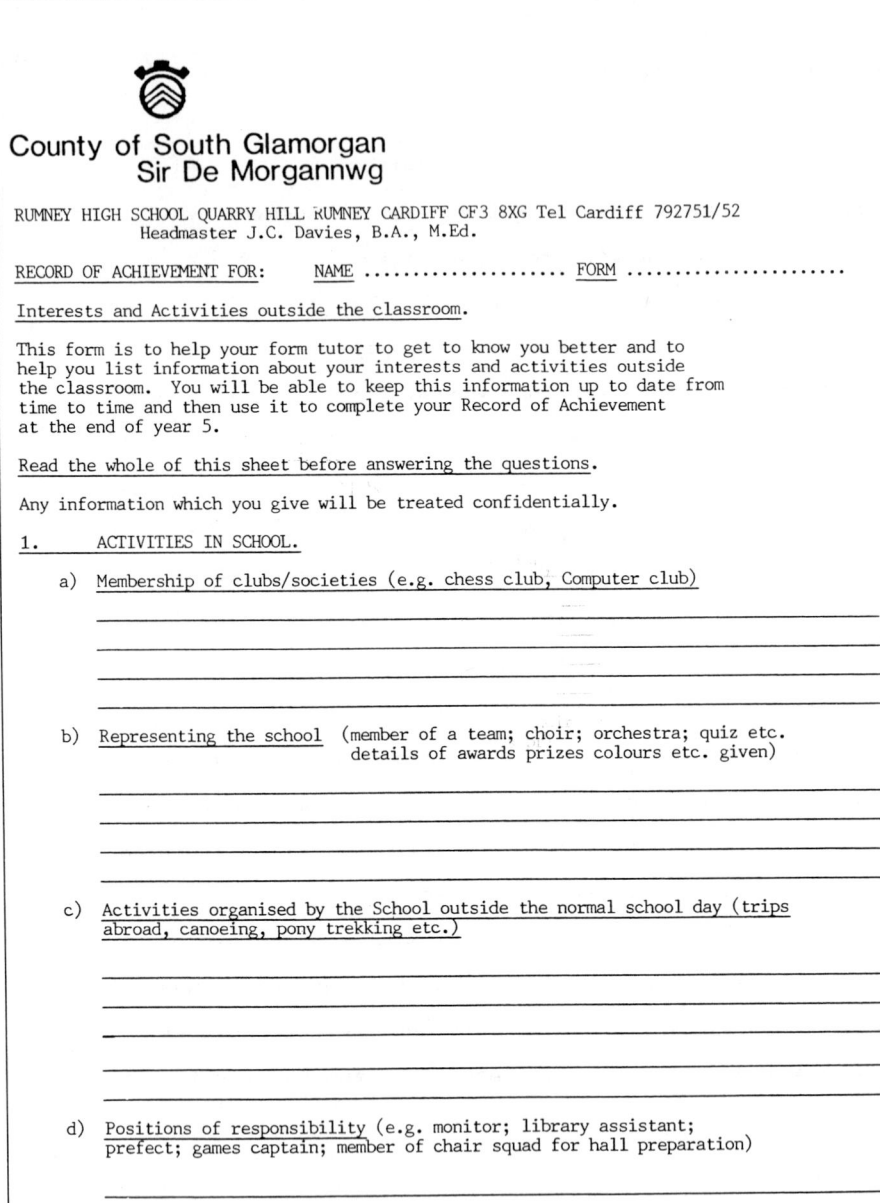

Fig. 6.14: Personal achievement from, Rumney High School, Cardiff

Any other activities in school.   (e.g. fund raising events, sponsored walk
                                  or swim or silence; school fete; taking part
                                  in assembly, carol service etc).

_____
_____
_____
_____

2.   ACTIVITIES OUT OF SCHOOL.

   a) Hobbies/Interests (e.g. music - playing an instrument, sport,
                         dancing classes etc).

      _____
      _____
      _____
      _____

   b) Membership of recognised organisations, clubs or societies (Church Sunday
         School; Youth club; Scouts; Guides etc., positions of
         responsibility held)

      _____
      _____
      _____
      _____

   c) Charity Work (Raising money for appeals visiting elderly people or
                    handicapped).

      _____
      _____
      _____
      _____

   d) Work experience (Saturday job, paper round, milk round etc.)

      _____
      _____
      _____
      _____

   e) Helping at home (e.g. with younger children or aged relatives or any
                        other way).

      _____
      _____
      _____
      _____

f) Any other activities.

_____
_____
_____
_____
_____
_____
_____
_____
_____
_____
_____
_____
_____
_____
_____
_____
_____
_____

Any details of your out of school activities which you may wish to include in your Record of Achievement will have to be confirmed by the person in charge of the organisation, or a parent or employer etc. Special forms will be made available for this purpose.

E.G. '86

Fig. 6.14 (cont.)

RUMNEY HIGH SCHOOL

PUPIL RECORD OF ACHIEVEMENT

Pupil's Name _____ Form _____

Date of Birth _____

The above pupil is compiling details of achievements and interests which take place outside the classroom and the school. This information will be used in the pupil's Record of Achievement which is to be presented at the end of the fifth year of secondary education.

Please sign below if you agree that the following statement concerning the above pupil is true.

_____
_____
_____
_____

Signature of verification _____ Date _____

Tel·No. _____

Position (i.e. club leader, vicar, parent, teacher etc.)................................

E.G. 1986

Fig. 6.15: Verification slip for personal achievements, Rumney High School, Cardiff.

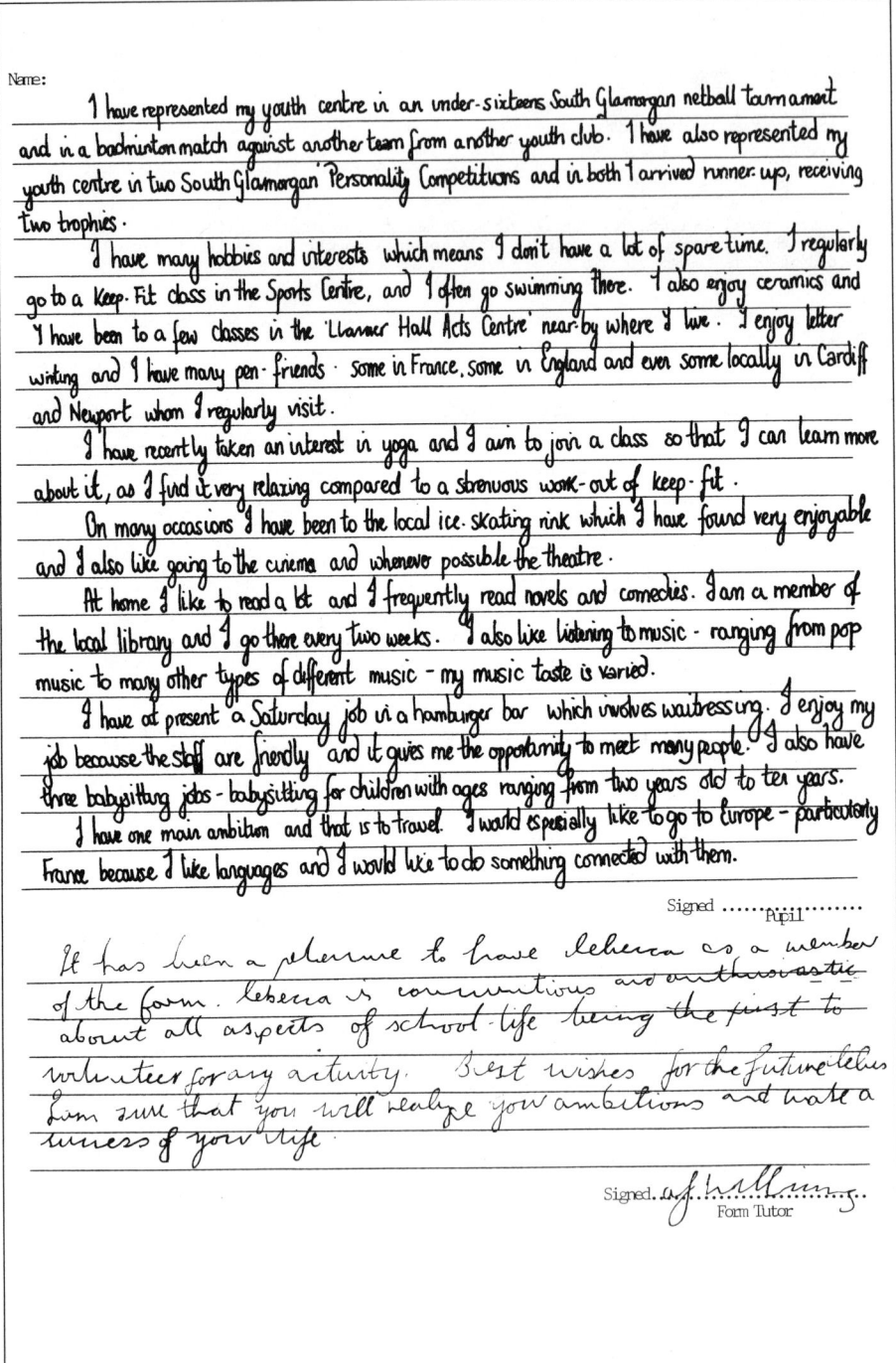

Fig. 6.16: Student's personal statement in a summative record of achievement, Rumney High School

f. Reactions to records of achievement

i. Teachers have been enthusiastic and co-operative. Without their co-operation it would have been impossible to have made progress. The project co-ordinator commented on 'a new air of confidence amongst staff who see that a revolutionary initiative is beginning to pay dividends'. One of the principle benefits acknowledged by teachers is the significant difference in their relationships with students.

ii. The response from students is very positive. They are motivated and interested in their own profiles. Those who have received the summative record of achievement have been delighted to have something of which they could be proud. An illustration of their involvement was the fact that on the first day of the autumn term, a number of the new Fifth Year students had been to the co-ordinator asking for verification slips, saying: 'We've done a lot in the holidays, we want to put it into the Record.'

Students particularly appreciated the individual interviews, where they could 'really talk to the teacher for the first time'.

iii. Strong links with further education and employers have been forged at Rumney, which is reflected in the enthusiastic response of both sectors. In fact they have amalgamated, in some cases, with the local FE college inviting the school co-ordinator to explain the record of achievement to its own employer groups. Perhaps this marketing on a local basis is what is needed to inform and convert employers to the benefits of records of achievement.

iv. The response from parents has been overwhelmingly favourable. In the words of the co-ordinator, parents were interested and supportive during the formative process, but were 'over the moon' when they saw the final record of achievement. Comments included, 'we have never had so much information', and 'it is so nice to have something to be proud of'. It was clear that many parents had no idea of the extent of their children's activities within the school. Figure 6.17 illustrates one parent's response to the initiative.

Contact:
Elizabeth Green
Deputy Head
Rumney High School
Newport Road
Rumney CARDIFF

Summary

It is clear that despite the demands which are made of teachers, of senior management in schools and colleges, and of the students themselves, the benefits of ROA are significant.

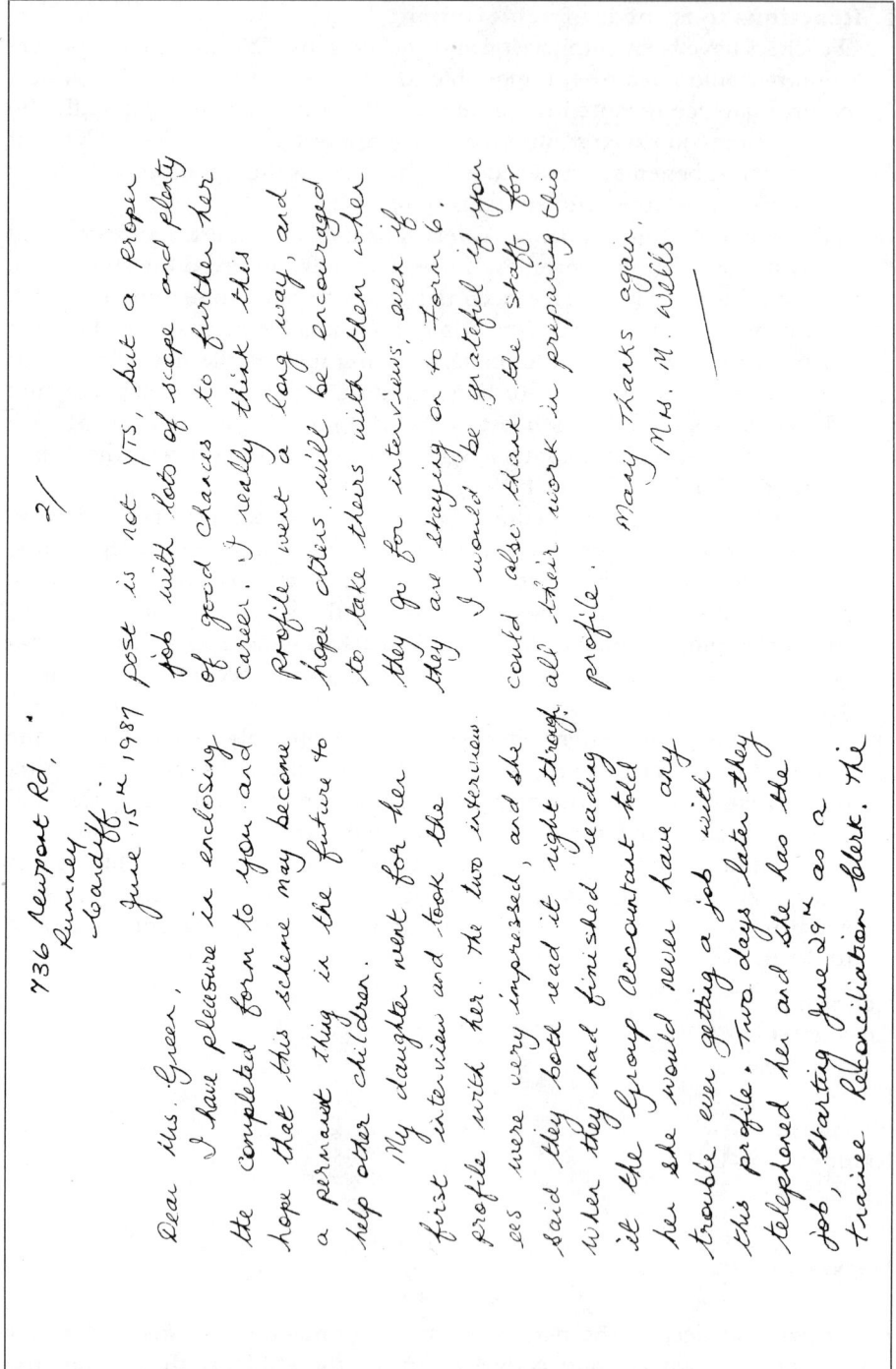

Fig. 6.17: Parent's response to a record of achievement, Rumney High School, Cardiff

The move towards the inclusion of the whole curriculum, and in many cases extra-curricular activities is healthy and encouraging.

Profiling unites all the initiatives decribed in the first section of this book; it forms an integral part of the assessment, and in some cases the certification of all except GCSE. The similarity in approach even in this case means that they are mutually supportive, rather than conflicting.

Early findings in the schemes which have been underway for some time indicate that there is a significant increase in the degree of 'engagement' of students in their life and work at school, greater commitment from teachers, and improved relationships between the two.[11] It is to be hoped that the difficulties can be overcome, and that this major new direction in educational assessment will continue to grow with the vigour which it has displayed over the last decade. In order for this to happen, and to avoid it being marginalised as a pre-vocational activity, one cardinal principle will need to be emphasised: profiling is about the WHOLE curriculum, and it is for ALL students.

Notes

1. Further Education Unit, *A Basis for Choice*, FEU, 1978.
2. DES, *Records of Achievement: a statement of policy*, HMSO, 1984.
3. Hitchcock, G., *Profiles and Profiling: a practical introduction*, Longman, 1986.
4. See 2.
5. See 2.
6. Hitchcock, G., 'Implementing Profiling within a School' in *Profiles and Records of Achievement*, ed. Broadfoot, Holt Rinehart, 1986.
7. HMI, *Curriculum 11–16: towards a statement of entitlement*, HMSO.
8. See 1.
9. See 2.
10. Welsh Joint Examination Council, 'Records of Achievement' *Newsletter* (ed. Bowring) WJEC, 1985.
11. See 3.

Chapter 7

The modular curriculum

A module is a means of re-structuring work into shorter learning packages, with short-term learning objectives and accompanying assessments. The module may either be free standing, or linked to other modules to form the basis of a longer course.

7.1 Background

Since 1982, modular developments have gained ground as a means of re-organising the secondary curriculum, particularly in the 14–18 age range. Initiatives such as those described in earlier chapters of this book have helped to encourage their growth, particularly in the 14–16 sector where they enable the curriculum to be tuned more finely to meet student needs.

Origins can be traced back through a number of initiatives, some national (the Scottish Action Plan)[1], some LEA-based (e.g. Oxfordshire, Coventry), some school-led (e.g. Peers School, Oxford; Greendown School, Wiltshire; Ysgol Emrys ap Iwan, Clwyd[2]), and some stemming directly from 14–18 initiatives, most notably TVEI.

7.2 Aims

The most common aims of modular courses are connected with the need to provide flexibility and variety within the curriculum. It may be that teachers wish to provide a more individually student-centred programme, to provide the opportunity for cross-curricular learning through complementary modules, or to give students the chance to taste and explore courses without the risk involved in a two-year commitment.

The context in which these aims are made explicit varies. In the Scottish Action Plan[3], for instance, the aims are to allow:
  i. *Mainstream* linear progression
 ii. An element required to *service* other disciplines
iii. An *optional component* related to mainstream activities
 iv. Opportunities for the *development of personal interests* or leisure pursuits

The modular curriculum 153

The aims expressed in the influential Hargreaves report[4] identify the role of modules in aiding the setting of short-term targets which would engage students' interest, and encourage the development of four aspects of achievement which Watkins[5] summarises as:

i. *The capacity for self-expression through writing*: the capacity to retain propositional knowledge, to select from it and the ability to memorise and organise.
ii. *The capacity to apply knowledge*: ability which is practical rather than theoretical, oral rather than written and which involves problem-solving and investigating skills.
iii. *Personal and social skills*: the capacity to communicate with others, to cooperate, initiate, display self-reliance and the ability to work alone, show skills of leadership.
iv. *Motivation and commitment*: to accept failure, to persevere, to learn in spite of the difficulty of the task.

The aims of many of those initiating modular developments are often concerned with the need to find space within an already overloaded timetable to incorporate new options for students. This applies to many pre-vocational courses where the opportunity to offer a wider range of options is made possible. It is particularly true of TVEI schemes where the need to enhance existing curricula and to provide students with experience in areas such as technology, micro-electronics and computing is paramount.

Most modular schemes aim to provide flexible courses with wider options which engage students' interest and enhance motivation.

7.3 Structure

Modules are vehicles for the delivery of a more flexible and innovative curriculum, not a prescriptive scheme with centrally devised criteria. (There are similarities with records of achievement which are not in themselves assessments, but which enhance and improve the assessment process.) There is no one structure which can be identified as 'the modular curriculum' or which defines the length of modules; a modular curriculum may consist of many short or a few longer modules. In some instances the entire curriculum of an organisation has been devised within a modular framework; at the other extreme, modules may simply form part of an option package within a traditional curriculum.

Modules have developed idiosyncratically; the structure depends upon the purpose for which they were introduced and on the philosophy of the innovators. Practical considerations have also played an important role. Some school-based developments are designed to provide courses of study which will interest students and reflect the concerns of the school and the surrounding area, without necessarily leading to national certification. Others are designed with the aim of producing stimulating, short-term learning targets, yet at the same time offering young people the chance to capitalise on their experience and gain external certification. Purpose largely determines the design and structure of modules and the framework within which they are set.

One definition of modules[6] contains implications for structure. It suggests that:
- A *module* is a free-standing unit of learning which may be grouped with other modules to form an educational programme.
- A *scheme* is a total set of modules from which a student may select a programme of study.
- A *programme* is a group of modules which together offer sufficient depth, rigour and quality to make the programme suitable for single subject qualification.

The Southern Examining group[7] suggests that a modular structure consists of three main models:

  i. *Complementary*
     This structure implies that modules are usually aimed at foundation level or are of a general nature. The performance in one module is not related to performance in another.
 ii. *Sequential*
     Sequential structures indicate a set of modules which can be taken in any order, but are not organised in any predetermined hierarchy
iii. *Articulated*
     In this model there is a clear order for the completion of modules; it is necessary to complete one before progressing to the next.

The structure adopted in the Oxfordshire Examination Syndicate[8] (see Figure 7.1) modular framework is designed to enable students to use modules (identified as 'credits' in this scheme) to count towards GCSE certification:

  i. A *GCSE credit* is a free-standing unit of learning. Credits can be combined in groups of five, which then become eligible for accreditation as one GCSE.
 ii. A *programme* is a number of credits (usually five) which offer the breadth, depth and quality required to qualify for GCSE accreditation.
iii. A *scheme* is the total number of credits that are associated with a specific GCSE title.

Each credit, which usually lasts for 20–30 hours, is assessed on completion and each credit carries the same weight in contributing to the GCSE certificate.

Two main alternative approaches to modules are emerging; the structure of the modular course depends largely upon which of these two predominates.

One approach seeks to amend existing practice, in which case modules tend to be:
- based upon existing syllabuses
- articulated (must be followed in a specific sequence)
- parts of single subjects
- compulsory within subject areas
- assessment concentrated near the end of a course

The modular curriculum 155

– made up of large segments of a subject

In the case of the second, or more innovative approach modules tend to be:
– different from existing syllabuses
– discrete – they can be taken in any order
– cross-curricular and inter-departmental
– used as part of several different subjects
– optional within a subject area
– assessed at the end of each module
– made up of large numbers of small segments of a subject

Although modular developments are still in their infancy, it is clear that with the involvement of examination boards and the use of modules in designing GCSE courses, more rigorous structures are already beginning to emerge.

7.4 Criteria

Again, there are no nationally prescribed criteria for the development of modules. Individual schools and colleges have frequently devised their own criteria in line with their particular philosophy. On the other hand, modules developed as part of the TVEI programme must meet the criteria laid down by TVEI. In this case, the ever-present consciousness of a contract with MSC ensures that criteria are clearly identified before a course is approved. Other school-based developments, which may be designed to motivate students through vocationally oriented courses have devised criteria relevant to those courses.

It is when the question of external accreditation becomes paramount that more rigid criteria emerge. TVEI courses must seek accreditation and GCSE modules must meet National and possibly Subject Criteria.

One example of the criteria laid down by an examining group can be seen in the Welsh Joint Examination Committee (WJEC) guidelines[9] which state that each modular unit within a scheme must be specified as follows:
– title of modular unit
– general aims of modular unit
– assessment objective
– proportion of marks allocated to the various objectives
– scheme of assessment, including the weighting given to each component, the subject, content and range of skills to be assessed
– illustrative examples of the assessment tasks (e.g. practical tests, problems, specimen papers) and associated marking criteria

Although modules are most commonly designed by practising teachers to fit the needs of their particular students (and this is perhaps one of the greatest attractions offered by a modular curriculum), this would seem to have a great deal to offer as a framework for devising criteria for school-based modules as well as those to be submitted for external accreditation.

Figure 7.1 provides an illustration of a submission conforming to the criteria laid down by the Oxford Examination Syndicate.

As might be expected, as modular developments become more complex and more concerned with external accreditation, criteria relating to assessment are becoming more stringent, although the methods by which the assessments are carried out retain a great degree of flexibility. Assessment objectives generally include such requirements as students being able to demonstrate ability in:
- identification (of problems and suitable responses)
- recall (of information, skills, and concepts)
- application (of information, skills and concepts)
- communication
- evaluation

Assessments are frequently combinations of coursework, assignments, oral work, fieldwork, folios, case studies and projects. Assessment criteria reflect this diversity and foster the link between modular developments and records of achievement by spelling out the same assessment goals. They recognise the positive achievements and successes of young people as they happen and not merely at the end of a two-year course.

It is likely that as experience of modular developments becomes more extensive, criteria governing their implementation will increasingly become centrally controlled as the influence exerted by examination boards becomes more powerful. It is to be hoped that the new flexibility and the opportunity for cross-curricular learning will not be compromised.

7.5 Impact

It is immediately apparent that the introduction of a modular curriculum has significant implications for organisations. Unlike some of the new approaches to learning described in this book, the very nature of a modular curriculum means that it impinges on the management and structure of the organisation, and upon the daily experience of staff and students.

The most noticeable effect is upon the timetable. Unless modules are to be only one step removed from the traditional curriculum in an unadventurous division of existing teaching blocks, the timetable will need considerable restructuring. Those who have committed themselves to a radical new approach have found that the destruction of conventional blocks of time has opened up new opportunities and revitalised 'tired' and unproductive periods of time. For instance, it is easy to recognise the lack of drive and urgency operating during the last few weeks of any term, particularly if school examinations have been completed.

Peers School, Oxford, is one establishment which has recognised this effect, and has taken a deliberate decision to operate modules across holiday periods. This removes the problem of 'winding-down' and 'starting-up' and ensures that students are engaged from the beginning to the end of every term. It also

The modular curriculum 157

		OES A.1.	
OXFORDSHIRE EXAMINATION SYNDICATE		SOUTHERN EXAMINING GROUP	

GENERAL CERTIFICATE OF SECONDARY EDUCATION

	CREDIT DESCRIPTOR		
Credit Title	In depth study - Nazi Germany		
Credit Code		Scheme Title(s) HUMANITIES	Scheme Code(s)
Preferred entry level	Candidates may take this unit at any stage when constructing a course in History or Humanities.		
Rules of Combination/ Module Map	As for the scheme as a whole. Only one In Depth Study may be offered as part of a course of five Units leading to a certificate in History or Humanities.		
Aims of Credit	To acquire knowledge and understanding of the Nazification of Germany in the past linking, as appropriate, with the present. To ensure that the candidates' knowledge and understanding is rooted in an understanding of the nature and use of historical evidence about Nazi Germany. To develop essential study skills such as the ability to locate and extract information from primary and secondary sources; to detect bias; to analyse this information and to construct a logical argument. To promote an understanding of the nature of cause and consequence, continuity and change, similarity and difference. To stimulate interest and enthusiasm for a study of the past, providing a sound basis for further study and for an informed and balanced approach to economic, political and moral issues.		
Assessment Objectives	1. (a) To recall, evaluate and select knowledge relevant to the context and to deploy it in a clear and coherent form. (b) To make use of and understand the concepts of cause and consequence, continuity and change, similarity and difference. 2. To demonstrate the skills necessary to study a wide variety of historical sources, such as primary and secondary written sources, statistical and visual material, artefacts textbooks and orally transmitted information. 3. To demonstrate the ability to look at events and issues from the perspective of people in the past.		
Content and Context	The context of Post 1st. World War - Germany. The economic, political and social effects of defeat - Weimar Republic. The growth of extreme political parties and the role of an individual or individuals in this i.e. Adolf Hilter. The world recession and its social, economic and political effects on Germany. The rise of Hitler, his motivation, impact and factors influencing this. The Nazification of Germany and the methods and tactics used to create a totalitarian dictatorship. The impact of Nazification on the state, institutions, sections of society, families and individuals.		

Fig. 7.1: Credit descriptor for a module in the Oxford Examination Syndicate Credit Bank

gives more meaning to a modular curriculum than is apparent when it is merely half-term blocks slotted into the old timetable.

For students, the most immediate impact is upon the curriculum, with new subjects becoming available, particularly in the area of high technology. These new subjects often mean the appointment of new staff to service the modules.

Teachers may have to face huge demands, including the need to:
- develop new teaching styles appropriate to the delivery of a modular curriculum
- devise and keep to tight schedules
- devote more time to organisation of their course in order to ensure that the whole course can be covered in the allotted time
- monitor absentees – absence can have a critical effect upon a student's chance of receiving credits which may be essential for the award of GCSE
- engage in development work in order to bring new topics into the curriculum

These demands appear to be accepted by most teachers already working with modular curricula – perhaps because the more positive impacts such as the opportunity to explore their own enthusiasms, to innovate and to see young people becoming actively involved in their work is highly satisfying.

7.6 Benefits

Many teachers who have developed modular courses argue that they lead to:
  i. Improved motivation: it is easier for students to maintain enthusiasm and motivation when presented with short-term goals than with two-year traditional courses. This has been found to have a corresponding effect on behaviour and attendance.
  ii. Leaving options open: students have the opportunity to 'taste' a number of subjects which would not otherwise have been available to them.
  iii. Cross-curricular implications: modules allow greater inter-subject and cross-curricular work than is possible under traditional systems. This re-inforces the move to cross-curricular developments identified earlier and in chapter 11 of this book.
  iv. Flexibility: modules allow greater flexibility in curriculum structure. Peter Watkins[12] cites Holyrood School, Chard, which offers thirteen humanities courses constructed from twenty-five modules. (See Figure 7.2)
  v. Equal opportunities: it is easier to encourage students to avoid gender stereotyping if they can opt for subjects on a short-term basis rather than being committed to a two year course.
  vi. Assessment: modules have facilitated the move towards profile assessment which encourages students to set targets, to assess their own progress and to be involved in recording their own assessment. It places

	Subjects	017	019	020	021	060	061	062	063	064	065	066	068	069	070	071	072	073	075
306	Economics	✓	✓	✓	✓														
317	History		✓			✓	✓	✓											
318	Geography								✓	✓		✓							
319	Social Studies								✓	✓	✓		✓	✓	✓	✓			
320	Family and Community Studies												✓		✓				D
321	Religious Studies																D	D	
325	Humanities A						✓		✓		✓	✓							
326	Humanities B						✓		✓					✓	✓				
327	Humanities C						✓	✓									D		
328	Humanities D										✓	✓			✓	✓			
329	Humanities E				✓				✓		✓		✓		✓				
330	Humanities F						✓				✓								
331	Humanities G			✓	✓				✓		✓								

	Module title	Other subjects to which the module may contribute
017	Business Organisation	Business Studies
019	The Framework of Business	Business Studies
020	Overview of the Economy	
021	What is Economics?	
060	Medicine through Time	
061	Victorian Britain	
062	Modern World Studies	
063	Local Study	Environmental Studies/Rural Studies
064	Earth Science	
065	Urban and Industrial Studies	Environmental Studies

	Module title	Other subjects to which the module may contribute
066	The Developing World	
068	The Individual and the City	Media in society/Drama in society
069	Power, Authority and Social Control	Media in society/Drama in society
070	Problems of Society in Britain	
071	Controversy and Conflict	
072	The Origin and Practice of Christianity	
073	Comparative Religion	
075	Family and Community Care	Family and Community Studies B and C

Fig. 7.2: Humanities subjects and their constituent modules at Holyrood School Chard

assessment at the heart of the curriculum, a concept which is advocated in Chapter 6.

vii. Negotiation: the wider range of options offered through a modular curriculum makes it more feasible for students to re-negotiate their own curriculum as they progress through the available routes.

viii. Teaching styles: new styles of teaching are made easier by the introduction of modules. Many modular schemes stress the importance of student involvement in problem-solving approaches, rather than a teacher-led emphasis on content. This is in line with thinking in GCSE, CPVE and TVEI.

7.7 Drawbacks

There are, however, counter arguments. Some of the disadvantages associated with a modular curriculum include:

i. Fragmentation: critics point to the dangers of fragmentation of the curriculum as it is broken down into seemingly unrelated sections.

ii. Coherence: fragmentation can lead to a lack of coherence in the secondary curriculum as a whole.

iii. Absence: the absence of either teacher or pupil for even a small part of the modular syllabus can have more serious consequences than a corresponding absence during a two-year course.

iv. Skills: it is more difficult to ensure that each student is given the chance to build up a range of appropriate skills within subject areas.

v. Boredom: while students may have great variety in their learning, teachers can become trapped into repeating the same, possibly narrow range of subject content which can lead to boredom and a lack of vitality in both content and process.

vi. Time: preparing a greater number of modules and the accompanying assessment is a serious problem. Some teachers complain that they spend a disproportionate amount of time on assessment of modules.

vii. Age and maturity: the fourth year student tackling a specific module is at a different stage of maturity from a student approaching the end of the fifth year. This can lead to a disadvantage in the accompanying assessment.

viii. Superficiality: it is possible for the curriculum to be split into a number of modules, none of which ensures a deep or searching study of the subject.

ix. Unstructured programmes: it is difficult for students to choose a clear, coherent route with recognised progression through systems which adopt a modular scheme not based on a linear progression.

7.8 Political rationale

There is no one political thrust identifiable in the move towards a modular curriculum. Impetus appears to have been generated through a number of different routes, often differing widely in political philosophy. On the one hand HMI[10] drew attention to the damaging results of many option schemes where students of fourteen could be forced to drop major curriculum areas, resulting in unbalanced subject choices that frequently closed off career choices. The difficulty of including new subjects in the curriculum structure was also recognised.

Another major influence arose from some of the socio-educational studies of the early eighties, most notably that of David Hargreaves[11]. This drew attention to the need to improve the diet offered to young people in secondary schools by recognising and giving credit for practical application of knowledge, for personal and social skills and for motivation and commitment, in addition to what was gained from the traditionally valued academic curriculum.

Hargreaves recommended the re-designing of the fourth and fifth year curriculum into six to eight week learning units, which would enhance motivation and stimulate the interest of young people.

It could be argued that the political implications of TVEI apply to much of the modular development; TVEI has been a major catalyst and political influences certainly affect this initiative (see Chapter 1). TVEI's main reason for involvement in modular developments stemmed from the need to expand and enhance the opportunities offered to young people while at the same time grappling with the problems of an over-full timetable. TVEI's emphasis on technical and vocational options led to an almost inevitable engagement in modular developments. Not only was this the ideal way to incorporate areas such as computing, information technology, technology and vocational experience, but it strengthened the TVEI philosophy in countering gender stereotyping in subject choice. Both male and female students are more likely to attempt options traditionally regarded as being the province of the opposite sex if they are only committing themselves for a short period, rather than a two year stretch, particularly if they are guided towards experimentation by their teachers.

All of these factors, together with the impetus created by classroom teachers seeking more flexible approaches to the curriculum, have influenced the development of modular curricula, but it is clear that there is no overriding, central political drive.

As was the case with records of achievement this does not mean that central forces have not been quick to recognise the strength of the movement and to become involved, in some cases even directing, development. This is particularly evident through the activities of the SEC and the Examination Boards seeking to create criteria and structures for modular accreditation through GCSE.

An addition to the political dimension has been created with the publication of proposals for a National Curriculum. These proposals, grounded in a subject-based curriculum, appear to be directly at odds with modular developments which are frequently characterised by their cross-curricular approach. However, the clash of two apparently irreconcilable political influences is not necessarily inevitable. It could be that the modular route may prove to be the most viable method of incorporating the range of foundation experiences advocated in the national curriculum (for example, modular humanities can incorporate history, geography and industrial studies). This solution would leave room for the inclusion of many of the experiences which have been prominent in the initiatives described in this book, and which many teachers feel have led to a more lively, interesting and relevant curriculum for young people.

7.9 First-hand experience of a modular curriculum

7.9.1 The Oxfordshire Examination Syndicate Credit Bank

The syndicate was set up in 1986 as a means of allowing schools and teachers to exert more control over the curriculum than appeared possible in the early days of GCSE.

The idea originated with local Heads, teachers and advisers, who submitted a proposal to the Southern Examination Group (SEG) for accreditation of the modules (or credits). The result is a working partnership with schools, LEAs and the SEG to develop an over-arching framework for curriculum developments and accompanying assessments.

One of the main objectives of the bank is to build up a number of modules from which teachers can either withdraw, or into which they deposit new modules. These should match the criteria laid down by the Syndicate. Guidance is offered to teachers planning new credits. An example of the help provided is illustrated in Figure 7.3.

The guidelines are still in the process of development; it is this dynamic process which characterises the scheme and which contrasts with the old, somewhat rigid interpretation of assessment routes available under GCE. It is particularly relevant for exploiting the wealth of new curriculum thinking which is currently taking place. The opportunity to include credits developed through TVEI and for GCSE means that the two initiatives can be genuinely complementary rather than competitive. Credits can be banked until they are required: five credits are needed to gain one GCSE qualification.

HOW TO WRITE A CREDIT

Aims   Think carefully about the learning which the credit is
               designed to promote and the activities which are appropriate
               to that learning. Remember that the stated intention of GCSE
               is to make the important measurable and not the measurable
               important. This should be foremost in your mind when
               devising the aims of a credit. When you are clear about the
               aims of the credit and have checked that they concur with the
               aims of the scheme, set them down in a few simple sentences.

Scheme of   Assessment means receiving the evidence of learning in a
assessment   credit. When you assess a student's performance you will look
               at the evidence and infer from it what the student "knows,
               understands and can do". As a credit writer you decide on the
               kind of evidence required for valid and reliable assessment
               to take place. The kind of evidence you select is called the
               assessment component. You need to select an assessment
               component which is fit for the purpose of assessing the
               learning in the credit. Some assessment components and
               their most common uses are listed below to help you.

Assessment Components

End of credit tests   :   tests taken under examination conditions
practical or written   towards the end of a credit.

Coursework tests   :   short tests taken under examination conditions
practical or written   at specific times during the credit.

Practical assignments   :   assessments of practical skills conducted
                               during the course of the credit.

Fig. 7.3: Part of the advice to teachers on the writing of credits in the Oxford Examination Syndicate Credit Bank

	Assessment opportunities are provided, often closely articulated with the learning process.
Planning tests	: tests of design and planning undertaken during the credit.
Oral tests	: tests of oral skills conducted at the end of a credit.
Oral assessments	: assessments of oral skills during the credit. Assessment opportunities are provided, often closely linked to the learning process.
Written assignments	: assignments undertaken during the credit, in response to specific instructions from the teacher.
Assessment of performance skills	: assessment of performance skills developed during the course and continually assessed.

Evidence may take the following forms:

Short answer questions	Sculpture
Structured questions	Artefacts
Free response questions	Pictures
Data response questions	Posters
Open ended writing	Films
Essays	Videos
Reports	Photographs
Investigations	Decorations
Critical evaluation	Graphs
Projects	Charts
Stories	Print-outs

Fig. 7.3 (cont.)

Questionnaires	Performances
Letters	Role play
Diaries	Recorded discussions
Logs	Interviews
Magazines	Debates
Storyboards	Radio programmes
Notes/draft	
Models	

Assessment Objectives

Assessment objectives give a general indication of the abilities to be tested. You need to look at the assessment objectives of the scheme as a whole and at the module map and be certain whether you are addressing all the assessment objectives of the scheme or a selection of them. The following explanation and diagrams should help you to think about this.

Each GCSE title has a number of assessment objectives and it is necessary to divide these and apportion them to credits. Over the complete programme of five credits, the assessment objectives for the title must be satisfied.

7.9.2 Cherwell School, Oxford

a. Background
Cherwell School is a 13–18 Comprehensive school with 750 students. The intake is mixed; parental expectations for examination success are a factor which the Head and staff need to take into account when planning innovation. The emphasis in the past, therefore, has been upon a 'traditional' curriculum.

The move towards modularisation of part of the curriculum gained impetus from a recent major curriculum review, together with the introduction of TVEI. It has been suggested earlier that TVEI has played a significant part in promoting a modular curriculum and Cherwell School offers a clear example of this trend. However, the facilities offered for innovation within a recognised accreditation system through the Oxfordshire Examination Syndicate means that modular developments are likely to extend well beyond TVEI options.

b. Organisation
TVEI options in Science and Technology, Business Studies and Services to People are all modular courses.

Students can choose six courses over a period of two years: each module is approximately 25–30 hours long and lasts for ten weeks.

Five of the six modules are sufficient to gain a GCSE qualification, which the school negotiates in two stages: first with the Oxford Examination Syndicate, made up of LEA advisers, Heads, teachers and SEG; secondly with SEG which accepts the modules, or credits, as the validating body.

The facility to obtain GCSE qualifications while participating in TVEI was a powerful influence in 'selling' TVEI to parents and students in the early stages. It is a pragmatic consideration which faces many schools and colleges trying to innovate in the face of traditional parental values.

c. Curriculum
While the main thrust of the modular developments at Cherwell centres around TVEI, and the Science and Technology, Business Studies and Services to People options, the variety offered by the Oxfordshire Credit Bank means that teachers are already looking to other curriculum areas. The approach is not to abandon the existing curriculum, but to look at ways in which the Credits available can lead to a better learning opportunity for students.

One possibility lies in the field of modular humanities[13], where there is the opportunity to combine modules from history, geography and economics, an area which is chronically overcrowded, and frequently results in students completely missing at least one topic. This system could allow everyone to have at least a taste of the subject, together with more detailed work in some areas.

Another area under consideration is that of Science, with the growing demand for students to experience a range of scientific principles and practice.

The modular curriculum 167

It might be that combinations of modules from physics, chemistry and biology will take the place of discrete science subject teaching.

A key factor in the development of modules at Cherwell school is that they should not be seen as the latest 'trendy' development, but that they should demonstrate a raising of skills, motivation and performance. They are there to serve the curriculum needs of the students and not to dictate the curriculum. To quote the Head

> *'It may mean that there needs to be a tighter definition of priorities – a ten subject curriculum could be transformed into 45–60 modules, offering greater flexibility in courses with clearly defined areas of experience.'*

d. Benefits

i. *Flexibility.* One of the greatest benefits identified by the school is the flexibility which was not available before. This is particularly noticeable in the way in which units are interchangeable.

ii. *Motivation.* Students are motivated by the short-term focus of their work – they appear to enjoy the fact that they can see the end of a particular unit, rather than the previous two-year stretch.

iii. *Higher standards.* Although it is too early to make a measured judgement, this appears to result from the fact that students work far more systematically. They are committed week by week over the whole period of the module. Indeed, it can have serious repercussions if that commitment is not present.

iv. *Recording achievement.* The link with records of achievement is clearly identified by the school. The regular monitoring of progress through ROA fits well with the awarding of unit credits at the end of each module, and helps to re-inforce the students' involvement in taking responsibility for their learning.

v. *Job satisfaction.* Staff have embraced the new developments enthusiastically. They have devoted their own time to writing modules and developing courses, and they constantly aim to improve the system. For instance, some staff have been concerned with 'getting the pace right'. In the initial stages of any module, some have finished ahead of schedule, while others need to rush to complete. It is this constant monitoring and sharing of professional expertise which reflects the belief of teachers in the development. The overwhelming majority of teachers at Cherwell School have adopted the use of modules as a significant aid to the delivery of a broad and relevant curriculum.

e. Drawbacks

i. *Organisation.* In addition to new demands for imaginative timetabling, there are logistical problems in implementing full module option choice across the six schools and one further education college taking part in TVEI. The difficulties of transporting students across the city through

busy traffic makes it impractical to share courses as originally planned.
ii. *Narrower options.* This organisational difficulty leads to a narrower range of modules being made available to students than the school would wish.
iii. *Over-assessment.* The move towards more frequent assessment, highlighted through records of achievement and the awarding of credits at the end of every module can lead to an over-emphasis on assessment. Some staff have commented that they seem to spend most of their time on this aspect, and have recognised that it is counter-productive to over-assess.
iv. *Over-conscientiousness.* Similarly, some teachers and students can become over-anxious and over-conscientious. While short-term targets may aid motivation, they can also exert considerable pressure on young people and teachers who feel that they cannot afford less than an unremitting effort.
v. *Excessive demands.* In an attempt to counter any accusations of modules being a soft option, there is a temptation for the most committed teachers to demand too much of themselves and the students. There is a fine balance to be achieved between maintaining standards and setting impossible attainment targets.

In conclusion

The way in which Cherwell School approached the introduction of a modular curriculum may well hold attractions for many schools seeking to accommodate the curriculum needs of students who face a rapidly changing world, while at the same time reassuring teachers and parents.

TVEI, as in so many cases, provided the ideal vehicle for experimentation and the development of teaching and curriculum development skills, while not threatening traditional parental expectations for their childrens' success.

Commitment to this approach has been built upon evidence which indicates that students are more motivated and attainment actually improved by a modular approach. It is upon this evidence that further developments using the Oxfordshire Credit Bank will be made.

Summary

Modular developments have, like many recent initiatives in the 14–18 field, taken an unsuspecting educational world unawares. In common with many of those initiatives, the modular curriculum has gained prominence as a direct result of a need identified by teachers and endorsed by students through their increased involvement and motivation. Fuelled by TVEI in particular, modular developments have helped schools and colleges to introduce greater choice into an already full curriculum.

The advantages associated with flexibility, motivation through the identification of short-term goals and greater choice must be weighed against the dangers of superficiality, fragmentation and lack of coherent progression. The close relationship between curricular learning through modules, and the recording of their assessment through records of achievement has been mutually beneficial. Increasing emphasis on the accreditation of modules for GCSE certification has added to their credibility as a viable alternative to the traditional curriculum.

Perhaps the greatest challenge lies in the extent to which modular developments can be accommodated within the framework and content of a National Curriculum.

Notes

1. Scottish Education Department, *16–18s in Scotland: an Action Plan*, SED, 1983.
2. Peter Watkins, *Modular Approaches to the Secondary Curriculum*, SCDC/Longman, 1987.
3. See 1 above.
4. David Hargreaves, *Improving Secondary Schools: Report of the Committee on the Curriculum and Organisation of Secondary Schools*, ILEA, 1984.
5. See 2 above.
6. Midland Examining Group, *Modular Curriculum: Working Paper No. 2*, 1986.
7. Southern Examining Group, *The Modular Curriculum: a Discussion Document*, July, 1986.
8. Oxfordshire Examination Syndicate, *Oxfordshire Credit Bank: Guidelines for Users*, Draft Working Paper, 1987.
9. Welsh Joint Examination Committee, *Guidelines for the Use of Modular Assessment Schemes*, 1985.
10. HMI, *Aspects of Secondary Education*, HMSO, 1979.
11. See 4 above.
12. See 2 above.

Chapter 8

Enterprise education

The idea of promoting enterprise, both in education and in the community, is one which has gained a new urgency with the advent of structural unemployment. Young people *need* to develop skills and attitudes which will enable them to identify and exploit opportunities which are not immediately obvious.

There are a number of agencies concerned with promoting enterprise amongst young people – a list of the major national initiatives can be found at the end of this chapter. This section will address the two main influences on the promotion of enterprise education in schools and colleges:
Young Enterprise – a national organisation providing fifteen to nineteen year olds with practical experience of running a company.
Mini-enterprise – a school-based activity giving pupils experience of running a business.

8A   Young Enterprise

8A.1   Background

Whilst the idea of enterprise education is gathering momentum, and is currently highly fashionable, *Young Enterprise* has actually been operating within the UK for twenty-five years. It has its origins in a movement known as 'Junior Achievement' which began in America in the 1920s, and which was introduced into the UK in 1962.

Young Enterprise offers students between the ages of fifteen and nineteen the opportunity to set up and run their own company for one year. The scheme is dependent upon the involvement of advisers from industry and commerce; it is seen as vital to the credibility of the operation that it should be industry-led rather than school-led, although teachers are also involved in an advisory capacity. In the year of its silver jubilee (1987), *Young Enterprise* catered for 21,000 Young Achievers, belonging to 1,271 Young Enterprise companies and overseen by 127 Regional Branches. Between 2,500 and 3,000 Advisers from industry gave up their spare time in order to assist the companies. It is a genuinely national initiative, with companies stretching from Tyree to St Austell, and from Jersey to Belfast.

8A.2 Aims

Probably one of the first advocates of 'experiential learning', *Young Enterprise* is definitely about helping young people to learn by doing. The aims are not that individual companies should make a quick profit, but rather that the individual should experience, over an extended period, how to organise and manage a company, to appreciate the different strengths of individuals and to capitalise on them. They also learn to communicate and work co-operatively for the overall success of the company, and the importance of elements such as effective market research, marketing, pricing and buying strategies. If at the end of the day the company makes a loss, then failing, and learning from that failure, can be as valuable as making a profit. In the words of the Director General of *Young Enterprise*: 'Better to be bankrupt at 16 and learn the lessons from it than to think that business is easy.'

The emphasis is on reality, and not on simulation. Whether Achievers are destined for the boardroom or the shopfloor in later life, they should have a better understanding of the processes involved in running a company, and of the importance and inter-dependence of each sector. They should also have gained sound practical experience to help them in their career decisions.

8A.3 Organisation

Each company is registered with the Young Enterprise Council as soon as it is formed. In order to achieve a successful launch, full co-operation between education and industry is essential. Industry provides a sponsor firm which possibly offers premises and certainly offers advisers to help with general management and accounting, production and sales. Advisers must not interfere or dominate. Making mistakes and rectifying them is part of the learning process. Schools and colleges also contribute, possibly with premises and the opportunity to publicise products.

The company is provided with an information pack containing advice on setting up a company, which usually consists of around twenty people. A typical skeleton for the organisation of the company is shown in Figure 8.1

The life of the company is limited to approximately eight or nine months, so that it easily falls within the scope of the academic year. This adds a touch of urgency to the proceedings and ensures that the tempo does not slacken. Winding up the company properly is equally important.

A managing director and staff are elected, salary scales determined, and shares up to the value of £150 at 25p per share are sold in order to raise capital. This capital must be returned to shareholders at the end of the venture, hopefully with a handsome dividend.

All posts are up for re-election half way through the year. One of the most interesting current statistics to emerge is that in 1987 60% of those

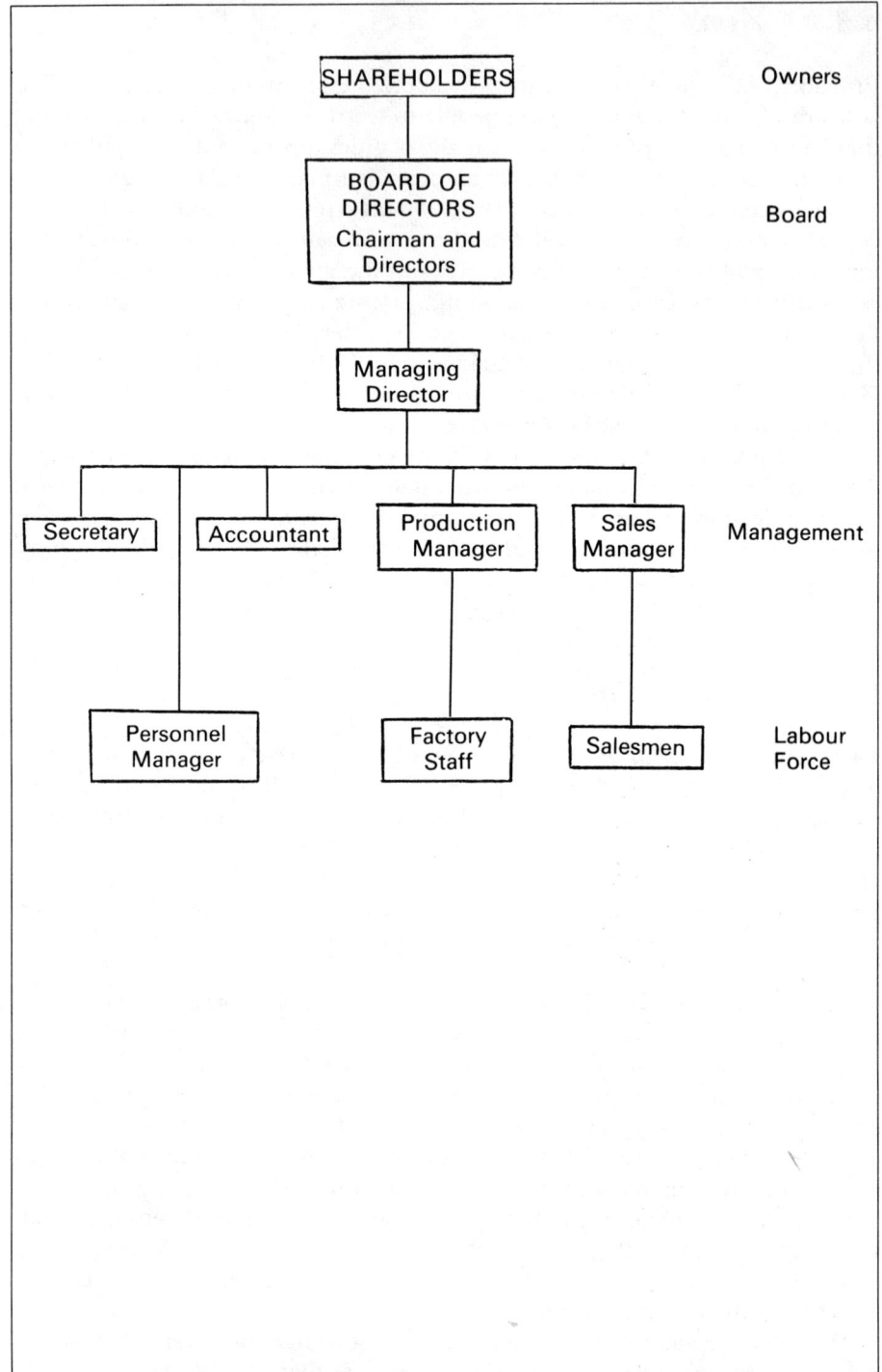

Fig. 8.1: Structure of a typical Young Enterprise Company

Enterprise education

participating in the scheme were female, but 60% of the companies were managed by males. By the end of the year this statistic had changed so that more than 60% of the companies were managed by females.

This demonstrates that *Young Enterprise* can act as a vehicle to overcome sex stereotyping, helping girls to recognise their strengths and qualities in a realistic, competitive setting.

8A.4 What do young achievers gain?

i. Genuine learning by doing.
ii. Feedback on practical performance and new-found skills, rather than the ability to use an argument or talk a way out of a problem.
iii. Enhancement of self-confidence and self-esteem through achieving success and learning how to work with others towards a common goal.
iv. Insight into the processes of management, industrial relations, marketing and the importance of wealth creation.
v. Recognition of the value of each member of the workforce, whether they are shopfloor or management.
vi. Development of the ability to present arguments in a reasoned way, through the regular board meetings.
vii. Appreciation of the importance of identifying people with the capacities to fulfil specific jobs, and the need to support those who are finding difficulties, and if necessary to supplant the managing director who can not take responsibility.
viii. Development of confidence born of experience, which is a very real asset when applying for jobs.
ix. The fact of having taken part in *Young Enterprise* is often a significant help in gaining employment.

8A.5 What's in it for employers?

i. It can be a valuable self-development exercise for young managers who are involved as advisers.
ii. It provides an opportunity for industry to influence the educational process and product.
iii. Young Enterprise is a rich ground for talent-spotting for recruitment.
iv. It enables industry to be seen to be making a contribution to the community within which it trades.
v. It helps young people to understand the importance of wealth creation.
vi. It can be a useful advertising vehicle, as well as a public relations exercise.

8A.6 First-hand experience of young enterprise: Mynx Enterprise, Sheffield

The variety of products and companies operating in 1986/7 included: the production of printed T Shirts at Balwearie High School, Kirkaldy; a range of wall clocks at Duston Upper School, Nottingham; and shell lamps and animals in Bolton.

The experience of the pupils of Eckington School, Sheffield, highlights some of the successes and problems associated with running a YE company.

Mynx Enterprise was established in October 1986 with a workforce of ten from Eckington School and the sponsorship of Noel Village Steel Foundry.

A fairly ambitious product was chosen: made-to-measure tracksuits which retailed at £21.99. It soon became clear that this price, even though it was higher than the cost of many YE products, did not adequately reflect the amount of work. Judging by the flood of orders based on word-of-mouth, which meant that no advertising was necessary, it was an attractive proposition for customers. Both sales and confidence were boosted by attendances at a trade fair at the Cutler's Hall, Sheffield.

a. Financial outcomes
The accompanying balance sheet (Figure 8.2) indicates the healthy nature of the company's end-of-year trading figures.

b. Lessons learned
The extract from the Company Report (Figure 8.3) indicates the lessons Young Achievers in Mynx Enterprise identified, and adds a little flesh to the bones of the 'advantages' section outlined above.

One of the misunderstandings from which *Young Enterprise* has suffered, is that it is solely an extra-curricular activity, taking place after school hours. In fact, by 1987 40% of the schemes were taking place within the school curriculum. The sole criterion imposed by YE is that the initiative should be employer-led, even if it is within school time. Another misapprehension concerns the ability level of Young Achievers; it is frequently seen as an activity for the high flier, but schools for the mentally and physically handicapped participate. The London School for the Blind carried out a successful marketing exercise in bottling smells which were labelled in Braille and sold to help blind people recognise substances by smell. It is initiative and perserverance which is needed, not physical or mental perfection.

Every Young Achiever successfully completing the project receives the Young Enterprise Achievement Certificate (Figure 8.4). Perhaps the last word should go to a Young Achiever who said:

> 'My experience has shown me the many different abilities called for to achieve a smooth and efficient running of business life. It is a lot more interesting and varied than I have been led to believe ... I now want to be part of it.'
>
> Sarah De Los Rios, Sheffield

Enterprise education

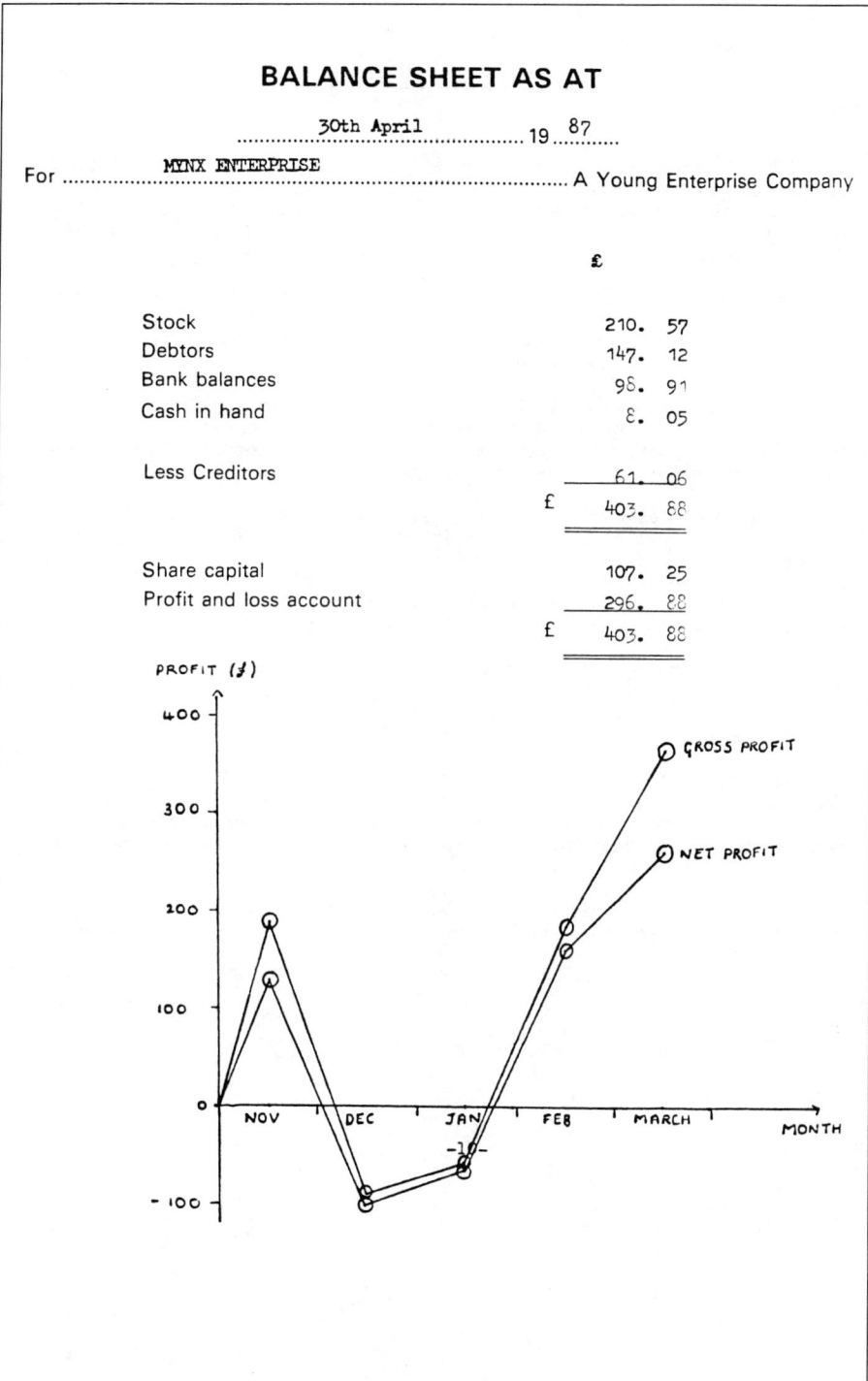

Fig. 8.2: Balance sheet end of year trading figures for Mynx Enterprise, Sheffield

IMPORTANT LESSONS LEARNED

Through experience we discovered that judging the suitability of company members for managerial positions is often difficult. An example of this was the appointment of our first Managing Director. His inefficiency and lack of interest soon led to his dismissal. We found that true managerial qualities may not emerge immediately.

The members of Mynx have also learned the importance of being honest with each other. When work was not up to the required standard it was, at first, difficult to make criticisms, as we were all good friends. Later on we came to regard all comment constructively.

In the early stages of the company, misunderstandings about times of meetings and the purchase of stock and materials occurred. This was due to a lack of communication. We found that good communication between workers and managers is essential for the smooth running of a company.

A personal lesson learned was that if you cannot do a job to company standards then you should not do it at all. If the correct tools or accessories are not available, leave the job until they can be obtained, and the job done properly. We have also found that if a member's work is below standard it is better to switch their task to another worker rather than waste valuable materials, and thereby profits.

Our company began sewing tracksuits in late January for a trade fair on 9th February. A valuable lesson learned was that production ought to have been started earlier to allow for many small problems encountered in the manufacturing process.

At the Trade Fair many of us found our personalities developing forcefully as we under took the role of salesmen. However, lack of confidence and experience in some quarters hindered our performance. It soon became clear how important the sales staff are and how necessary thorough training is.

Young Enterprise has been enjoyable, it taught us much about business under hectic and realistic conditions.

                                                              Sarah Broxholme

Fig. 8.3: Extract from company report, Mynx Enterprises, Sheffield

For futher information about Young Enterprise contact:
Derek Jackson
Director General
Young Enterprise
The Industrial Society
Robert Hyde House
48 Bryanston Sq
London WIH 7LN

8B The mini-enterprise in schools project

Mini-enterprise is not so much a scheme – more a way of life. Or to be more accurate, it is an idea, and a way of stimulating ideas relating to enterprise. There is no national organisation as there is in *Young Enterprise*, but national backing has been provided by the joint Department of Trade and Industry/ National Westminster Bank/Society of Education Officers project launched in Industry Year (1986). The project aimed to help every secondary and middle school in England and Wales to introduce mini-enterprise during Industry Year.

8B.1 Aims

There are three main aims associated with mini-enterprise:
 i. Education FOR enterprise which includes schemes promoting the development of entrepreneurial skills in young people. They seek to prepare them to set up their business or to identify opportunities for other forms of self-employment on leaving school.
 ii. Education ABOUT enterprise where youngsters engage in schemes which help them to understand the world of work, wealth creation, organisation, marketing and finance.
 iii. Education THROUGH enterprise where the emphasis is on education achieved through personal development, including through an enhanced ability to communicate and co-operate with others. The very fact of having a clear goal is a strong motivator, which leads to higher levels of attainment.

In practice it is rarely possible to disentangle these three aims; by running a company pupils learn about themselves, as well as about how industry and commerce work. One of the key features of both mini-enterprises and *Young Enterprise*, is that young people are involved in making decisions – decisions

YOUNG ENTERPRISE

This is to Certify that

_____

has participated in operating

_____

Young Enterprise Company

at _____

and thus has had an opportunity, through direct involvement and practical experience, of:

1. Acquiring a basic knowledge of the organisation, methods and practices of industry and commerce together with the skills needed at all levels to operate a successful enterprise.
2. Understanding the role of the employer and the nature of the mutual obligations that need to exist between fellow workers and employers to promote sound working relationships.
3. Appreciating the value and worth of creating profit and wealth in their own right to provide for the needs of individuals and the community.
4. Gaining a knowledge of the factors and personal qualities (particularly the generation of trust, acceptance of responsibility and the need for good communications) that enable effective teamwork.
5. Discovering the rewards of personal achievement and greater self knowledge that come through learning new skills and developing new friendships.

Date: _____

Sir David Checketts, KCVO
Chairman

BIM PUBLISHED IN INDUSTRY YEAR 1986 ON BEHALF OF YOUNG ENTERPRISE, BY THE BRITISH INSTITUTE OF MANAGEMENT.

Fig. 8.4: Young Enterprise Certificate

Enterprise education 179

which will affect themselves, their colleagues, and the success of their company.

8B.2 Funding

Schools wishing to embark upon a scheme in 1986 were eligible for a grant of £30, with the opportunity to apply for a low interest loan of £50. This was intended to help teachers research mini-enterprise before committing themselves to a particular project, to buy teaching materials, pay telephone or postal charges, or even contribute to in-service training (although this would actually pay for very little INSET).

In order to add a degree of authenticity to the venture, applications for loans were organised through NatWest banks on the basis of interviews conducted with representatives of the company, in exactly the same way as a 'real' business experience. The need to make a positive presentation to the bank, to repay the money at an agreed time and to decide on the distribution of profits are all part of the exercise.

Although the project was intended as a one-off investment, enthusiasm has been so great that a second phase was announced in autumn 1987, so that new schools can apply for grants.

8B.3 Organisation

Part of the brief of the Mini Enterprise in Schools Project is:

> 'to disseminate all existing approaches to mini enterprise, to foster and encourage co-operation between projects working in the field; and to encourage LEAs to include Enterprise training within their programmes of in-service work.'[1]

Although there is no national organisation along the lines of *Young Enterprise*, nevertheless seven Regional Co-ordinators appointed during Industry Year '86 ran over one hundred training courses involving 3,500 teachers. These in turn led to some 2,000 new mini enterprise companies.

Part of the dissemination has included work with mini companies organised through the Durham University Business School (DUBS), Young Enterprise, Schools Curriculum Industry Project (SCIP) and the very useful Longman Mini Company Kit.

Mini Enterprise in Schools has also launched a number of collaborative schemes (for example with CRAC and NICEC in the careers education field (see Chapter 10).

One of the most innovative developments is the setting up of a Teacher Company scheme, whereby teachers are the workers. Their personal involvement highlights the educational advantages of mini enterprise, and gives teachers confidence in their ability to manage companies with young people.

8B.4 First-hand experience of mini enterprise: Queen Elizabeth School, Corby, Lancashire

Unlike Young Enterprise, which is aimed at students aged fifteen to nineteen, mini enterprise companies involve students ranging from the age of seven up to nineteen. The types of company, organisation, products and experience vary widely. In Forge Lane Junior School, Middlesex, pupils set up a company selling apples which were bought at a discount from the local shopkeeper. Ellen Wilkinson High School, Ealing, set up twenty-four mini-companies selling products which included pot pourri, plant cuttings, catering and car washing services.

The Minitrix company was set up with the school's Low Attainment Project (LAP) group within the design department. Forty-six students took part in a scheme which was designed to: motivate; teach skills; develop skills of working together as a team.

It was agreed that all participants should be workers and directors, that each session would begin with a progress meeting, that a management team would be elected from the worker/directors, and that the company would run for ten months (Figure 8.5).

a. Finance
Initial funding was provided out of capitation, which was paid back as profits accrued. It was agreed that the company should work on a profit-sharing basis and salaries would be paid out at the end of the ten month life of the company.

Contracts of employment were drawn up and signed by the worker/directors.

b. Organisation
Policies were agreed at the initial meeting, and give an indication of the framework of the project.
  i. The company name was agreed after a small group brainstorming session followed by a large group vote. The name would be MINITRIX.
  ii. By the same method the logo was adopted (Figure 8.6).
  iii. The first sales would be through a weekly school shop run by the worker/directors on a rotation basis.
  iv. The company's first products were agreed from those presented by the staff and batches of twenty were commissioned.
  v. A managment team was appointed by the group. The officers were:
    Managing Director
    Secretary
    Finance Manager
    Production Manager
    Personnel Manager.
  vi. The break would be staggered from the main school break and would be

Enterprise education 181

```
                    CONTRACT OF EMPLOYMENT
                      (NOT A LEGAL DOCUMENT)

Dear Sir or Madam,

I am pleased to inform you that you have been appointed to the service of our Mini
Co-operative Company known as

                        _____

as a worker or Worker/Manager of our Co-operative you are also a Director and you
share in the decisions and profits of the Co-operative and are expected to attend
all monthly meetings of the Co-operative.

The terms of your appointment to the Co-operative are as follows:

1.    Your Name _____

2.    Place of Employment _____

      Section _____ Works Number _____

3.    Your hours of work will be as follows:

      Day _____ Start _____ Finish _____

4.    A proportion of the profils will be paid at the end of your appointment to the
      Co-operative according to the total hours worked. This may include any
      voluntary overtime when available.
      You are entitled to a 10 minute coffee break within your work hours (not overtime)

5.    If you are off sick you must provide a signed certificate (Note).

6.    If you are absent for other good reasons you should apply for leave of absence.

7.    If you are absent or late deductions will be made from your final pay.

* N.B. You will not be paid during holidays or when absent - only for the hours
       actually worked. Three minutes late loses quarter of an hour's pay.

The amount of your final pay depends on the following points:

1.    Co-operation of all members of the Co-operative.

2.    Good rate of productivity.

3.    Good quality, i.e. well made and well packaged items.

4.    Good ideas that will sell.

5.    Any special orders completed on time.

6.    Good market research.

   N.B. Substandard items reduce the profilts.

Signed _____ Personnel Manager.
Date _____

                                                            JM 86
```

Fig. 8.5: Contact of Employment, Minitrix Mini-enterprise Company, Corby

Fig. 8.6: Logo designed by students for Minitrix Mini-Enterprise Company, Corby

ten minutes long during which time coffee would be available in the Home Economics room, at a small charge.'²

c. Products
Four products, which could be completed relatively quickly in order to maintain interest, were selected: a toy lorry with removable bricks; a key rack; Christmas decorations; soft toys.

Students opted for the product on which they were to work.

d. Wages
Wages were distributed at the end of the project. The total profit was divided by the total number of hours worked by all the students. This gave the hourly wage rate.

The hourly rate was then multiplied by the number of hours worked by each student to give individual wages. These varied between £1.20 and £10.41, according to the number of hours the student had worked.

e. Benefits
In common with other enterprise education projects, the students at Queen Elizabeth School gained an insight into the working of the economy. The profit-sharing idea made the quality and marketing of their products a real issue, rather than a school exercise. More importantly, the work with this low

Enterprise education 183

attainment group highlighted the way in which enterprise education can develop personal and social skills. In the words of one teacher:

> 'Often the general manner of the students towards the public was harsh, disrespectful, and at times bad-mannered. This was not deliberate but reflected a deficiency in some of the students' basic social skills.'

On one occasion students spent a whole morning unsuccessfully attempting to sell products at a 'fayre'. A lunchtime meeting to discuss ways of approaching customers, accompanied by a brief practice brought a dramatic change in takings. The lesson learnt by the students were not merely financial – it was more long-lasting in terms of their personal development and social skills acquired in a real context. They also learned to work together co-operatively.

f. Drawbacks
Problems included:
- Some managers were unable to fulfil their role.
- Reliance on a small number of students to undertake out-of-school selling meant that staff became too heavily involved in marketing.
- Lack of training in selling was highlighted.
- Not all students were enthused by the idea of enterprise education – there remained a nucleus who caused some disruption.

g. Conclusions
Despite the problems, Minitrix was successful in interesting and motivating a group of students who had little previous experience of succeeding in their school lives. It indicates that enterprise education can be equally beneficial for all attainment levels.

Lessons learned for the future included the following:

i. A group of students should be attached to one member of staff and form a discrete company.
ii. Companies should be wound up at the end of every term and wages paid at that point in order to maintain interest.
iii. Selling for all the companies should be organised through the same shop or stalls.
iv. Students should be encouraged to take greater responsibility for running the companies.
v. Greater involvement across the curriculum should be sought – eg accounting, stock-taking, financing could all become part of the theory supporting the practical experience.
vi. Mini enterprise should be extended to other groups within the school.

Contact for MINI Enterprise In Schools Project:
Project Director
Mini-Enterprise in Schools Project
Centre for Education and Industry
University of Warwick
Westwood
Coventry CV4 7AL

Summary

Enterprise education is ideally suited to promoting the skills which young people need in order to cope with our rapidly changing society. It can develop problem-solving and creative ability; young people need to be flexible and to work co-operatively in groups if their company is to succeed.

It is, perhaps, these aspects of Enterprise that are more important even than the aquisition of knowledge about the way the economy works.

The benefits are not only for the students: a recurring theme has been the need for teachers to develop new skills. These include:
– developing a student-centred approach
– exploring contacts with local industry and the community
– flexible use and design of resources
– ability to allow students to take responsibility for their learning
– debriefing and reflective skills, to help students realise their experience is transferable[3]

All of these outcomes have implications for easing the transition which is taking place within schools and colleges today.

For Enterprise Education to work most successfully it should become a fully integrated part of the curriculum, and available for all young people. It is already seen as an essential component of most TVEI and CPVE courses.

One possible model for ensuring progression would be for mini-enterprise to be a part of primary pupils' experience; for the Longman Mini-Co Kit to be used in the Secondary Curriculum; and for Young Enterprise to be available in the 15–18 age range.

This proposal does have certain drawbacks; no matter how good the scheme, there will always be some students who are uninspired by the idea of business. It would be counter-productive to turn what should be an exciting experience into a compulsory chore.

Enterprise Education shares many of the aims and develops many of the skills outlined in the main 14–18 education initiatives. There is a strong case for making it an integral part of every student's educational experience.

Notes

1. Kevin Crompton, Mini-Enterprise in Schools Project, Article in *Life Force*, 1986.
2. John Merry, *'Minitrix': a company in the making*, unpublished dissertation, 1987.
3. Kevin Crompton 'A Curriculum for Enterprise: pedagogy or propaganda, *School Organization*. Vol 27, No. 1, 1987.

Chapter 9

Education – industry links

9.1 Background

The thread of education-industry links is woven into the fabric of all new curriculum initiatives; in some it features more prominently than in others, but it is always present. This indicates the increasing importance of education-industry liaison.

The idea of establishing closer links between education and employers is by no means new. As long ago as 1926 the Hadow Report[1] called for closer co-operation between the two. However, it was not until the 60s that any real increase in general interest can be detected. The cynical might link this to the growth in Further and Higher Education which creamed off a high proportion of industry's recruits.

In 1965 the newly-constituted Confederation of British Industry (CBI), in conjunction with the DES, Ministry of Labour, the Central Employment Executive and the Trades Union Congress endorsed a scheme for seconding practising teachers into industry. Other bodies expressing interest included HMI and the Schools Council. By 1975 the Schools Council Industry Project (now Schools Curriculum Industry Project), SCIP, was born; this involved collaboration between Schools Council, CBI and TUC.

This was particularly timely, for in 1976 James Callaghan (then Prime Minister) delivered what has become regarded as the most influential pronouncement on the development of closer links between education and industry at Ruskin College Oxford. He drew attention to the quality of schools' preparation of young people for the world of work, and reiterated the complaint of industry when he said: 'I have been concerned to find that many of the best-trained students have no desire or intention of joining industry.'

He also suggested that teachers lacked experience of trade and industry, that curricula were not related to pupils' work after leaving school, and that pupils left school with little or no understanding of the workings or importance of the wealth-creating sector of the economy.

Callaghan criticised industry in equally strong terms when he claimed that employers often lay down unrealistic standards of academic attainment for school-leavers which were not required for performance of the job. He also stated that they did not make allowance for the fact that more school leavers

Education – industry links

were entering Further and Higher education and that companies bore a responsibility for making their careers more attractive to school-leavers.

Controversy surrounding these remarks led to the 'Great Debate', which in turn supported the efforts of those already committed to bringing education and industry closer together. The trend has continued and most recently has been given added impetus by the identification of 1986 as 'Industry Year' (see 8.2), and by the publication of the Government White Paper, *Working Together – Education and Training* (1986)[2] and *Working Together for a Better Future* (1987)[3].

In common with YTS (Chapter 4) the threat from overseas competitors in the marketplace is used as an argument for strengthening the links between industry and education. Emphasis is placed on preparing students for a place in the competitive world of work in order to assist in the country's economic recovery.

The announcement[4] of the national extension of TVEI, commencing in 1987 was one recent move to make education/industry links an integral part of the curriculum. This is a major step towards giving education/industry liaison greater status.

Although legislation and Government statements seeking a change in practice has no doubt advanced the cause of closer co-operation, it is in the growth of communication, understanding and collaboration at local level that the most fruitful education/industry liaison is found. Whilst the impact of a massive increase in youth unemployment could have been expected to adversely affect liaison initiatives, in fact the opposite is true; every LEA in the country now has an identified officer responsible for education/industry links. The trend appears very likely to continue.

9.2 Some major participants in education-industry liaison

9.2.1 *National initiatives*

a. Confederation of British Industry (CBI)

CBI represents around 250,000 firms employing more than half the country's workforce. Although its main function is to represent its members' interests to Government, it is also involved in school-industry liaison. Activities are primarily concerned with teacher/industrialist exchange visits. It also organises occasional conferences which bring together students and industrialists.

Contact:
Head of Education Department
Confederation of British Industry
Centre Point
103 New Oxford Street
London WC1A 1DU

b. Understanding British Industry (UBI)
UBI is a registered charity sponsored by the Confederation of British Industries Education Foundation. It aims to improve understanding of industry and wealth creation in schools, to influence school curricula and to improve understanding of the education system amongst industrialists.

More than sixty-five LEAs run collaborative schemes with UBI, and 750 companies were actively involved by 1987. Activities include teacher placements in industry, industrialist placements in education, management training for headteachers, in-service training courses, initial teacher training and information services.

Contact:
Information Officer
Understanding British Industry
Sun Alliance House
New Inn Hall Street
Oxford OX1 2QE

c. Understanding Industry (UI)
The Understanding Industry programme has been operating since 1976 and aims to:
– provide sixth form students with an understanding of industry and commerce
– present this understanding in a regular, structured pattern through the medium of the school timetable
– involve teachers in the vital subject of creating this country's wealth

The emphasis is on bringing information about industry to sixth formers. Young managers will undertake a series of talks, discuss industrial issues and help with vocational information. The presentations are usually of a high quality, but a fee is charged for the service.

Contact:
Director
Understanding Industry
91 Waterloo Road
London SE1 8XP

Education – industry links

d. Young Enterprise (YE)
Young people between the ages of fifteen and nineteen can, with the benefit of advice from industrialists, set up and run their own company for one year (see Chapter 8). They learn how to operate a business, handle money, produce goods, and take decisions.

Contact:
Director General
Young Enterprise
Robert Hyde House
48 Bryanston Square
London W1H 7LN

e. Mini-Enterprise in Schools Project (MESP)
This scheme was launched by the Department of Trade and Industry in September 1985. A major contribution to Industry Year, it was jointly sponsored by the NatWest bank. Pupils of all ages, including primary pupils, set up and run small businesses, selling services and products both within school and in the community (see Chapter 8).

Contact:
Project Director
Mini-Enterprise in Schools Project
Centre for Education and Industry
University of Warwick
Westwood
Coventry

f. School Curriculum Industry Project (SCIP)
Originally the Schools Council Industry Project, SCIP supports seconded teachers within LEAs by involving industrialists and trades unionists in curriculum development.

Contact:
School Curriculum Industry Project
School Curriculum Development Committee
Newcombe House
45 Notting Hill Gate
London W11 3JB

g. Centre for the Study of Comprehensive Schools (CSCS)
CSCS has, in collaboration with BP, published a number of useful broadsheets on links with industry. Extracts from its advice to teachers and employers are included in Figure 9.1.

Action For Firms

Here are some guidelines for personnel linking with schools.

● **Contact:** meet the headteacher and ensure school senior management support. Work with a named key contact on the staff.

● **Your firm's commitment:** ensure the support of your own company's senior management, and clarify the firm's view on time off and induction for link work.

● **Communication:** clear and full briefing and preparation by both sides for all staff involved is essential.

● **Evaluation:** all schemes should build in their own evaluation and publish results at intervals, ensuring that the feedback is used constructively.

● **Networks:** plug into all possible networks; identify useful ones, and exchange ideas and examples of good practice.

● **Inservice:** get involved with school inservice work and offer joint opportunities; use teachers to inform industry about education.

● **Contribution to industry:** identify ways in which the scheme benefits the firm and see that this information is widely publicised.

● **Management Practice:** be prepared to focus on management practices and not just curriculum; offer yourself as a member of school working parties.

● **Projects:** set up small, self-contained manageable projects. Approach a school with your "community" hat, not just with your firm's hat.

● **Ownership:** ensure that teachers feel their projects and developments belong to them and that credit accrues to their school as well as to the firm.

Action For Schools

Here are some guidelines for teachers linking with industry.

● **Contact:** a school should name a key member of staff for local firms to contact and through whom other teachers can link.

● **Support:** talk with your headteacher and senior management staff; gain their commitment to the scheme. Involve the pupils, parents and governors of your school.

● **Communications:** publicise the scheme well and keep everyone fed with current information.

● **Evaluation:** work with your industry link to set up an evaluation and use its outcomes.

● **Networks:** Identify your contacts and find out all the possible networks you can use.

● **Inservice:** Involve the industry link in school working parties and school inservice days.

● **Contribution to school:** identify ways in which the scheme benefits the school and see that this information is widely publicised.

● **Projects:** select and design one small project to build upon.

● **Initiate:** don't wait for industry to approach you; go out and find contacts; have expectations beyond financial benefits. Remember that change in school comes from contact with the outside world.

● **Continuity:** tie your initiative or project into the work and curriculum of the school, so that its survival is not dependent on only one person's enthusiasm.

Fig. 9.1: Extract from CSCS Bulletin 6 *School-Industry Links*

Education – industry links

Contact:
The Director
CSCS
Wentworth College
University of York
Heslington
York YO1 5DD

h. Industrial Society
The Industrial Society is an independent organisation which receives funds from both employers and Trades Unions. Its aims are:
– to teach companies how to get their message across to their employees and the community to promote closer schools-industry links

It devotes considerable resources to the strengthening of school-industry liaison, including the joint in-service training of teachers, lecturers and employers.

Contact:
Press Officer
The Industrial Society
3 Carlton House Terrace
London SW1Y 5DG

i. Industry Year
1986 was designated 'Industry Year'; the aim was to encourage a better understanding of industry and to promote a better image. In relation to education it aimed to:
– link all secondary schools, and as many primary schools as possible, with local companies
– encourage organisation of Industry Weeks in schools and colleges, providing a focus for industry-linked activities
– involve industrialists in in-service training
– encourage involvement in initial training
– improve links and exchange personnel with Further and Higher Education establishments.

Activities associated with Industry Year were varied: schools and companies devised their own schemes, in addition to national initiatives. One example of a company attempting to link with every secondary school in the country is the Woolworth 'Leadership' competition. Schools were asked to nominate entrants for the competition which looked for: leadership qualities in commerce and industry; invention and design; community work; environmental work; personal development; music and the arts; or sports.

Every interested headteacher in the country was visited by a Woolworth manager. Activities included a large number of caring and community help projects. One boy set up a newspaper, obtained a bank loan and sold advertising to raise revenue whilst another organised an exchange visit to Africa to help handicapped children.

Winners received an award (see Figure 9.2) and a place on an Outward Bound Course.

'Industry Matters' is the extension of Industry Year and is continuing to promote the same aims.

Contact:
Education Adviser to Industry Year
RSA
8 John Adam Street
London WC2N 6EZ

j. Local Employer Networks (LENS)
One of the more recent attempts to rationalise education-industry liaison is the national training initiative launched in 1987. LENS is sponsored by the Association of British Chambers of Commerce, the Confederation of British Industry and Manpower Services Commission – a powerful team.

It is intended that the country will be covered by a network led by a Base Organisation which co-ordinates operations within its area. Tasks include surveying existing training provision, producing a directory of actual and potential participants in liaison activities and an analysis of employment patterns. The aim is to draw together, build upon and extend existing education-industry liaison; it also seeks to influence the planning and provision of vocational education and training.

Schemes agree to operate a three year franchise, the first year of which is funded externally. The subsequent two years must be self-financed.

Contact:
Project Administrator
Local Employer Networks
UK Network Head Office
33 Earl Street
Sheffield S1 3FX

9.2.2 Local initiatives

Local initiatives are many and varied; some of the strongest and most long-lasting effects are achieved through personal contact between local firms and schools. The extent of commitment on both sides and the resulting enrichment of the curriculum is most noticeable in these links.

One illustration of the strength of local links in the secondary sector is that of Norton Hill School, Bath, which has built a 'working partnership' with local companies. Thirty-eight companies took part in the school's Industry Week (as part of Industry Year '86) and £1300 of sponsorship was provided.

Fig. 9.2: Woolworth's 'Leadership Award' sponsored for Industry Year 1986

Over one thousand members of the community visited the Industry Week activities, which was described as:

'serving notice of the school's intention to devise and deliver a long-term programme of close and mutually beneficial links with industry.'

Figure 9.3 illustrates the range of activities in which the school and local employers engaged during their 'Industry Week'.

A common example of locally-based liaison is that of area groups of schools and employers, usually led by one teacher and one employer. Organisation of joint activities, both in curriculum support and exchange visits of teachers and employers are more successful when channelled through local agencies.

It is most effective when groups are chaired by representatives with high status within their organisations, eg headteachers and directors, who can both encourage and facilitate involvement.

The scale, scope and nature of activities varies according to local conditions. What is admirable in a high density population with a mixed economy will be inappropriate in a remote rural area. In an Authority which places education-industry liaison high on the list of priorities, one of the first School-Industry Liaison Co-ordinating Panels was set up in 1975. It brought together representatives from commerce, industry and education to co-ordinate initiatives taking place within the Authority. It has served as a forum for the exchange of ideas, information and contacts, and has influenced the development of policy in this field within the LEA.

9.3 What can education gain from links with industry?

There are three main areas in which schools and colleges can benefit from linking more closely with industry:
– Resources
– Vocational Preparation
– Curriculum support

9.3.1 *Resources*

a. Materials
Many industrial and commercial concerns have surplus material which they are only too pleased to donate to schools if they are approached. This can range from end-of-roll paper in a printing works (often of a very high quality which schools would otherwise be unable to afford) to dress material or metal for engineering projects.

Education – industry links

	Year
Session One: 9.30–11.00 a.m.	
1. I.B.M. — Computers in the Office	6
2. Demonstrations and games led by I.B.M.	1/2
3. The British Aerospace/Avon Hi-Tech Bus	3
4. British Aerospace — an audio-visual presentation	3
5. British Aerospace Lorry	3
6. British Gas — Craft skills	5
Session Two: 11.30–1.00 p.m.	
As above (except for 6) plus	
7. A Bank Loan Simulation led by B.I.S.	4
8. Money Management — B.I.S.	5
9. Visit to Pauls Agriculture	4
10. Visit to Blatchfords	5
11. Visit to Horstman Defence	6
Session Three: 1.55–3.25 p.m.	
1. I.B.M.-led demonstration/games	1/2
2. Money Management — B.I.S.	5
3. Bank Loan Simulation — B.I.S.	4
4. The Hi-Tech Bus	3
5. British Telecom — a general presentation	3
6. Wessex Newspapers — competition results	
7. Surveying/Architecture — Beazers	4/5/6
8. British Aerospace — an audio-visual presentation	3
9. British Aerospace Lorry	3

Evening Session: 7.30–9.00 p.m.

For parents and pupils of all years at Norton Hill. In addition to exhibition stands the following will also be taking place:
— "Working Parnership" video (Unilever)
— Educational Support — British Telecom
— Owen Owen — "Any Questions?"
— Employers Expectations — F. W. Woolworth
— Careers with I.B.M.
— A Working Stand — Clarks Shoes Ltd

Fig. 9.3: School-industry liaison programme, Industry Week, Norton Hill School, Midsomer Norton

b. Equipment

Enterprising schools and colleges have already tapped the resources of industry for equipment which they are able to provide for their students. In some cases firms changing their computing system have donated old (but by no means obsolete) computers. Even if gifts are not available, most companies are prepared to make loans of quite expensive and sophisticated equipment in order to support specific projects within schools.

This is not a new idea but it does rely upon teachers having the initiative to go out and ask. Perhaps the ultimate example occurred when a number of schools in the Manchester area were each given an obsolete *Meteor* jet. Aeronautical studies were suddenly re-vitalised!

c. Sponsorship

Sponsorship of individual students in higher education is well established in some industries, but what is less often recognised is that companies can be persuaded to sponsor projects within schools and colleges. Employers and companies which are well disposed towards supporting education/industry liaison, but are not sure what is required, are often only too pleased to be able to identify with and support specific projects.

d. Personnel

One of the most useful resources which industry can offer to schools is that of personnel. With the right relationship and a clear brief as to what they can contribute, firms are often a surprisingly generous source of voluntary helpers. In cases where a successful scheme has been established as many as fifty or sixty volunteers have been identified to spend time with students. The range of activities is enormous, including specialist help with computers, contribution to engineering foundation courses, assistance with mock interviews, and even the exploitation of personal interests such as sculpture and ballet dancing. The involvement of 'adults other than teachers (AOTs)' has become increasingly important in new approaches to the 14–18 curriculum.

e. Accommodation

This does not refer to the provision of mobile classrooms – although anything is possible! More realistically, industry can be persuaded to make facilities available both for the training of young people, who are exposed to an adult learning environment, and more frequently for the use of teachers' in-service training. Two examples of this can be seen in links arising from the School-Industry Liaison Co-ordinating Committee described earlier. Two large companies represented on the Committee, and consequently familiar with the aims of the group, regularly make their training facilities available to teachers. These facilities, and the opportunity to hold joint training sessions, are appreciated by both education and industry. It is a resource which can be tapped on a wide scale across the country.

f. Money

Many teachers are reluctant, or never consider approaching employers for hard cash to buy equipment, sponsor projects, or provide special materials for particular activities which cannot be funded under normal capitation restrictions. It is surprising how often firms approached for cash are willing to contribute – possibly to provide a Sixth Form brochure, to fund a pre-vocational activity, or residential experience.

g. Work experience

This is one of the most widely-used and sought after facilities offered by employers. The opportunity for young people to gain first-hand experience of life in the working world is invaluable both for personal development, self-confidence, social and coping skills, and a realistic understanding of working conditions. In order for students to gain these benefits, an extensive preparation programme is necessary, in which teachers talk to and brief employers (and employees) about what a young person on work experience can properly expect. They also familiarise themselves with the employers' demands.

h. Work shadowing

This is a less widespread activity, but one which is increasing in popularity. Young people with an interest in a particular career are given the opportunity of following, or 'shadowing' someone in order to gain a flavour of the type of work, social contacts and skills which make up the fabric of the job. It is more commonly a feature of professional or highly skilled occupations, where it is not possible for the student to obtain realistic work experience.

i. Visits

Visits to industry are one of the most well-established forms of liaison; in the earliest days even those institutions with no commitment to bridging the gap between school and work, between education and industry, organised the perfunctory 'careers visit', where young people trailed around in a guided tour gaining very little.

Visits to industry, and the corresponding visits of industrialists into schools have increased in recent years. At their best they offer a new insight and form the basis of a new relationship for many individuals. They may be organised by the CBI, by the LEA, or by local organisations. They are probably most successful in the area of teacher/employer exchange and in cases where a careful programme with clear objectives is established in advance of the visit. Some LEAs have a good record of supporting such programmes which can have a marked effect on classroom teachers with no previous interest.

j. Teacher industrial secondment

Sponsorship or more prolonged visits of teachers into industry, through such avenues as Goldsmiths Fellowships, Understanding British Industry projects and CBI sponsored schemes has grown in recent years. These secondments

Guidelines for managing long-term teacher secondments to industry

Pre-Secondment

LEA

- Devise/Review/Modify, where appropriate, policy aims of Education/Industry liaison, preferably in consultation with representatives from schools/industry organisations, local companies, elected members and institutions of Higher Education which could support developments.
- Appoint and define where appropriate, the role of an Education/Industry liaison officer.
- Establish a responsibility in the Directorate for Education/Industry liaison, e.g. Assistant Director.
- Establish a network of personnel who have a shared interest in the curricular implications of Education/Industry liaison, e.g. Assistant Director, TVEI Co-ordinator etc.
- Establish the relationship between secondment and other strategies for Education/Industry liaison.
- Decide on the length, number and frequency of secondments.
- Decide on the target group(s) for secondment, e.g. School Head, Deputy, Teacher, LEA Administrator, Adviser.
- Decide whether and how to use the secondee(s) across the LEA.
- Investigate ways in which secondment could benefit current initiatives in the LEA, e.g. CPVE, TVEI and management development.
- Devise, where appropriate, the selection criteria for secondment in consultation with Schools/Industry organisations, local company representatives, elected members.
- Organise an awareness raising seminar on long-term secondments to industry for key LEA representatives and Head teachers.
- Identify the particular opportunities in local companies.
- Advertise and encourage Heads to respond to secondment programme.
- Establish with the company the consultation mechanism for selection of the secondee, including who will be the final arbiter.
- Appoint an educational tutor for the secondee(s) to provide professional support.
- Decide on the mechanism for the monitoring of the secondee(s). A monitoring group should consist of representatives from the LEA, School and Companies involved; the Group should meet on a regular basis.

Company

- Devise/clarify, where appropriate, policy aims of Education/Industry liaison.
- Identify and publicise specific areas in the company which would be particularly suitable for secondment.
- Provide briefing papers on the company.
- Establish and brief senior staff on the aims of long-term secondments.
- Notify all personnel of the company's support for secondment.
- Take an active role, in consultation with the LEA, on the selection of the secondee.
- Identify and brief an industrial tutor to support the secondee.
- Arrange a preliminary meeting of the industrial tutor and secondee to identify objectives.
- Communicate negotiated programme and brief staff who are likely to be involved.

Fig. 9.4: 'Teacher Secondments to Industry', UBI/British Telecom

Headteacher
- ▶ Establish the school's policy for liaison with industry of which the secondment should be part. Communicate this to the staff.
- ▶ Establish whether the School can contribute to, and benefit from, the LEA secondment programme.
- ▶ Select a potential secondee with the personal and professional qualities, and with a high degree of credibility with colleagues, who will be able to influence the curriculum on return. Such a person should be able to maximize his/her opportunities and have high credibility in industry. A person in a senior position is most likely to be a suitable candidate.
- ▶ Establish broadly how the secondee would be used on return to School.
- ▶ If the application is successful, brief staff, students, governors and parents.

Individual
- ▶ Be aware of the potential impact on the total curriculum of Education/Industry liaison.
- ▶ Clarify aims/objectives of the secondment in consultation with the Head and LEA representatives.
- ▶ Prepare for the interview; investigate relevant background information. This could include general information about industry.
- ▶ If accepted, establish personal needs to prepare for secondment.
- ▶ Negotiate secondment objectives with industrial tutor.

During the secondment
LEA
- ▶ Educational tutor should arrange to meet with secondee(s) on a regular basis to provide support and review progress.
- ▶ Make arrangements for secondees to meet to share experiences.
- ▶ Be prepared for inappropriate objectives to be modified.
- ▶ Decide on post-secondment objectives.
- ▶ Educational tutor should be involved in preparing the secondee, and the School, for the post-secondment period.

Company
- ▶ Facilitate meetings with key personnel.
- ▶ Arrange visits, where appropriate, to give the secondee a wider view of the company; e.g. suppliers and customers.
- ▶ Ensure that the placement is weighted towards an active involvement rather than observation in the company; the degree to which this can be implemented will depend on the length of the secondment.
- ▶ Devise a structured programme but allow enough flexibility to enable the secondee to re-negotiate objectives and respond to developments.
- ▶ Provide support and advice where appropriate.
- ▶ Provide a base in the company for the secondee.
- ▶ Decide how the secondee can be used in a consultancy capacity, e.g. update on recent developments in education.

Headteacher
- ▶ Arrange to visit the teacher on secondment.
- ▶ Prepare for the return of the secondee, e.g. create/modify management structures which can facilitate change.

inevitably reach a smaller proportion of the teaching force, but this is more than compensated for by the value of the in depth, first-hand experience which individual teachers gain by working within a company for a prolonged period. These benefits will, however, be limited if they are not effectively disseminated to other teachers and schools within the LEA.

An example of the preparatory work necessary is outlined in the extract from the UBI/Telecom teacher secondment programme (see Figure 9.4). The most common form of secondment is that of teacher into industry; the corresponding exchange of industrialist into school or college is notoriously difficult to arrange. Where it has taken place there has been a marked increase in industrialists' understanding of, and respect for, the work carried out in schools. One British Aerospace manager, who spent only three weeks in a comprehensive school was enthused by the commitment and dedication of the teachers, commenting on the fact that even in their free time conversation generally centred around pupils' needs and work.

9.3.2 Vocational preparation

a. Careers talks and general information

This is the resource with the longest history. Even the most insular schools or colleges have instituted occasional talks by membes of industry and the professions. Such talks can be counter-productive unless they are undertaken by skilled communicators. However, the chance to talk to someone actually doing a job can be a most valuable source of information for young people making career choices. It is even better if the speaker is young, so that the gap in experience and perception is minimised.

b. Careers literature

One of the most difficult tasks facing careers teachers is that of maintaining an up-to-date information library, with attractive, well-presented literature. Industry and commerce can be invaluable in providing relevant, eye-catching material. Admittedly they are part of an attempt to attract suitable recruits, but teachers are well able to sift the information and advise students.

An interesting new development is emerging with the availability of 'ACCESS' careers information on the TTNS database. This information is available to any school or college throughout the country which subscribes to TTNS: it is partly sponsored by industrial and commercial concerns, and provides the latest information at the touch of a button, making much of the paper information obsolete.

c. Careers conventions

A more sophisticated version of the straightforward careers talk, or provision of literature, is the careers convention. Organisation can be a major undertaking. Schools and colleges which offer this facility to their students usually

Education – industry links

mount a convention every two years. A range of professional, industrial, commercial and service occupations are represented, and contributors usually agree to set up an exhibition and provide a representative to answer young peoples' questions. It can be a very effective way for students (and teachers) to gain first-hand information about a variety of occupations in a familiar and stress-free environment.

d. Work experience

The value of work experience as a means of enhancing students' self-confidence and fostering personal development has already been discussed. However, it also has a part to play in vocational preparation; the opportunity to experience working situations at first hand before irrevocable decisions have to be taken is a great help to many young people. It may be that the individual is undecided, and a chance to sample two or three jobs can play a vital part in choosing. The benefits are equally valid whether a career choice is confirmed, or whether the individual with a life-long ambition to become a nurse finds that he cannot face the sight of blood. The opportunity to change paths is still open.

e. Challenge of Industry conferences

Organised by The Industrial Society, these two-day conferences for sixth formers bring industrial managers and trades unionists into schools where they have the opportunity to discuss issues facing industry today. The conferences aim to increase understanding of the wealth creation process, to emphasise the need to manage by persuasion, and to understand the rights of employees to be represented by trade unions. They also encourage young people to see a career in industry as challenging and stimulating.

The conferences are highly participative, with managers attached to a group of sixth formers working on a series of problems and hopefully hammering out their own solutions (see Figure 9.5). Clearly the success of such conferences depends upon the hard work and enthusiasm of the organisers together with the commitment of industry, but they provide a useful focus for building and extending liaison, and for offering sixth formers an insight into the world of industry. The main drawback is that these conferences are expensive – schools are charged approximately £350 per conference.

f. Practice interviews

The chance to experience mock interviews with employers who give constructive feedback is invaluable for students of all academic abilities. Most employers are willing to contribute their time to help in this exercise.

NEWSPAPER TEARING EXERCISE

LEADERS BRIEF

Resources: 3 sheets double page size newspaper(e.g. Times)

For each group : 1 roll of sellotape
                 1 ruler

1. You have a team of 5 people. You have one sheet of newspaper and some sellotape. Using these resources, you have to produce a continuous length of material shich should be as long as possible and must be suspended at least two feet above ground level. The longer the paper, the greater the profit you will achieve. Your purpose is to achieve maximum profit.

2. The exercise will take place in two stages.

   a) The Planning Stage

   This will last for 20 minutes. You may do whatever you wish during this period, and will have 2 extra sheets of newspaper to develop your prototype. At the end of 20 minutes, you must write down for your group adviser, the profit you aim to achieve in the completion stage.

   The profit arrangements are as follows:

   - you earn £50 for the first five feet assembled.
   - and then £20 for each extra foot

   Constraints

   - each piece of sellotape you use must be no more than 2" long
   - subtract £10 for every join sealed with sellotape
   - subtract £10 for every point the material is supported off the ground (this inculdes the two ends).

   b) The Completion Stage

   Time: Normal time taken for the completion stage is five minutes. For every second inside five minutes, add the sum of £1.00 to your profit. Subtract £1.00 for every second above five minutes.

   Your target profit is £500. (Maximum that has been achieved is £1,300).

   The completion stage will last as long as you require.

Fig. 9.5: Example of an exercise used in Challenge of Industry Conferences (Industrial Society)

Education – industry links

9.3.3 Curriculum support

a. Enterprise education
Enterprise education, particularly through the channels of Young Enterprise and the Mini Enterprise in Schools Project, has played a large part in the integration of links with industry into students' curriculum (see Chapter 8).

b. Projects
Project work is an increasing part of student activity, particularly in preparation for GCSE. The majority of projects can be made more realistic and have greater impact on students if they can visit industries using processes which they are studying. This can range from chemical engineering and welding to surveying and construction or catering. Almost any project can be illuminated by first-hand experience.

One student interested in electronic engineering was able, with the help of a local firm, to work through all the stages of designing an integrated circuit: preparing the chip and producing an end product – a set of flashing disco lights. She gained more from this experience than could conceivably have been offered in a school sixth form alone.

c. Business games and simulations
This is an excellent way of introducing awareness of commerce and industry into the curriculum. CRAC and Longman publish a number of business games and simulations which teachers have found useful.

d. Worksheets
A new flavour is added to the use of worksheets if they are prepared by employers. Most industries and commercial enterprises can produce a worksheet relating to their company for students to use in school. The most dedicated teacher cannot hope to compete with the range of experience which can be drawn upon. It is not confined to older students, but is equally relevant for primary pupils.

e. Integration across the curriculum
The move towards an integrated, cross-curricular approach to teaching and learning has been a recurring theme. Industrial liason and support is an ideal vehicle for promoting this idea. Simulated business games, work experience and Young Enterprise all emphasise the need to use a variety of skills in real situations. Experience of using a variety of skills to solve problems is a most effective way of demonstrating the value of cross-curricular learning.

f. TVEI/CPVE
These two initiatives (Chapters 1 and 3) have seen the introduction of education-industry liaison into the mainstream curriculum of schools and colleges.

In both cases the need for work experience and for involvement of employers in curriculum work is an identified part of the course. Whilst there is still some way to go before this is fully achieved, it has given credibility to the idea of integrating industrial liaison into the curriculum.

g. Current industrial practices

Use of industrialists to assist teachers in keeping up-to-date on the latest industrial practices is a particularly valuable contribution. Technology changes so rapidly that teachers are inevitably left behind in maintaining current knowledge. It not only helps teachers, but re-vitalises the curriculum for students and ensures that they are aware of new developments.

9.4 What can industry gain from links with education?

Employers' interest in education-industry liaison can be summarised under four main headings:
- service
- publicity
- understanding wealth creation
- recruitment

9.4.1 Service

a. Helping young people

There is no doubt that a major part of the motive of many employers involved in education-industry liaison is a genuine desire to do something to help young people. This is evident not only in the willingness of managers to take students into the firm for work experience or work shadowing, but also in the attitude of the other employees. During many years of visiting students on work experience placements varying from stables to electronics industries, there was a common response of, 'well I wish that someone had done this for me, I'm only too happy to help'.

b. Community conscience

Firms often wish to present their corporate image as being one which cares from the community, has a conscience about the welfare of the community and its needs, and fulfils a role in helping the local area. This can either be a genuine sense of moral obligation, or an astute public relations exercise.

c. Closer communication and understanding

Employers may be disillusioned with the recruits they are taking from schools and college, or they may simply feel that it is counter-productive to criticise without making a positive effort to both understand and contribute to what is happening in education. Certainly more employers are engaging in the development of the curriculum within schools; they contribute expertise and a knowledge of the skills and problems facing young people in the world of work.

Some schools have included employers in the planning both of new curriculum initiatives such as TVEI, and in the expansion of more traditional areas such as mathematics teaching. In return, employers gain a more realistic idea of the work taking place in schools and colleges, and are more readily able to build on students' experience. The emphasis is on liaison, communication, increased understanding and less mutual criticism.

9.4.2 Publicity

a. Profit

It is, perhaps, unrealistic in a time of high unemployment and increasing pressure on the resources of both large and small firms, that they should devote manpower, money and time to an activity which is entirely benevolent, with no corresponding 'pay-off'. Many firms might harbour, as at least a part of their interest, an awareness of profit. It is particularly evident in the activities of some of the large banks which sponsor a variety of collaborative projects. It is clear that if they can establish their name in the minds of students, they have an advantage in attracting future customers. This concept of liaison as part of the marketing policy can be equally useful for the committed training officer to sell the idea to the directors of the company.

b. Public image

Establishing a company name within schools and colleges also enhances the image of a firm with the local population. Large employers in particular need to build up good relations with the local community; being seen to take a caring, positive interest in the development of the young people can only help to foster that image. It also helps in the case of employees' attitudes to the firm; they have their own children at local schools, and are likely to react favourably to evidence of company help.

c. Improving occupational image

Some employers become involved not merely to improve the image of the company in the locality, but in order to enhance the image of the profession in the eyes of young people. An example of this can be found in the energetic campaign and high profile involvement of the engineering industry, which strenuously attempts to raise the image and status of engineering in the eyes of able youngsters.

d. Advertising
Publicity through sponsorship of competitions or involvement in activities such as Young Enterprise can provide a cost-effective source of advertising.

9.4.3 *Understanding wealth creation*

a. The contribution of wealth creation
A large part of the motive of many industrialists, and of the Government's promotion of education-industry liaison, lies in the attempt to explain the importance of the wealth creation process. This is spelt out in the White Paper *Working Together – education and training*[4]. It is an idea which is strenuously promoted, particularly by employers engaged in the manufacturing industry. They draw attention to the role of manufacturing and wealth creation in providing resources with which to fund the service sector. It is probably a justifiable complaint that too many people call for improved services without understanding the source of revenue which pays for the service.

b. How industry works
Allied to this is the desire to introduce young people to an understanding of how industry works. It is helped by the sort of experiential, participative learning which has been outlined. This is especially true of business games and of involvement in mini-enterprise and *Young Enterprise* where individuals adopt the roles of directors, shop floor workers and trade union officials; all these provide an opportunity to experience at first hand the interactions, demands, constraints and responsibilities of business and manufacturing.

9.4.4 *Recruitment*

a. Identifying potential employees
Initially it was true that what most employers wanted was access to opportunities to recruit the 'best' candidates for jobs. Motives are now more comprehensive, more directly related to educational experiences, and more altruistic. Nevertheless, there is still an element of enlightened self-interest in employers' involvement. It may be that the local laundry hopes to identify a willing and cheerful shopfloor worker, or that an engineering firm is looking for potential recruits to sponsor through university. Recruitment does still play a part in what employers expect to gain from liaison, although at a time of high unemployment and reduced recruitment, it is inevitably a much smaller part.

b. Extending awareness of local employment
There is an expectation that students will be more aware of the local work situation, and will more readily adapt to the transition from school to work.

c. Reducing employee wastage
There is less chance of costly wastage through young people opting for a job about which they are ignorant.

Summary

Education-industry liaison has grown significantly in the period since 1976. There is every sign that it is likely to continue to occupy a prominent place in new curriculum developments, particularly in the field of 14–18 education. There has also been a growth in employers' contribution to the management of schools, through their new role on governing bodies.

The advantages of liaison to both education and industry have been discussed: there are benefits to be gained for students and institutions within the education system. If full advantage is to be taken of these opportunities however, it is essential that the process is genuinely reciprocal, and that industry becomes more familiar with what is *really* happening within schools, and with what education is trying to achieve.

Notes

1. The Hadow Report, *Education of the Adolescent*, 1926.
2. Department of Education and Science, *Working Together: education and training*, HMSO, 1986.
3. Department of Education and Science/Department of Employment, *Working Together for a Better Future*, HMSO, 1987.
4. See 2.

Chapter 10

The careers contribution

10.1 Making sense of the confusion

The first part of this book is devoted to an examination of new curriculum trends in the field of 14–18 education and training. Whilst many of these trends are admirable and are concerned with seeking a better deal for young people, the result is frequently one of confusion.

The student is faced with a mass of what may seem to be contradictory and competing claims. Teachers themselves are often confused and may be unfamiliar with developments in which they are not directly involved.

Some way has to be found of making sense of new developments for the student, and of co-ordinating innovations so that they are integrated into the fabric of the school or college.

10.2 What should be done to rationalise the new trends?

Is there a need for a new post within schools and colleges geared specifically to the job of co-ordinating 14–18 curriculum developments, or is there perhaps a mechanism already established which can fulfil these functions?

It might be helpful to identify exactly what ARE the tasks which need to be performed in order that the benefits of the new curriculum initiatives may be fully mobilised for the benefit of the student.

i. Firstly, it is clear that there must be someone, or some group of people within the school that is well informed about the variety of opportunities available and able to disseminate details clearly and comprehensively.

ii. Secondly, a key requirement is for trained personnel in a position to offer sound guidance on the most appropriate route open to young people and on who can help them to recognise the implications of their choices.

iii. Thirdly, if there is one thing above all others required in order for schools, colleges and individual students to be able to take full advantage of the new developments, it is that there should be full and effective liaison between teachers, students, parents, further and higher education, managing agents, employers and the individuals responsible for organising each initiative. If these three tasks associated with information, guidance and liaison are accepted as being necessary for the co-ordination of 14–18 developments, then the next step is to consider whether there may not already be in existence a pool of expertise which can be tapped within the school or college.

One obvious option is to investigate the role of careers education with particular reference to the part it plays in:
– preparing young people for life after school
– acting as a co-ordinating mechanism for new 14–18 developments

10.3 The role of careers education

Careers education has a vital role to play in preparing young people for adult life. This does not mean that it is confined to a narrow, mechanistic 'job-matching' function. On the contrary, good, well-thought-out and co-ordinated careers programmes touch every aspect of the young person's experience and development.

Careers teachers have long been concerned with helping students towards realistic self-assessment of their strengths and weaknesses, towards setting achievable targets to which the individual can aspire, and towards gaining practical, first-hand experience. The aim is to help students to develop interpersonal and practical skills which will enable them to make the best use of their individual aptitudes and talents on leaving school. In other words, careers education has concerned itself with many of the areas of knowledge and skills which are now achieving prominence under initiatives such as TVEI and records of achievement. It also helps students to gain an understanding of the rapidly changing educational, training and occupational opportunities open to them, and should offer sound guidance so that they can make informed decisions about the best route for them.

In addition, careers teachers help students towards an understanding of the economic basis of society, the importance of wealth creation, their role as adults in society, and the quality of personal relationships both in and out of work.

10.4 Functions of the careers teacher

There is a distinction to be made between the complementary roles of the careers teacher and careers officer. The careers teacher is a member of the teaching staff of the school who comes into contact with students over a long period of time. The careers officer works for the Careers Service, visiting a number of organisations to give specialist vocational advice and guidance, offer impartial information on local and national training and employment opportunities, and provide a direct link between schools, colleges and employers.

This chapter addresses the work of the careers teacher or lecturer, who is an integral part of the teaching force of the institution.

The very diverse tasks of the careers teacher can be summarised under three main headings:
– information
– guidance
– liaison

a. Information
This covers a wide and ever-increasing range of topics, including:
 i. the gathering, classifying and display of information relating to specific job and training opportunities
 ii. maintaining and up-dating careers libraries
 iii. providing information in a digestible form and making use of modern information technology (eg ACCESS careers information on TTNS)
 iv. information about other institutions – primary, further education, higher education, training agencies
 v. organising careers conventions to disseminate a range of information to students and parents
 vi. gathering and providing information *on* young people, as well as for them

b. Guidance
'If decisions are to be properly informed, full and reliable information and sensitive guidance must be available at the right times for all.'[2]

Careers guidance includes:
 i. personal guidance aimed at helping the individual to recognise strengths, to build and capitalise on these, and to identify areas which might be developed
 ii. helping the young person to identify intrinsic interests, and occupational interest areas – often with the assistance of a computer based guidance system such as JIIG-CAL (Job Ideas and Information Generator)
 iii. development of self-assessment and decision-making skills
 iv. presenting alternatives in terms of courses and educational experience available within the school and in further and higher education
 v. help with job seeking skills and strategies
 vi. identifying positive alternatives to employment and to traditional routes on leaving school
 vii. guidance on choice of work experience and helping the individual to make the most of that experience

c. Liaison

The key to the work of the careers department in schools and colleges lies in effective liaison. This includes liaison with:

i. *other teachers within the school*

   One of the prerequisites for a successful careers teacher is the ability to gain the co-operation of other members of staff, so that information flows freely

ii. *the careers service*

   It is essential for there to be a good, trusting relationship between careers teachers in schools and colleges, and the careers service which has responsibility for advising young people on the choices open to them on reaching sixteen and for placing them in jobs or training. (Some LEAs foster this by organising joint training sessions.)

iii. *parents*

   The importance of involving parents as partners has long been recognised by careers teachers.

iv. *industry and commerce*

   The thrust of many of the initiatives described in this book has been a concern with preparing young people to cope in an increasingly competitive and technological society. The careers department is the front line link with the world outside school. For example, schools organising work experience for two hundred pupils must develop links with a great number of employers.

v. *further education colleges, polytechnics and universities*

   The careers department is the first point of contact with these institutions and provides a comprehensive picture of the range of courses available locally and nationally.

vi. *training agencies*

   These may fluctuate and change, but it is in the careers department that up-to-date information on training provision can be found, and it is through personal contact and liaison that the most fruitful results are obtained.

vii. *the community*

   This includes a great variety of local organisations: one example is Rotary, which has a long history of being willing to provide members who give up their time in order to help students with mock interviews and applications.

viii. *schools/industry liaison*

   See Chapter 8 for full details, but one important aspect is the encouragement of industrialists' contribution to curriculum developments within the school and college.

ix. *co-ordinator/team leader*

   This essential over-arching role involves co-ordinating the work of the careers team, teachers involved in pre-vocational work, and the wider team of teachers responsible for the guidance of students. This reinforces the point made in *Working Together for a Better Future* – that careers education is part of the role of every teacher.

d. The role of careers as a possible co-ordinating mechanism for 14–18 developments

The tasks required in order to make sense of the initiatives with which schools and colleges have been inundated in recent years has been spelt out in 10.2. It is clear, from the analysis of the role of careers education in helping students to prepare for adult life, that there is a close correlation between the experience, tasks and roles already carried out in this area, and the new demands being made for rationalising developments in the 14–18 field.

There is, then, a need for someone skilled in information gathering, guidance and liaison to make sense of the variety of opportunity offered to students.

These requirements accord so closely with the functions undertaken by careers education, that there is a strong argument for building upon this experience and expertise, and for placing the task of co-ordinating and drawing together the strands of the new trends under the aegis of the careers department.

10.5 The counter argument

The idea that the careers department should carry responsibility for co-ordinating 14–18 developments would not, however, win universal support. It could be considered positively undesirable. For instance:
  i. It has been suggested[1] that it is a mistake to continue the practice of having a separate careers department; that it is better for children if careers becomes a part of the mainstream activities of the school and a generic task of all teachers.
 ii. Even if a separate careers department is maintained, it may not be appropriate for that department to manage the new initiatives. Careers could be (and is, in some schools and colleges) seen as a marginal activity; co-ordination of these new trends should be central to the organisation and curriculum.
iii. It may be that the needs are, in fact, very different from those fulfilled by the careers teacher – that it is essentially a central management issue, and that their co-ordination is not, therefore, an appropriate function of the careers department.
 iv. The Deputy Head with responsibility for the curriculum, or the Vice Principal in a college, is in a far better position to have an overview of the provision available within the school, and has the status to ensure that the perspective of the organisation is represented.
  v. With the advent of a national curriculum, the need for specialist advice of this nature will be diminished, and careers work, together with choice

in curriculum options, will be subsumed into the national, prescribed framework.

10.6 First-hand experience of the Careers Department in a co-ordinating role: Castleford High School, West Yorkshire

Many careers teachers throughout the country already have responsibility for co-ordinating 14–18 developments. One example of the skills required and the tasks fulfilled illustrates the contribution which can be made by the trained careers specialist.

Castleford High School is a mixed, 12–18 Comprehensive school with 1050 pupils, serving a small West Yorkshire industrial town.

A review of the responsibilities of the Head of Careers gives an indication of her experience, which has prepared her for the role of TVEI Co-ordinator.

a. Head of Careers
This post involves the tasks outlined in 10.4 including: information seeking and dissemination; guidance of students and parents; liaison with students, parents, teachers, careers officers, employers.

It is concerned with the individual student and the need to offer appropriate guidance, the need to work closely with other teachers in order to gain co-operation and establish lines of communication, and the need to form a network of contacts beyond the school.

b. Work and residential experience co-ordinator
From tentative beginnings, where students contacted employers and made their own arrangements, work experience has become an organised scheme, designed in collaboration with a neighbouring school, as an integrated part of the curriculum.

This has extended to planned residential experience, where the students' experiences are used as a basis for real learning, and are not merely isolated activities.

c. Pre-vocational education
The Head of Careers collaborated with the pre-vocational Co-ordinator who developed this course for sixth form students. The aims are presented to students, teachers and employers in the form of a statement attached to any final certification. (See Figure 10.1.)

In addition to work experience, experiments with work across the curriculum, involving teams of teachers working together have been trialled. It is significant that the co-ordinator drew attention to teachers' feelings of guilt

AIMS OF THE COURSE

1. To promote personal and social development.

2. To give responsibility to learners that will reflect and promote status changes (pupil to worker, child to adult, minor to citizen).

3. To devise learning procedures that promote self confidence, self esteem, responsibility, autonomy and solidarity, in addition to offering technical or academic competence.

4. To develop the ability to work effectively with others.

5. To reflect the realities of young people's lives and prospects in the 1980's.

6. To develop skills which are transferable between a variety of settings.

7. To discover and use the talents of the pupils to achieve these declared aims.

SIGNED...... M.V. Butler

Fig. 10.1: Aims of a pre-vocational course, Castleford High School, Wakefield

The careers contribution

that they were not 'teaching' but were acting as facilitators in an active learning environment.

Links with the community were promoted through this course, and the co-ordinator needed to have a well-established network of contacts.

One of the community projects undertaken on the course was the construction of playground seating for a neighbouring primary school. See Figure 10.2 (an extract from one student's profile).

d. Enterprise education
Another consequence of experience gained through the pre-vocational course was the development of Enterprise Education (Chapter 8).

Students set up and ran a school bank, in collaboration with the local branch of Midland Bank. This involved decisions on location, opening days, and advertising. After testing consumer response by organising a market research survey, the bank opened on two morning breaks each week and attracted fifty members.

e. Profiling
This was an integral part of the pre-vocational course and later of TVEI. It served not only as a means of accrediting the work undertaken by the students, but contributed to the growing confidence in new relationships which were emerging between teachers and students as a result of the initiatives already underway. It was described by the co-ordinator as one of the main thrusts for developing teaching skills.

It also strengthened links with the Careers Service by involving them in the use of profiles for guidance and counselling purposes.

f. Personal and social education (PSE)
Building on the success of earlier initiatives, the Head of Careers became convinced of the need to develop a wide-ranging PSE course for middle school students, to prepare them for the choices that they would face, to enhance their personal development and to help them look at themselves as individuals.

Careers work involving self-assessment played a large part in the course. It focused on concern for the individual, and also helped to build up teachers' counselling skills.

g. Links with industry
The contacts made through careers education formed the basis for extending links with industry through other areas of the curriculum. The school became involved in the Schools Curriculum Industry project (SCIP). As part of this project, third year pupils worked with professional editorial staff on the local *Castleford and Pontefract Express* and prepared the centre pages for one week's circulation.

The school is twinned with a local clothing manufacturer, and has worked with the firm to give students an understanding of how a business produces,

```
Community Projects

    A group of six students undertook the construction of playground seating
for the pupils of Smawthorne First School. The project was initiated in
November and completed by Easter. Chris was involved in the following:

    Planning...   preliminary meeting with client, outlining a brief,
                  appraising clients needs, drafting of sketches, deciding
                  upon the most suitable design.

    Materials..   purchase of materials - sand, cement, wood, collection of
                  materials from Selby, planing of wood to size, co-ordination
                  of material delivery on site.

    Construction  marking out of site, laying foundations, modification of
                  plans, use of tools - trowel, spirit level, plumbline,
                  mixing cement, bricklaying.

    Organisation  coping with kids, working on Sundays, use of staff room,
                  liaison with staff, managing of colleagues, meeting deadlines,
                  contact with local press, appraising the finished product.
```

Fig. 10.2: Illustration of a community project undertaken by pupils at Castleford High School, Wakefield

markets and advertises its goods. It is also developing industrial links on control technology with another local firm.

These are only two examples of the varied links which have been established between the school and local industry.

h. TVEI
In the words of the Head of Careers:

> *My job as TVEI co-ordinator seems a natural extension of all the other work in which I have been involved. It calls on the full range of skills which I have built up through the other initiatives, needs a network of contacts in the community outside school, and the ability to counsel students on the variety of options open to them.*

Principal requirements for working as a co-ordinator of the 14–18 developments offered within (and outside) an institution were identified as:
  i. concern for, and ability to communicate with individual students, teachers, parents
 ii. experience of working with teams of staff
iii. liaising with teachers across the school and with employers and the community outside the school
 iv. co-ordinating teachers in work across the curriculum, ranging from performing arts to information technology
  v. ability to organise work experience and residential experience, and to ensure their integration into the curriculum.

It is not only in schools like Castleford High School that the contribution which can be made by careers education in co-ordinating 14–18 developments is recognised. An increasing number of LEAs are appointing advisers with overall responsibility for careers, school-industry links and 14–18 initiatives.

Contact:
Barbara Thomson
Castleford High School
Castleford
West Yorkshire
WF10 4JQ

Summary

There are a number of alternatives available for handling the diverse initiatives in the field of 14–18 education. This chapter has been concerned with the way in which careers education is geared to helping students to prepare for life after school, and towards making decisions which are best suited to their needs. It has also considered the way in which this function might be harnessed in order to adopt a unifying role, and to make sense of the options facing young people.

The drawbacks and counter arguments to such a proposal have been outlined, but despite these very real objections, I would suggest that there is a good case for retaining a strong, separate careers department. Careers teachers can take a broader view of the curriculum than subject teachers, can provide students with all the relevant information and offer impartial, objective advice. It makes good sense to build upon and extend an existing source of expertise and experience.

However, if this approach is adopted it is absolutely vital that steps are taken to ensure that the quality (and quantity) of provision is enhanced in order that all students throughout the country have access to comparable levels of provision. There is a route through which this can readily be achieved. In April 1987 the Government published the document, *Working Together for a Better Future*, aimed at improving provision of careers education in schools and in the Careers Service through a major joint exercise. This went beyond the bland declaration of 'desirable provision' to the instigation of a searching survey of careers provision in schools and colleges throughout the country. Every institution was required to respond to a detailed questionnaire and LEAs were required to report back to the Government.

The recommendations of the document match very closely what needs to be done not only to enhanace careers provision, but to establish a strong base from which the co-ordination of 14–18 initiatives can be organised. These recommendations include:

i. identification of 'individuals to ensure that careers education and guidance, related activities – including pre-vocational education, school/industry links, work experience, personal and social education – are of a satisfactory standard across the whole of the Authority's area'

ii. acknowledgement of the importance of relevant and practical approaches to learning through GCSE, TVEI, CPVE, work shadowing, work experience, mini-enterprise and records of achievement in meeting students' educational needs and developing knowledge and skills which can be applied in the adult world.

iii. recognition of the importance of ensuring that students are on appropriate courses, that they have adequate support to successfully complete their studies, and that they progress smoothly to the next stage of training, or to employment.[2]

iv. allocation of adequate time and facilities to carry out the work effectively

The recommendations support the argument that developments aimed at offering students a more relevant, practically oriented and problem-solving approach to learning, are linked to the support which can be offered by the careers department.

In order to ensure effective implementation, an enhanced level of resourcing for training and administration is needed (but this should already be in hand in order to meet Government requirements), and the principle that the Head of Careers makes a contribution to the management team should be established.

This model for the co-ordination of 14–18 developments is only one possible strategy; the disadvantages have been outlined, and there are certainly alternatives. What is not in dispute is the fact that there needs to be *some* way of ensuring that all staff and students within an institution can turn to a central source where the full range of information is readily available, where they can receive advice and guidance, and where they can be sure that liaison with all relevant agencies is a matter of routine.

Notes

1. Baroness Hooper 'Careers education likely to lose status in national curriculum' *The Guardian*, 29 July 1987.
2. DES/DofE *Working Together for a Better Future*, Department of Education and Science and Department of Employment, 1987.

Chapter 11

Common themes

Many of the initiatives described in this book have common roots; others originate from widely differing backgrounds. Whether individual schemes are employer-led or education-led, pre-sixteen or post-sixteen, a number of themes have emerged which are common to all. It is these common themes which highlight the direction in which 14–18 education and training has developed in recent years, and which draw together the ideas and philosophies of what might otherwise appear to be a disparate collection of conflicting programmes. The developments which can most easily be identified include:

11.1 Experiential learning

Experience-based learning has featured in every one of the initiatives described in this book. It is characterised by a reversal of the traditional practice of teachers dictating the content and methods of learning, and where any practical experience is an adjunct to rather than a central characteristic of the course.

Learning by doing puts experience first and builds upon this experience. The earliest example of this approach is probably that of *Young Enterprise* (Chapter 8) which has been in operation for over a quarter of a century. It attracted more widespread attention through YTS, and the idea that students could be motivated to learn by helping them to use experience in their lives and work gradually gained recognition. It was extended into TVEI and CPVE; both of these initiatives influenced the development of experience-based learning. Teachers accepted that it was possible to motivate young people by exploiting their interests and experience. TRIST took this one step further by adopting the same strategy for the in-service training of teachers, in the hope that students would benefit from the repercussions.

A significant advance was achieved with the emphasis on a problem-solving, experiential basis for GCSE – the first time that it had been advocated within an academic public examination system.

The growth of experience-based learning in all of these initiatives culminates in the assessment of students' attainments through profiling and records of achievement. The involvement and participation of students advocated in records of achievement is a natural consequence of the experience-based learning undertaken by the student. It heralds a major shift in learning strateges in schools and colleges.

11.2 Changing teaching styles and student/teacher relationships

Experience-based learning has implications for the associated issue of the teaching styles necessary to accommodate new methods of learning. An experiential, problem-solving approach and individual learning must entail different teaching strategies. None of the initiatives outlined earlier can succeed with didactic methods. Teachers are called upon to act as facilitators, to develop support materials for individualised learning programmes, and to organise work periods so that students can build upon practice to understand the associated theory.

Even GCSE, which operates within a prescribed framework and national criteria which determine syllabuses, requires new teaching styles. Demands upon teachers for flexibility and innovative techniques are greater than ever before. Teachers accustomed to traditional delivery find it difficult to adjust to a less structured, more informal ethos.

Nevertheless, those who have successfully made the transition are unanimous in acknowledging the advantages which quickly become apparent. Improved motivation and growth of student autonomy are foremost among the benefits.

Perhaps the most significant change is that found in the evolving pattern of student/teacher relationships. Students and teachers are talking to each other as individuals in the course of reviewing their work, setting targets, negotiating learning objectives and jointly assessing work.

Beneficial results have been obvious in the profiles and records of achievement movement, even in situations where there has been no accompanying curriculum initiative; it has become a characteristic of CPVE and TVEI schemes.

Major changes demanded of teachers cannot be achieved without appropriate supportive INSET. The TRIST programme administered an effective 'short sharp shock' which influenced large numbers of teachers. It aimed to create a body of teachers prepared to experiment with new teaching styles; whilst not reaching every teacher and lecturer, it nevertheless succeeded to a large extent.

CPVE also concentrated on experiential INSET designed to promote experience-based learning and participative teaching strategies. Records of achievement depend for their success on the participative, active engagement of students and teachers, leading to a change in student-teacher relationships.

11.3 Cross-curricular issues

A consequence of the new teaching and learning styles is that learning is beginning to take place across the curriculum, and not merely within separate subjects. Each of the major initiatives encourages the development of cross-curricular work: even GCSE, which was initially conceived as a single subject examination, has bowed to consumer pressure and now offers a range of modules which can be grouped together to provide certification. Inclusion of cross-curricular skills in records of achievement recognises their importance, and helps to encourage their inclusion in the curriculum.

It is not easy to create a climate where cross-curricular work is incorporated into the fabric of the curriculum. It demands more of teachers and of the organisation, but it does give students the opportunity to develop skills and to gain knowledge which relates more closely to their life after school.

11.4 Links with industry

The value of education and industry working together has become increasingly accepted in the last decade. Some of the ways in which this is achieved have been outlined in Chapter 9, but the need for employers' participation has been specified in TVEI, TRIST, CPVE, YTS, records of achievement, and even GCSE. Employer participation is a pre-requisite of enterprise education, and the relationship with careers education is evident.

There is still a long way to go before all the misconceptions are removed, and employers are persuaded to make sustained contributions to the curriculum. 14–18 developments have encouraged a movement which was already taking place, and have put the issue of industrial liaison firmly on the agenda of those involved in the education and training of young people.

11.5 Modular developments

Since 1982, modular developments have gained ground as a means of re-organising the secondary curriculum, particularly in the 14–18 age range. A module is a means of re-structuring work into shorter learning packages, with short-term learning objectives and accompanying assessments. They may be either free standing, or linked to other modules to form the basis of a longer course.

TVEI (Chapter 1) has been one of the greatest influences on the growth of modules; the demand for enhanced curriculum options in hi-tech areas such as microelectronics, design technology and computing meant that they could often only be included through short courses. Many TVEI schemes, such as that devised in Somerset, relied upon a modular curriculum operating not only in these specialist options, but also in the mainstream general education sectors.

11.6 Integration

Despite the common themes shared by 14–18 initiatives, teachers, educational managers and politicians have all become aware of the need for greater integration and liaison. There have been moves to link CPVE with both YTS and TVEI and there are signs that TVEI is actively seeking a closer partnership with GCSE in order to provide certification for courses. Records of achievement spans all the intiatives.

The need for integration of the wide range of pre-vocational and vocational developments led to the establishment of the National Council for Vocational Qualifications (NCVQ) in 1986. The NCVQ is a body initially funded by the Government, but expected to become self-financing after 1991. NCVQ has a remit to:
– secure standards of occupational competence and to ensure that vocational standards are based upon them
– design and implement a new national framework for vocational qualifications
– approve bodies making accredited awards
– obtain comprehensive coverage of an occupational section
– secure arrangements for quality assurance
– set up effective liaison with bodies awarding vocational qualifications
– establish a national database for vocational qualifications
– undertake or arrange to be undertaken research and development to discharge these functions
– promote vocational education, training and qualifications.[1]

The proposed National Vocational Qualification (NVQ) will initially have four levels: Basic, Standard, Advanced and Higher. The possibility of extending the range to include professional qualifications is being explored.

The recommendations of the NCVQ will have implications for many of the initiatives and curriculum developments in the 14–18 field. Figure 11.1 illustrates a typical model for NVQ qualification.[2]

It is expected that NVQ will be fully implemented by 1991. It is likely to have a significant effect on the 14–18 developments outlined in this book.

Conclusion

Apparently disparate initiatives have revealed a number of common threads including: experiential learning; new teaching styles; cross-curricular work; links with industry; new approaches to assessment. All of the new developments require informed and appropriate guidance and co-ordination, as advocated in Chapter 10.

Common themes

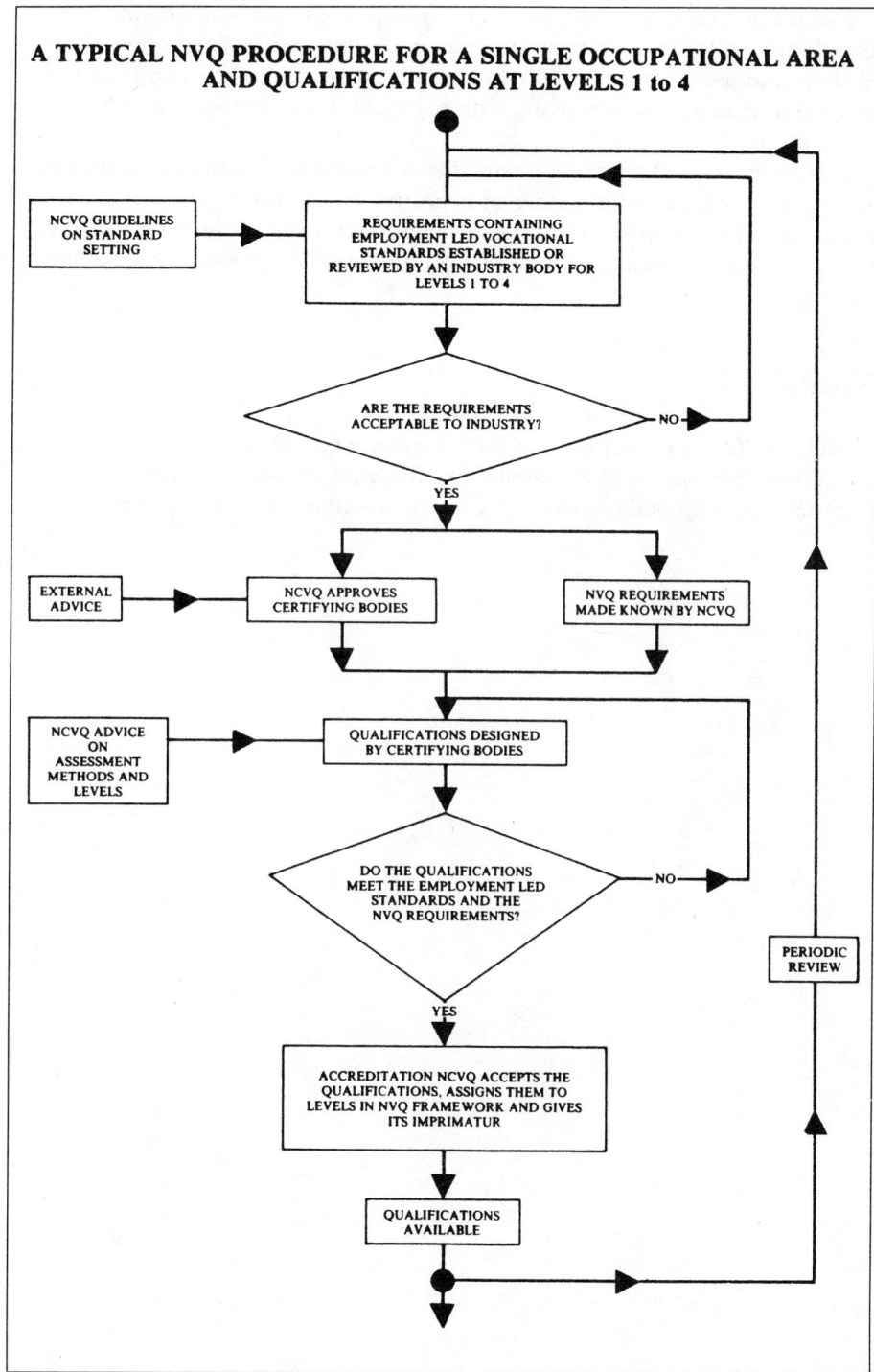

Fig. 11.1: National Vocational Qualification procedure

Taken together it is clear that a new atmosphere is gradually taking hold in schools and colleges. Emphasis is more on process and less on product; more on skills and less on content. There is some evidence that the pendulum may have commenced its return swing with proposals for a content-based National Curriculum.[3]

It is to be hoped that the desire for a prescribed National Curriculum accompanied by periodic testing of cognitive skills and attainment does not undermine the advances which have been made in offering young people a more relevant, dynamic curriculum, better able to produce self-sufficient adults.

Notes

1. NCVQ, *The National Council for Vocational Qualifications*, HMSO, 1987.
2. NCVQ, *The National Vocational Qualification Framework*, 1987.
3. DES, *The National Curriculum 5–16: A consultation document*, DES, 1987.